ALL TO PLAY FOR

ALL TO PLAY FOR

HOW SPORT WILL REBOOT OUR FUTURE

MATT ROGAN

WITH KERRY POTTER

EBURY
PRESS

1

Ebury Press an imprint of Ebury Publishing,
20 Vauxhall Bridge Road,
London SW1V 2SA

Ebury Press is part of the Penguin Random House group of companies
whose addresses can be found at global.penguinrandomhouse.com

First published by Ebury Press in 2021

This edition published in 2021

www.penguin.co.uk

A CIP catalogue record for this book is available from the British Library

ISBN 9781529148138

Typeset in 10.5/14.5 pt Corbert
by Integra Software Services Pvt. Ltd, Pondicherry

Printed and bound in Great Britain by Clays Ltd, Elcograf S.p.A.

The authorised representative in the EEA is Penguin Random House
Ireland, Morrison Chambers, 32 Nassau Street, Dublin D02 YH68

For Conor and Niamh
Work hard but play harder

CONTENTS

PROLOGUE: Sport is Special

Something strange was going on in London. As any Londoner knows – and any tourist swiftly discovers – the first rule of the Tube is that you don't talk to anyone else on the Tube. Or indeed acknowledge them in any way. Eyes averted, silence maintained, own business minded. But during the summer of 2012, when the London Olympics were in full, glorious flow, the usual rules did not apply.

At ten o'clock on a balmy Saturday night, I took the Underground from one side of the city to the other, with my five-year-old and two-year-old in tow. We'd been watching the men's modern pentathlon at Greenwich Park, the climax of the Games, and were dashing to catch the last train back to our home in the countryside. It was the kind of schlep I'd usually endure rather than enjoy – it was *way* past everyone's bedtime for a start – but these were not normal times. The sweaty, crowded carriage had a carnival feel. People fell over themselves (literally) to give up their seats for the children. Others offered them packets of Haribo. We chatted happily to strangers, swapping memories of our days and discussing the magical fortnight of sporting alchemy we'd collectively witnessed. Everyone was beaming.

Such was the power of the London 2012 Olympics; such was its transformative, stardust-sprinkling effect on the national

1

psyche. And it wasn't an outcome many had predicted. As Simon Barnes wrote in *The Games*, *The Times*' retrospective book about London 2012:

> London had spent seven years being wooed by the Olympic Games and had been difficult to please, seeing only the defects of a too-ardent suitor … Overnight everything changed. After this ardent but one-sided courtship, London and Britain fell without warning, fell like a ton of bricks, and the next 16 days were full of the euphoria of love requited.

It felt like a watershed moment for sport. Not just the action playing out on the pitch, track, or in the pool, but also the sense that sport as a movement could make special things happen, and that we should hold that feeling in our hearts no matter what the years ahead might throw at us. There was a precedent to these moments throughout history. When researching my previous book, *Britain and the Olympic Games: Past, Present, Legacy*, with my co-author (and dad) Martin Rogan, we heard stories about the 1948 Olympics and a similar feeling washing over the city, then newly scarred from the Second World War: a collective drawing of breath and of reconnection.

Somehow in the process of falling in love with London 2012 – its enthusiastic volunteer army, its multiculturalism, its flood of gold medals for Team GB – we'd managed to break away from the drudgery of daily working life and live in the moment. We might not have officially taken those two sun-drenched weeks as annual leave, but, boy, did it feel like it. Emails went unread, feet were up on the desk, eyes glued to the TV screen rather than the computer. Weekdays may have blurred into the weekends but everyone remembers where they were on Super Saturday; that joyful summer evening when Mo Farah, Jessica Ennis-Hill and Greg Rutherford all won athletics gold after Team GB secured two in rowing and one in track cycling earlier in the day. What could be more perfect?

Moments of national cohesion and collective joy were in short supply in Britain in the years that followed. Talking to strangers on the Tube once again became a bad idea. Two referendums – the Scottish independence vote in 2014, when the Scots narrowly voted to remain part of the UK and the Brexit vote in 2016, which was another close one that led to us severing ties with the European Union and had a seismic impact on the national mood. Views became increasingly polarised, with social media acting as the battleground for raging culture wars. Punches were thrown, teeth were gnashed and families argued, while economic and political uncertainty swirled all around. Social, class, wealth, generational and regional divisions became more entrenched than ever before.

And yet, it was possible to escape. While the good times had left town, sport hadn't. It was possible to dip back into that euphoric Super Saturday feeling now and then. A TV audience of 17.3 million watched the nail-biting final set of Andy Murray's first victory at Wimbledon in 2013 as Britain lay claim to its first men's winner in 77 long years. In 2018, Prince Harry and Meghan Markle's wedding attracted an audience of 18.7 million, but that number was dwarfed a month later by the 20.7 million who saw England's men narrowly exit the 2018 football World Cup at the semi-final stage.[1]

Live sport's power to pull in mammoth TV crowds is no mean feat when you consider the rise of other options – catch-up, YouTube, Netflix – in recent years. With audiences increasingly fractured and attention spans ever decreasing, it's even tougher to hold the whole nation in thrall. Yet sport continues to magnetise us, and in relative terms is revelling in a golden age. Of the top-ten most-watched shows in the 2010s, eight out of ten were sport-based, with the 2012 Olympics closing ceremony top of the tree, pulling in 24.5 million (a staggering 51.9 million people watched at least 15 minutes of coverage during the Games – that's 81.5 per cent of the population). By comparison, turn the clock back to the 1990s and sport featured only twice in the top-ten rated shows, once for football and then for Torvill and Dean's 1994 Olympic bronze performance.

We still watch sport together, at the same time, and dissect it with our colleagues the next morning. Sport and its stars unite us and give us something to pull together for. It can even make us believe that wearing a waistcoat is a wise sartorial choice, as England men's team manager Gareth Southgate showed in those heady days of the run up to the semi-finals of the 2018 World Cup. England finally won a penalty shootout, and Marks & Spencer reported a 35 per cent increase in waistcoat sales based on Southgate's sharp dressing. Weird and wonderful times, indeed.[2]

And when we're not just watching it, we're doing it. And this is despite the fact that, like live sport, participation sport has faced a host of challenges in recent years. Financial austerity has limited investment in public facilities, at a time when the inequality gap between rich and poor has refused to budge.[3] But although there are fewer facilities and people have less money in their pockets, there has actually been a modest increase in the number of active adults in the country, according to Sport England's final data available before the COVID-19 pandemic hit in early 2020. Numbers rose from 28.2 million (62.7 per cent of the adult population) to 28.6 million (63.3 per cent) in the 12 months from November 2018.[4] These increased activity levels were particularly marked among women, older people and those who are disabled or suffering from long-term health conditions. Sport was finally making progress in drawing in those who are traditionally hard to reach, thanks to a range of initiatives, from the lauded 'This Girl Can' campaign (we'll come to that later) to the FA investing in walking football for older players.

Of course, it's not all been positive. If sport is a key factor in pulling society together, then that comes with a deeper level of scrutiny and examination. The COVID-19 pandemic and its subsequent shutdown of sports clubs, gyms, playing fields and pools has forced us all to re-examine our relationship with sport and fitness – as the adage goes, you don't know what you've got till it's gone. The industry has frequently been dragged from the back pages of newspaper to the front when things have gone awry. Some athletes have taken drugs, some have forgotten their standing as role models to our kids, some coaches have pushed their charges beyond acceptable boundaries. Several football teams have priced their tickets out of the reach of locals in their own home town. There has been corruption in the corridors of sporting power. Successive governments have sold off our playing fields to build housing estates. Britain still has a reputation for winning Olympic medals at predominantly posh, White middle-class sports (this isn't actually the case but reputations linger). This doesn't make sport a failure or a bad influence. It just means that we need to treat it carefully, understand why it's such a potent tool, and unpick how we can use it as a force for good in challenging times. To do this, we also need to look at sport in the round – at struggling schoolchildren as well as gold medallists; at cash-strapped community clubs as well as Wembley and Wimbledon; at GP surgeries as well as fancy private gyms.

Now the good news. There are an awful lot of reasons to be cheerful. They're just not always easy to spot if you don't know where to look. That's where this book comes in.

It unearths stories, both from within the industry itself and from grassroots level, that to date have gone largely unshared. When we weave these narratives together we see that sport and fitness are undergoing a huge evolution in Britain, and mostly for the better. Considered in the round, the future looks bright.

Let's briefly return to those TV viewing figures. In 2019, a year after Gareth Southgate's England men's team had fallen in the FIFA World Cup semis, a massive 11.7 million people watched England's women reach the same stage of their tournament. In fact, England women's match against the United States was the most-watched TV programme of all of 2019, until the return of BBC comedy *Gavin & Stacey* pinched the trophy on Christmas Day. And this was no one-off. England's women sold out Lord's Cricket Ground in 2017 as they won the Cricket World Cup. In 2016 the British women's hockey team won a penalty shootout for Olympic gold at the Rio Olympics – and in doing so, delayed the *News at Ten*. After decades of incremental changes, women's professional sport suddenly became big news, bigger even than The News, in this case.

We'll tell lots more stories like this in the pages ahead. The pioneering football club that's become an NHS clinic. The professional footballer who was once too ashamed to admit to being one. The woman who is helping generations of mums start moving again after childbirth. The charity supporting kids' mental health by launching a new approach to movement. The passionate ultra-runner trying to overhaul his almost exclusively White sport. The creator of the commercial model for the Olympic Games explaining how it will change with the times.

The new generations of sportswomen and men who aren't prepared to play by the previous generations' rules.

Although the pandemic caused gyms and stadium to be shut, it was also a chance to reconnect with the rituals we hold most dear in our society and reflect on how much they mean to us. The stories we share in this book are each individual pieces of the complex jigsaw puzzle that is Britain's relationship with sport and exercise. It's such a complex puzzle that few have tried to piece the whole picture together from pre-school to podium, surgery to stadium – but that's the unique challenge I have taken on for this book.

I discovered that a discussion about professional football actually fits neatly alongside one about mental health, which in turn slots into a debate about our responsibility to create happy, healthy kids. That a conversation about generational change merges into one about the creation of new sports, and in turn the way that we need to think about designing our cities. Building the whole picture has helped me understand the true influence of sport in this country in our post-pandemic world. This is the story of how one of the longest-standing and last-remaining collective rituals in our country can help us see a path to a happier and healthier future.

CHAPTER 1 / Back to the Future

It probably seems a little strange to start a book about the future of sport by looking at its history.

But with sport, as with many things, it's important to understand a little bit about the past to understand why things are the way they are today – and why now might be the time they change for good. Context is key. Many of the debates we find on the front and back pages of newspapers today are actually repeating from previous generations. The difference is that now Britain is at a point where permanent change is not only possible, it's extremely likely.

Let's start at the beginning. It may come as a surprise, but we didn't always have a divine right to play or watch sport. For centuries, sport was the preserve of the rich and famous – and participants were often less than volunteering to be involved in the action. In Roman times, emperors and the affluent filled the Colosseum to enjoy their sport while gladiators, simultaneously heroes and slaves, were fed to the lions. Even then, the real power and influence were in the stands. Knights competing in tournaments throughout England during the thirteenth century took their lives in their hands to win events for rich benefactors who were financially backing their respective teams. We may think elite sport is a ruthless business at times today, but it's *nothing* compared to 800 years ago.

WHY THE BUCOLIC VILLAGE GREEN WASN'T ALL IT SEEMED

There is an awful lot of sentimental nonsense talked about the early days of sport, when (we are told) sport was a world of fair play and amateur ideals, and far less competitive both on and off the pitch. In truth, sport was never like this. Cricket being a case in point. Many have a utopian dream of a gentle summer's game on an idyllic village green, the kind of quaint scene you might expect to see at the beginning of an episode of *Midsomer Murders*.

However, cricket was never really anything of the sort. By the eighteenth century, it was a massive gambling sport with match formats being regularly changed to create new betting markets. And how they tweaked those formats – a team of 11 players once played a less able one with 22 players to create a 'fair' competition. Players were able to receive goods, if not money, for their performances as the betting industry exploded, creating a world ripe for corruption. Firm rules for the game were only instituted in 1744 to reduce the number of gambling-related disputes. This certainly puts into perspective the furore that erupts nowadays among cricket's hardcore if a new competition is launched.

As cricket spread across the country, highly competitive aristocratic landowners with money and time to spare would employ the men on their estates who were the best cricketers to join their teams. This was a rare moment of class integration for England in the eighteenth century. Although the divides were clear again the moment players stepped off the pitch and saw the very different quality of catering facilities for lunch or tea, the on-pitch action had at least begun to break down some barriers. As we shall see, sport continues to find itself at the centre of a debate on class in Britain.

Public schools were a huge influence on the development of sport in Victorian times, for both good and bad. These schools were the only ones that gave boys the opportunity to participate in sport at school, a concept that did not hit state-school education until far later. Forward-thinking girls' public schools followed suit to significant criticism from those who believed sport was not ladylike. The early headmistress of Cheltenham Ladies' College, Miss Dorothea Beale, was one who ignored the barracking and noted how, having exercised, her girls were much more focused in the classroom. Active children were – and remain – more effective learners.

Once they had left, public school alumni set about writing down the rules of the games they had enjoyed and launching formal associations to govern them. They tried to reinforce the idea of amateurism to do so – sport, they claimed, was imbued with Victorian values of Corinthian spirit and fair play. Any payment of athletes, they argued, would sully that relationship. What this meant in practice was that working women and men could not take time out to compete, and could not even be paid to take roles that were aligned to their sport (for example, boat building for a rower, or teaching rugby in a school). By insisting on amateurism as a guiding principle, the upper classes restricted access to their sports.

This was controversial in a confident, bustling Britain in the throes of the Industrial Revolution. Each sport handled this challenge differently. Rugby's governing body the Rugby Football Union (RFU) voted to keep rugby strictly amateur. The impact of this was that keen, talented working-class players from northern industrial towns could not miss work to play. Unwilling to be dictated to, northern teams broke away and formed a new code – now known as 'rugby league' – with a key principle from the start being 'broken time', which meant that players could be compensated financially for missing work. 'Rugby union' pursued amateurism for almost another hundred years in Britain until finally relenting at the end of the twentieth century. However, the impact of the RFU's decision remains with a divided sport, and one in which the union code is still perceived as the more 'upper class' of the major team sports in Britain.

COMMUNITY, COHESION AND CASH

Football, conversely, made a very different decision in the late nineteenth century. The reduction of the industrial working week from six to five and a half days created a window for watching and playing sport. Local industrialists were keen to fund teams as they noticed the key role they played in gelling together communities. Very quickly football teams, as well as rugby ones, started to pull in tens of thousands of spectators. As well as all the benefits of community cohesion, which also created a commercial opportunity for the industrialists to recoup some of the money they were paying their workers – they could sell tickets and then use some of those funds to search for better players to grow the profile of their teams. Rather than fight a losing battle to supress the commercial growth, administrators of the game begrudgingly allowed the sport to become professional, and football has been a business ever since. By the turn of the century, football clubs were limited liability companies and competing for the best talent the British Isles could provide, with proud, proactive owners at the fore.

Amid the steady development of sport for competition and commerce's sake, it took a brave maverick to think more broadly about the wider benefits of sport for the general population beyond the power of a community getting together to cheer on their local team. It wasn't in the hubbub of London or in the industrial north that something more important had been stirring, but in the sleepy village of Much Wenlock in Shropshire. Local GP Dr William Penny Brookes decided to focus on the prevention of physical illnesses, such as lung disease, instead of simply treating their symptoms. He saw exercise as the principal way to achieve this, encouraging people to take part in physical activity. In 1850 he launched the Wenlock Olympian Games – inspired by the tradition of the Greek Olympic Games. This event was unashamedly open to all classes, ages and genders, which was a brave commitment from the doctor in what were still deeply conservative times. It was a roaring success, although Penny Brookes refused the offer of developing a national equivalent at Crystal Palace when told by the powers that be this would have to be an amateur competition.

Brookes's emphasis on sport and exercise for all through the Games played a significant role in the improved health and wellbeing of his local population. He also opened a local library to encourage reading, and significantly improved the sanitary conditions in the area. Having seen the benefits of physical activity on learning, he focused his efforts on getting 'physical training' as a compulsory school lesson. This finally became law shortly before his death in 1895.

Brookes's pioneering innovations in linking together physical health, mental health and education were not his only legacy. In 1890, the sleepy village of the Olympian Games had a special visitor in the shape of Frenchman Baron de Coubertin. He wanted to inspire the French to become more physically active (and never again lose a war). De Coubertin took inspiration from the time he spent observing Brookes's British Games, and many of the features informed his vision for the first modern Olympic Games in Athens in 1896. The biggest international sporting event was born with British innovation and the broader value of sport at its heart.

DOORS OPEN TO WOMEN

While the first Olympic Games in 1896 were a modest success, unlike in Much Wenlock women had to wait to take part. They participated for the first time at the 1900 Paris Olympic Games, competing in lawn tennis and golf, with women's athletics and gymnastics debuting in 1928. By this point female athletes (professional and otherwise) were performing feats of endurance that proved ridiculous any notion they needed protecting. In 1926, 19-year-old New Yorker Gertrude Ederle made history by becoming the first woman to swim the English Channel – and in a faster time than the five men who had already achieved the feat.

Similarly, in Britain, it was a case of two steps forward, at least one back for women's sport. Employers such as Cadbury, Boots and Rowntree's started to build playing fields for use by female and male workers alike, which normalised the sight of women playing sport. At the time, there were around 150 industrial towns with women's football teams, the most famous of which were Dick, Kerr Ladies emanating from Dick, Kerr & Co. in Preston. During and after the First World War they played in charity fixtures around the country and raised money for injured servicemen. On Boxing Day 1920, their match against St Helens Ladies at Goodison Park drew a crowd of 53,000 spectators, a world record for women's club matches that lasted for 98 years. The team were featured regularly in the Pathé newsreels and their star players became well-known. The fame was short-lived. Less than a year after this match, the FA banned women's football from their members' grounds. While they claimed women were not up to the physical nature of football, in reality they saw women's football as a threat to the growth of the men's game, in particular now the men were back from the war.

Despite setbacks of this nature, women's understanding of the need for physical exercise continued to grow thanks, in no small part, to the pioneering efforts of Prunella Slack who was the driving force behind the Women's League of Health and Beauty, an organisation that encouraged women to exercise as a means towards physical and mental health. The League gave a generation of women whose fathers, brothers and husbands had been killed during the First World War the opportunity to exercise together in classes of varying levels of difficulty. Slack used activities such as Pilates, aerobics, dance, yoga and much more to encourage women to find comfort and confidence through the catalyst of movement.

After the horrors of the Second World War, in summer 1948, war-torn, cash-strapped Britain was in need of a boost. In response, London managed to put on an exceptional Olympic Games. The genius behind it, Sir Arthur Elvin, also reinvented the blueprint for a sports event – selling broadcast rights, sponsorships and tickets in order to cover the cost of hosting the Games. He happened to be the owner of Wembley Stadium at the time and turned a tidy profit along the way, in the best traditions of the early football team entrepreneurs.

British women's and men's amateur athletes performed at an incredible level given that access to enough protein and the right types of carbohydrate for elite performance was hampered by rationing; a reality for several years after the war. The 1948 Games medal table showed clearly which nations' athletes had been worst affected by rationing and nutrition problems. This signalled the beginning of the modern understanding of the ways in which diet and nutrition impact human performance.

The British female medal winners in particular produced achievements against the odds. Unlike many of the male athletes, they were typically unable to access coaching through the Armed Forces. Having driven trucks and buses during the war, high-jumper Dorothy Odam became a typing temp to give her the flexibility to both train and also look after her two children. Hurdler Maureen Gardner was a ballet teacher, which didn't contravene the rules of amateurism but kept her fit, while sprinter Dorothy Manley fitted her training into the weekends and evenings after work. This immense juggling act meant it was possible to prepare and compete in her home nation for the 1948 Olympics. When she was was selected for the Commonwealth (then 'British Empire') Games in New Zealand in 1950, however, her work and home life had to be put on ice for a while, as she embarked on what was then a five-week boat trip to the other side of the world.

The year 1948 also saw a major breakthrough for inclusivity with the birth of the Paralympic Games in Stoke Mandeville. At the time, casualties of war were too often left on the fringes of society for the rest of their lives. However, the Stoke Mandeville Games showed very clearly the role sport could play not only in rehabilitation, but also reintegration of the less fortunate into modern life.

ATHLETES TAKE CENTRE STAGE

As the world slowly righted itself in the second half of the twentieth century, sport continued to provide a release to the challenges of daily life. However, there was one major inequality in the system. While sport was becoming bigger business, still very little financial gain was filtering down to the players themselves, even those lucky enough to play in 'professional' sport. It took until 1960 for players to be properly looked after. It was a man named Mark McCormack who created the first genuine business to recognise the true value of the athlete in the US, initially in golf. TV at the time was booming, athletes becoming stars, and McCormack's big golfing names were worthy of the fair returns McCormack negotiated for them.

Not satisfied with simply selling his athletes, McCormack sold the television programmes of the events his athletes competed in, the Championships and British Open Golf being early customers. Not wanting to leave any money on the table, his production company made the actual programmes that he sold. He even invented the show *Superstars* – a big hit in Britain in the 1970s and 1980s – which pitted his now megastar athletes against each other outside of their chosen sport. He created the idea, owned the athletes, ran the event, produced the TV show and then sold it to sponsors and broadcasters. Little surprise his business, IMG, became the most powerful in sport as it was more professional on and off the pitch. Meanwhile, the athletes he represented became household names with manicured images and attracted brands happy to pay them to advertise their products.

That's not to say that all athletes became poster boys and girls. As the profile of sport grew, some athletes took a stand to make key points about changes they wanted to see in society. Some of the earliest athlete-activists drew global attention at the 1968 Olympic Games in Mexico City as African-American athletes Tommie Smith and John Carlos performed a controversial raised-fist salute on the podium. This was a symbol of Black Power and the wider human rights movement, raising awareness of the social unrest in North

America at the time, just months after the assassination of Dr Martin Luther-King.[5] The two were suspended from the US Olympic team and faced a significant backlash on returning home.

Away from the world of protest, the early 1980s saw the running boom of the United States arrive in the UK, as the London Marathon took place for the first time in 1981. This was about more than running itself, however, more a recognition that sport could and would need to fit around increasingly busy lifestyles. People could go for a run at a time that suited them. Home aerobics became a staple on breakfast TV, with its instructors becoming stars in their own right (remember Mr Motivator?). *Fame*, the US drama about young professional dancers in New York City, burst on to British screens in the early 1980s, showing glamour and sweat could co-exist.

As the 1980s rolled on, and MTV's videos killed the radio stars, the worlds of sport, music and entertainment began to merge even further. Stars of fast-growing US basketball league the NBA became music artists. LA Lakers player turned rapper Shaquille O'Neal sold a million copies of his first album, *Shaq Diesel*, and brought out enough music to justify a greatest hits compilation. The most famous of all, Michael Jordan, became a movie star while his Nike trainers became global fashion statements as well as on-court kit. The boundaries between sport and pop culture dissolved. Saturday-night TV in Britain included the show *Gladiators*, a hugely popular format that made no apology about sport being first and foremost entertainment. Sport started to become part of showbiz, carried along in the heady affluence of the end of the twentieth century. Fame has advantages and disadvantages, of course. Ben Johnson's positive drugs test as 100-metre

Olympic champion in 1988 sowed a seed of doubt in the public conscience, which remains to this day.

The digital era dawned at the beginning of the twenty-first century and sport in Britain came coughing and spluttering into a new dimension. Satellite TV financed the creation of a new top football division, the Premier League. British sportsmen and women started to cut through in the way Jordan had in the US; David Beckham being the first. Private gyms began cropping up, although those company playing fields that had been so key to spreading the message of sport for all were increasingly sold off to the highest-bidding housing developer. Britain produced a conveyor belt of eloquent, ethnically diverse, world-beating female Olympians, yet the doors through to fair levels of media exposure and financial reward were at best only slightly ajar. Or, in the case of several private golf clubs, remained shut.

A GLIMPSE OF THE OPPORTUNITY

More often than not, history is the best guide to the future. It hints at opportunities, and warns of the pitfalls. In writing this book, I've learnt sport is no different. So, what does the history of sport, from gladiators in the Roman arena to *Gladiators* presented by Ulrika Jonsson and John Fashanu, teach us to look out for in the years ahead?

Let's start with the tough stuff. The sad truth is that much of sport's history is tainted by prejudice. The sporting world many of our grandparents or great-grandparents hark back to would have excluded much of the population – by virtue of either gender, race or class. History shows that consistent repression of athletes (whether gladiators, female footballers or lower-class cricketers) can reinforce class divides. It suggests that real change comes from inclusion – and that we need people like William Penny Brookes at the helm. He was brave enough to resist his Olympian Games moving to Crystal Palace as he didn't want to lock out anyone from competing. We are also likely to need to continue his struggle to emphasise the importance of physical exercise in cash-strapped schools.

While there are threats we need to navigate, there is plenty in the history of sport to hint at the opportunity and empowerment sport can offer society. Cricket was breaking down class barriers on some level in the eighteenth century, long before the need to do so was on any wider social agenda. The modest Wenlock Olympian Games showed the benefits of exercise on the physical health of a local community. Women have achieved excellence to contest and challenge the compromising agenda of the male establishment for centuries, whether filling stadiums for football matches or swimming the Channel at pace.

History also tells us sport has been a business since the very earliest of days. Commerce was the enabler for the creation of the very first high-profile football teams to excite Britain's new factory workers. Commercial acumen enabled Britain to put on a 1948 Olympic Games and boost a country ravaged by the Second World War. Great entrepreneurship has often freed up our view of what sport actually consists of in the first place. If an 11-a-side game isn't your thing, then join a gym, a yoga or Pilates class – just as Prunella Slack's League was advocating 100 years ago. Entrepreneurs have enabled athletes to receive fair payments for their talent, while enabling them to have wider platform to make their voices heard.

As film director Danny Boyle's showstopping opening ceremony for the London 2012 Olympic Games told the story of Britain growing up with sport at its core, it felt like we were entering the teenage years of the twenty-first century. Could

London 2012 give us the boost that the 1948 Games did, and the sustained jolt to our health and happiness that Penny Brookes delivered? Would it help us recognise the diversity of our nation, with a new breed of multicultural athletes at our core? Perhaps, just perhaps, now was the time for sport to realise the potential it had long promised.

CHAPTER 2 / The Difficult Teens

As the torch went out on the London 2012 Paralympic Games, having been lit at Stoke Mandeville just ten miles away from my house, it felt that Britain was bouncing back from recession in style.

As we know, with the benefit of hindsight, it wouldn't be many years before the mood in Britain was to take a turn for the worse. The twenty-first century's teenage years would feature many of the same growing pains as human adolescence. It would feel like new issues were hitting us from all sides. But what pride we had before our fall! The Games themselves were undeniably brilliant. In the run-up, after much initial sniping about cost and logistics, the critics lay down their arms. By the time rowers Helen Glover and Heather Stanning crossed the finish line to win Britain's first gold medal, there was a palpable sense of excitement pulsing through the nation.

Glover and Stanning were just the start. London 2012 brought more Olympic gold medals for Team GB than ever before in both the Olympic and Paralympic Games, with Britain's women at the fore. Day after day, Jessica Ennis-Hill, Laura Kenny, Charlotte Dujardin, Nicola Adams, Ellie Simmonds, Sarah Storey, Katherine Grainger, Jade Jones and many more were front- and back-page news. The men were no slouches either – Mo Farah, Chris Hoy, Andy Murray and Co also won their fair share of a total of 29 British gold medals.

Even if the difficult teenage years that lay ahead demonstrated many areas where Britain's old intolerances were laid bare, that was definitely not true of the inclusivity and warmth of the London 2012 Paralympic Games, which had been a triumph in their own right. Britain remains today the only nation in the world that has attracted 60,000-plus people per day to watch disability sport. Ellie Simmonds, Sarah Storey and David Weir took their place among the Games-related nominations for BBC Sports Personality of the Year, and nobody batted an eyelid. London 2012's successes remain big news to this day. In 2020, Dame Jessica Ennis-Hill was awarded the title of providing Britain's best-ever women's sporting moment by BBC Sport for her London 2012 heptathlon victory.

Another British athlete whose achievements stand the test of time is rower Greg Searle, who won gold in the coxed pairs final at the 1992 Barcelona Games with his brother Jonny; the duo famously snatched first place at the finishing line. Twenty years on, Greg, by then a married dad of two children, decided to come out of retirement (well, a successful career in business consultancy) to pursue his 'comeback dream' at London 2012. He won bronze in the men's eight, at the ripe old age of 40.

'My attitude was very different second time round,' he says. 'When you're given a chance to do something a little later in life, you really appreciate the opportunity and work hard to make the most of it. I noticed my body wasn't as powerful and strong as it used to be but I recognised what a privilege it all was. All that training is a choice rather than a sacrifice.' It wasn't just the 'mature student' of rowing who had changed, the culture had too. 'The awareness of mental health is much greater now. Back then it was much more: "Pull yourself together, man."

When I started out, you would see the sports psychologist if there was something wrong with you. Now we use psychology in a positive way to get more out of ourselves.'

What's more, back in the early 1990s there was 'no concept that rowing was a job' but, when Greg returned in the late 2000s, he found a very different outlook among his young teammates, thanks to National Lottery funding. 'Everyone now is a full-time rower and paid a grant so they feel they're starting their working life as an athlete. This means they don't have distractions and they can focus 100 per cent on the sport.' This Lottery funding for elite sport started in 1997 and was a key reason why Team GB were able to go from scraping just one gold medal at the Atlanta 1996 Games to winning 28 more in 2012.

INSIDER INSIGHT: GREG SEARLE

One of Britain's greatest ever rowers, Greg Searle, won Olympic gold at just 20 years old when, along with his older brother Jonny, he came first in the 1992 Barcelona Olympic Games' coxed pairs final. He was awarded an MBE in 1993, won bronze in the Atlanta 1996 Games and also competed in Sydney in 2000 before retiring. He became a partner in performance consultancy Lane4, alongside Olympic gold medallist swimmer Adrian Moorhouse. In 2012, aged 40, he came back to win bronze at the London Games in the men's eight.

You've been in the Olympics both pre-and post-Lottery funding for athletes. Has that funding helped make Olympic sport more democratic? You don't need parents with money to facilitate your training now, do you?

Yes, it's been fantastic for elite-level performance. The Lottery has also provided funding for the system so coaches and equipment are in place and it's also done an incredible job for grassroots facilities. There are not many tennis courts, cricket pitches or rowing clubs that haven't benefited from grants in the last 20 years or so. It's been game-changing for British sport at a time when playing fields have been disappearing to become housing.

When you returned to rowing did you find the younger rowers more serious than when you started out, because they're being paid to do a job now?

There was definitely a serious-minded approach with the twentysomethings. That's largely good for the performance but I'm not sure if it's good for the person. They end up being quite one-dimensional, which is a worry because you're not going to be a rower forever. It's quite useful if you've got some other strings to your bow. Talking about transition [from elite sport into normal life] is more of a thing than it used to be. In fact, the concept didn't used to exist. Before, you were, say, a teacher who did some rowing. Now you're a rower who retires so you have to work on that transition. That is changing though. Rowing's performance director Brendan Purcell is interested in athletes being rounded people and has put in place a mentoring system using former athletes. He looks at things in a more holistic way, which I think is healthy.

When you've been an elite athlete, is it difficult to enjoy playing sports for fun, at a lower level? Have your Olympic achievements 'ruined' other sports for you?

No, because I'm not sure performing sports at a higher level makes you happier. Sport at any level makes me happy. I rowed in the Olympics but now I love playing cricket in the same side as my son in the Marlow 2nd XI cricket team. My enjoyment of those things is similar.

You've got two sporty children: are you a pushy parent?

I recognise that my role is to facilitate their performance and their enjoyment of sport. There's a balance to be struck – an optimal level of pushiness! I don't want them to underperform because they've been lazy or turned up with the wrong kit but at the same time, having achieved other things in my own life, I'm able to keep in perspective what my children are doing. Kids shouldn't be made to feel that parental love is conditional on performance. I do understand why parents really want their children to do well in their sport though: you feel like you've made all these sacrifices, you haven't gone on holidays, you've had to get up early and sit in sweaty sports halls on weekends and missed going for your run or whatever sport you want to do, you've spent loads of money on kit ...

What do you make of the rise of the ultra-competitive parent?

When we were younger, parents were so much less involved in our sport. Mine had no concept of what rowing was. Participation was largely driven by the child, teachers and coaches. Now parents are much more involved. They think, 'If I'm not getting my child 10,000 hours of gymnastics training I'm failing them, so how can we fit that in?' And sports clubs rely more on volunteers who are inevitably parents. As a parent, you are then inextricably linked, you are part of the sporting experience.

Your predictions – and hopes – for the future of sport?

I feel fairly positive about its role over the next few years. One of the consequences of the pandemic is that being healthy was put on a higher pedestal, people have reassessed their priorities around fitness, so therefore will there be better support and better facilities? That said, I fear what will happen with money disappearing from sport. For example, we've made great progress recently with women's sport – if you put grassroots development in place, the sport does well and then the commercialism comes in. But if that money disappears, say, due to the vagaries of commercial sponsorship, is that worse than the sport never having the money in the first place? You've created a generation of players who expect to be paid but then you can't pay them. It's difficult.

My own sporting journey of 2012 was more of a mixed bag. A keen runner, I'd spent most of the Olympics period itself with an ankle injury, hobbling around the events for which we were lucky enough to have secured ballot tickets. It was terrible timing as I was building my running up for a crack at the San Sebastián Marathon in the autumn, with the intention of trying to qualify for the Boston Marathon in 2014. To do that, I needed to run a marathon in under 3 hours 10 minutes. I'd been originally targeting the Boston 2013 race but had missed the target and put my plans back a year.

While I did manage my own qualification gold medal that autumn, the warm glow of anticipation for Boston 2014 didn't last long. As I watched the 2013 race, shortly before three o'clock Boston time, two homemade bombs exploded near the finish, killing three people and injuring several hundred others. The bombs were instigated by two terrorist brothers, acting apparently alone in protest at American involvement in Iraq and Afghanistan. If I had qualified for that year's race as originally planned, I would likely only have been half an hour past the finish line that day. The next day, I chaired a breakfast meeting for many of the leaders of Britain's biggest sports at Lord's. Our minute's silence was incredibly moving. We stood overlooking the empty home of cricket, which had brought communal joy to so many people from around the world, in complete shock that anyone would want to bring harm to people in Boston – or anywhere around the world – celebrating collective sporting achievement.

THE FALL AFTER THE PRIDE

It didn't take long for Britain to come back down to earth as 2012's highs became 2013's angst.

Teenage life typically involves the thrills of a new sense of freedom and possibly budding romance offset against the inevitable periods of awkwardness, arguments and phases of identity crisis. The teenage years of the new millennium followed exactly the same pattern. British society and culture plunged into the doldrums, plumping for a glass-half-empty approach, garnished with a particularly large dollop of conflict and crisis.

Each year dictionary.com publishes a 'word of the year' based on search trends on the site during the year in question and the news events that drive them. That decade's list makes for sobering reading.

2012: Bluster
2013: Privacy
2014: Exposure
2015: Identity
2016: Xenophobia
2017: Complicit
2018: Misinformation
2019: Existential

Were things really that bad? Well, yes. If you spool back through the news stories of the day – austerity, Brexit, Grenfell and the *Windrush* scandal are your starters for ten – the truth is, it was a grim time. So how did this all impact on sport? The best place to start with that is with another word, one which encapsulates the desire of Sebastian Coe, chairman of the Organising Committee for London 2012, to achieve something far deeper and more important than merely putting on a sporting party: legacy

EXAMINING THE LEGACY

If you get into the reeds on the question of legacy from London 2012, you'll see the organisers of the Games did a terrific job of delivering on everything that was under their (and only their) direct control. They built a whole new area of vibrant London on a polluted wasteland. Created a defining moment for the integration of disability into society. Delivered more British sporting role models than we could ever have dreamed of. Helped Britain fall in love with attending live sport all over again.[6] All of which, with the Games themselves paid for in full by Britain's biggest businesses, despite a domestic recession, and with the public purse paying for the regeneration, will pay back for generations to come.

It wasn't all good news, however. Where the 2012 Olympics legacy hasn't gone to plan is with the most challenging of its ambitions – to make Britain more active as a result of London 2012. This was the part of the jigsaw where London 2012 could not do it on its own; it required cooperation right across the system for decades to come. Not easy to do under any scenario but particularly tricky when the Games organisers stepped down at the same point that public debt was £1.34 trillion. To put that in context, the banking crisis increased public debt by 300 per cent between London bidding to host the Games in 2005 and 1 January 2013.[7] The late Dame Tessa Jowell, who was one of the most influential people in making London 2012 happen, is on record as saying Britain would likely not even have bid for the Games had the decision been made after 2008's banking crisis. After the Olympics finished, whose job exactly was it to get Brits moving?

The hard truth is that London 2012 managed to keep sporting activity levels steady, with most recent (pre-pandemic) figures showing a miniscule rise in participation. But a truly meaningful, bring-out-the-bunting increase? That part of the legacy failed. But why?

It's all very well to create excitement and buzz around sport, but kids who haven't automatically fallen into sport are going to need somewhere to play. It's far easier to fall in love with sport because your parents are both besotted, or you attend a school with both the facilities and teaching commitment to help you try out different things. Not everyone is that lucky, and post-London Olympics, the obstacles to exercise for the less privileged were just getting bigger.

A significant challenge was that school provision for PE reduced after London 2012. The Institute for Fiscal Studies calculated total school spending per pupil in England fell by 8 per cent in real terms between 2010 and 2018. When school budgets are tightened, PE is particularly hard hit because it is more costly to provide than classroom-based activity. Polly Toynbee and David Walker's book *The Lost Decade* suggests one in three state secondary schools cut PE from pupils' timetables between 2012–19.

If schools are not providing as much sport, then children need to look elsewhere. Sadly, that's not been easy, either. While the torrent of playing-field sell-offs at the turn of the century slowed to a trickle as the Games approached, the upkeep of public facilities continued to be a challenge for cash-strapped councils. This meant those tempted into sport – on a pitch, court or in a pool – didn't always have the kind of experience London 2012 might have promised. It's not easy to play cricket if clubs are full and councils can't afford to maintain public pitches. Or to nip down to the park to play basketball if someone has snapped off the ring by swinging on it, and it has not been repaired.

Toynbee and Walker cite a finding by Sport England, the government body responsible for encouraging the nation to take part in sport and exercise, that public access tennis-court availability has fallen by 5 per cent since 2010 in addition to the availability of fewer school courts. Each court closure is a decision made at local council level as they struggle to balance their books. It's an impossible choice – tennis or social care? Football or potholes? Rugby or rubbish collections?

The challenge from London 2012 wasn't that people didn't want to play more sport, it was that it was getting more difficult to do so. In fact, without the London 2012 legacy effect sporting participation would likely have plummeted. Static participation numbers, in the context of austerity Britain's sporting cuts, are actually a major achievement, and I will argue forever and a day in London 2012's defence in that regard, without throwing the local authorities, who were forced into impossible choices, under a bus. The sad truth is that after London 2012 those who most needed sport to be an option for them were most likely to have been frozen out – whether at school or in the parks. At a local level rays of light existed – as we shall see later with the advent of Spencer Lynx Hockey – but they relied on unfailingly generous volunteers, and were the exception that proved the rule.

You are probably wondering how the overall sporting participation numbers managed to stay stable given there were fewer facilities available and much less provision in schools. Well, firstly, the remaining facilities got busier – as anyone who has tried to book a five-a-side football pitch, locate an indoor cricket lane or find a gymnastics class for their kids will testify. Secondly, more flexible individual sporting pursuits that didn't need facilities – the likes of running and cycling –

continued their inexorable rise, often at the expense of team sports like football and rugby.

Thirdly, private gyms filled the gap.[8] In 2012 there were 1,595 fitness facilities in the UK, and by 2018 that number had more than doubled to 3,419. Whereas council-run leisure centres offered a pay-as-you-go model, most of the new breed of private gyms with fancy facilities demanded a hefty monthly subscription fee (and often a joining fee), which only the affluent could afford. Although a sector of lower-priced private gyms emerged, costing £10 to £20 per month, that's still prohibitively expensive for many people. And if you live in an overcrowded urban area, the leisure centres are oversub-scribed, the private gyms are too expensive, and you have to travel miles to find grass, trees and space in which to safely run, workout or ride a bike, is it any surprise that being regularly active becomes simply too difficult? Throw in working long hours and kids who you can't leave at home but can't drag along with you either, and it's frankly impossible. As Sport England data from 2018–19 showed, inactivity was rooted in lower socio-economic groups, with the study noting that 'those in routine/semi-routine jobs and those who are long-term unemployed or have never worked are the least likely to be active'.[9] Affluent families, Sport England reported, are consistently more likely to bring up active kids. This isn't surprising when you consider the obstacles for the less affluent to play the games they love, let alone discover new ones.[10]

BRIDGING THE GENDER DIVIDE

The challenges we encountered in the teenage years of the century were not only at a class level. We've also come across consistent research suggesting some harder-to-attract groups

– in particular women – felt disenchanted by the sport they could access in their communities and found many of the opportunities open to them intimidating. Who wants to run in a badly lit park on a dark winter evening? Or attend a yoga class when you've never done yoga before and don't have a mat? One outstanding attempt at tackling this issue came in the form of Sport England's 'This Girl Can' campaign, which launched in 2015. The high-energy launch clip showed women of all different shapes, sizes, ethnicities, circumstances and ages being active in myriad ways. These weren't elite athletes, rather normal women with normal lives, all buzzing off endorphins. Tanya Joseph, a marketing and communications expert who had previously been Prime Minister Tony Blair's press officer, cooked up the idea on arriving at Sport England. 'I found a statistic that was really interesting – 70 per cent of women said they'd like to be active, yet they weren't,' she says. 'We thought, this is a massive market. We need to go after it because if *we* don't go after it, who will? This needs to be a behaviour-change campaign – we have people who say they want to do something and are not doing it. What is stopping them?' Sport England's research pinpointed three main barriers to activity: women worried about their appearance, their sporting ability (either that they weren't good enough or they were too good) and having the time to exercise. The campaign was designed to address these issues. 'We said, these are feelings that everyone feels,' says Tanya. 'You are not alone. Rather than make you feel bad for not exercising, let's show you women who face those same struggles and have found a way of being active. Let's show you women doing it on their own terms and for themselves.' It certainly struck a chord, with 2.8 million women inspired to become active. It was the most successful intervention that Sport England has ever made.

INSIDER INSIGHT: **TANYA JOSEPH**

During her time at Sport England, Tanya was the marketing whizz behind 2015's 'This Girl Can' campaign, which encouraged women to become active. It was the most successful intervention the organisation has ever made and continues to this day. Currently managing director at global PR firm Hill+Knowlton Strategies, her previous roles included four years as then-Prime Minister Tony Blair's press officer.

What sparked 'This Girl Can'?

When I got to Sport England I realised there was an inequity in the way the money, which comes from Lottery funds and taxpayers, was invested and the impact that investment was having. No matter what Sport England did, the gap between the number of men and women being active was always massive – 2 million fewer women than men each week. To me this seemed really bad from a public policy point of view – if you have an active woman in a household, the whole family is more likely to be healthy, the children are likely to do better at school and you're less likely to suffer from health conditions that burden the NHS. But also it was bad from an equity point of view – women play the Lottery and pay their taxes so they should get a share of the pie too. It took a long while to persuade the Sport England board they needed to venture into this territory. It was very new for them. They'd traditionally invested in *things* – places, kit, equipment – and people already interested in being active. But what we said to women with the campaign was: it doesn't matter if you run like Paula Radcliffe or Phoebe from *Friends*, the point is you're doing something.

It was a huge success, encouraging 2.8 million women to be active. Have those women continued to be so?

There was a huge cultural shift: women's attitudes to sport changed and sports providers have changed. The Rugby Football Union now know you can't wait for women to walk past a rugby club and venture in. You have to go to where they are and talk to them – so they go into nail bars and show their players having nice nails, subsequently busting the myth that you can't play sport and look good. The numbers of women being active had been sustained but we have seen that the pandemic hit women's free time harder than men's. I'm really worried about the impact on women's physical and mental wellbeing.

What still needs to be done to increase participation of hard-to-reach groups?

Every single sport needs to thinks about provision through the eyes of the consumer. Too often big sports organisations are run by people who are fanatical about sport and who don't understand why people wouldn't do it. Although it's very different now, Sport England used to be like this. When I joined, no one could understand me because I would say, 'I don't like doing sport, only watching it.' Running is the one thing I got into but when I told my colleagues, they immediately said, 'Ooh, we'll get you a place in the London Marathon!' I was, like, 'Why?! I like to go for half an hour, I can listen to music and no one nags me. That's all I want. I don't want it to be a competition, I just want to do it on my own terms.' But most of sport is run by people who are enthusiasts and they find it very difficult to put themselves in the shoes of someone for whom it's not the most important thing in their lives.

Your predictions – and hopes – for the future of sport?

We're seeing more sports getting it in terms of broadening participation. People like Chris Grant who sits on the board of Sport England are willing to take a stand and talk about the things that those of us who are non-White have been saying for a really long time. I really applaud him. Sport England did a great job in really difficult circumstances during the pandemic in encouraging people to keep active. I'd like to see a strategy to support activities that aren't club-based because I think that'd really support female participation. This could be a really exciting time for sport. We've realised how essential sport is when our mental and physical wellbeing are under attack.

What happened after London 2012, then, was that the public sector started to struggle with its side of the bargain to build and maintain the infrastructure that enables people to exercise. As a result, the right to be active began to veer away from being a fairly basic human right to something that could at times feel difficult to access, or intimidating, or came with a price tag, or all of the above. While the sporty got sportier and the fit got fitter, those on the periphery were pushed away through lack of exposure at school, booked-out sports halls and the unappealing and/or unaffordable notion of monthly commitments to gyms. Many women were finding it hard to find time to exercise. Race was also tied up in this, something we'll explore later on. Children weren't always getting their school PE fix, and the ones who particularly missed out were the ones whose parents couldn't get them to after-school clubs and who didn't have gardens in which to burn off energy. The sporting class divide widened.

Just like sport, health also felt the impact of public austerity at a level we have yet to truly comprehend. The NHS were struggling with the same per-head budget cuts as schools and so spent the millennium's teenage years stuck in a world of cure rather than prevention. This created a ticking time bomb. Analysis of data from the National Child Measurement Programme between 2006–17 revealed trends in severe obesity among primary school-aged children for the first time. In 2006, 2.6 per cent of Year Six girls were severely obese, rising to 3.33 per cent in 2016/17. The proportion of severely obese Year Six boys increased from 3.7 per cent to 4.78 per cent over the same time period.

This toxic combination of inactivity and healthcare budget decline doesn't, of course, mean that the game is up. People still play, just not evenly. So in order to be a force for good among new communities as well as existing ones, sport needs to work out how to succeed in a country where the inequality gap is stubbornly consistent, and at risk of increasing. We've done it before – but this time around, Cadbury and Boots aren't going to build new facilities for their workers, encourage women to exercise on their own terms or proactively educate the community as to how to stay healthy.

We need to be smarter and think harder. Not just to solve the class, ethnicity and gender divides but also because there is now another significant division in our nation – a generational schism. Towards the end of the twentieth century and at the dawn of the new one, generational change in Britain had evolved fairly gently. But that was about to change.

A GENERATIONAL TIPPING POINT

To understand how the generational divide impacts us all, we need to stop off at the Brexit 2016 decision and its immediate aftermath. Don't worry, we won't stay there long.

It's well-documented that younger generations were more inclined to vote for the UK to remain in the European Union rather than leave, with 73 per cent of people under the age of 24 voting Remain. By 2017, for the first time in Britain, age was more significant than income in predicting voting intention.

Just think about that for a minute. Despite the widening inequality gap in this country since 2008, the food banks and hospital waiting lists, age was actually a bigger driver of whether voters plumped to keep the Conservative Party in power to navigate the stormy post-Brexit waters. Mind the generation gap – it's so vast now you can easily fall into it and never clamber back out. But to unpick how sport can change this country, we need to understand the differences in generational perception and how this plays out in the sporting arena.

There are four main generational groups in Britain today:

Generation Z: Our youngest group, currently in their early twenties, teens or younger. They were born in 1997 or later.

Millennials: Those born between 1980 and the mid-1990s. Note the oldest millennials are now pushing 40, so when older people use the term, often derisively, as short-hand for 'young people' (e.g. to insult them for blowing too much money on avocados when they could be saving to buy a house), they're off the mark.

Generation X: Now middle-aged, they were born between the mid-1960s and 1980.

Baby boomers: Those born between the end of the Second World War and the mid-1960s, so many are now retired.

This manner of segmenting people is not an exact science and, by necessity, hugely stereotypical. My mum and dad, for example, buck almost every baby boomer pattern I am about to walk through. However, I know many other people (and in fact, far more) whose views, experiences and life-styles do broadly fit these categories. On balance, I think it's worth exploring these generational demographics because this insight is a useful tool to help us understand how and why sport will change.

The year 2017 did not just see a seismic shift in drivers of voting preferences. It was also the year that the millennials became the largest generation in the British workforce, as a record number of baby boomers headed to retirement. This millennial cohort is significant not only because this is the generation who are going to be leading our businesses and governments in ten years' time, but also defining the way in which sport develops. So to predict the future of sport, we need to understand them. Along with Generation Z, who will follow in their wake, they think and act very, very differently to previous generations.

The millennial worldview, so the story goes, is heavily shaped by recent global events – first 9/11 and then the 2008 financial crisis, around which time they likely entered the labour market. They're fortunate if they have yet managed to enter the property market at all. As a result, they've started to form a much broader worldview. Gathering experiences matters more to them than possessions. They don't tend to resent the baby boomers for retiring in their early sixties, understanding they grafted extremely hard to get there and often pushed the extremities of social mobility to do so (and those baby boomers will likely be their grandparents or parents). That said, they do question the implications of this. Even if they're not as strident as Generation Z around the legacy of climate change and failure to address the inequality gaps, they do feel some of the responsibility for action, and remain frustrated that they're unable to buy a house or move on up like previous generations. They're envious of the concept of retiring on a generous, state-supported pension and aware they're unlikely to see that future for themselves, thanks to a public debt they are not responsible for creating. At the same time, as and when they enter parenthood, they're extremely grateful for the additional childcare options baby-boomer grandparents might offer.

Given the pace of change in Britain over the previous ten years, you'd be forgiven for thinking the millennials followed on directly after the baby boomers, as an extreme reaction to the significant changes of the last decade. But actually, there's a quiet, well-behaved (at least now) generation that sits between the two noisier cohorts. Generation X is where I sit. I was born in 1975, which makes me slightly more millennial than boomer and scratching my head awkwardly (and yet ever so politely) at the social chaos before me.

My generation, at least among my peers, seems to be caught chasing an impossible dream. We want the work–life balance we are all too aware our parents didn't have, but many of us made commitments and built families before the banking crisis changed the rules of the game. While we are lucky to be the last generation to own our homes as a norm, we know that means we are set to work longer than our parents, which in turn entails managing the pressures of an increasingly digital working life, which comes home with us daily on our smart-phones. We were not brought up on the internet (the closest I got during my degree was dabbling with a temperamental word processor), but we have had to learn sharpish.

At our best, we can balance the worlds of boomer and millennials with aplomb – mowing the lawn, paying down the mortgage, and simultaneously work out how to operate the smart TV, support the kids' online learning, navigate five different recycling bins and try out this mindfulness lark. At worst, we're too busy to do any of them properly (hence that aforementioned quietness – we're too busy to speak out) and haunted by the feeling that we're simply marking time waiting for the millennials to appear. We are wracked by political inde-cision and overseeing a country we've only changed incremen-tally since our parents' turn. In our hearts, we know our pathetic tinkering will be to the detriment of ours and forthcoming generations. We're caught between two generations with huge personalities and wildly different preferences, attempting bravely but slightly forlornly to reconcile the two as we struggle to keep the corridors of power intact and mark time before the millennials and Generation Z will truly push things on.

WHAT GENERATIONAL CHANGE MEANS FOR SPORT

For all the division in British society, sport is one thing – maybe the only remaining thing – that our generationally divided nation agrees about. Sport is a platform, a theme, a metaphor. It can be whatever we want it to be. For every generation, it works and has a fundamental role to play.

Let's start with the baby boomers. For all the pressure it is under, the NHS continues to do a spectacular job. When Britain won the right to host London 2012 in 2005, life expectancy for men was 77.2 years and women 81.4. In the period up until 2018 (and pre-COVID-19), King's Fund data suggests it increased to 79.6 and 83.2 respectively.[11]

It's not only a case of this generation living for longer but being healthier for longer. As recently as 20 years ago, certain sports were perceived as 'for older people' – bowls and golf, for example. Today that is not the reality. Sport England's Active Lives survey suggests that 60.3 per cent of 65- to 74-year-olds do at least 150 minutes of exercise a week.[12] That is *a lot* more than many people I know of my age. Baby boomers have got time on their hands and are enjoying an active retirement. In fact, when you look at who does at least two lots of exercise per month, baby boomers are close to being the most active of all groups. In 2019, there were 12.5 million boomers active in the UK. No wonder we are seeing new formats of much-loved games being developed – walking football, for example. This generation are refusing to pull on their slippers and put their feet up in front of the fire.

Generation X, meanwhile, grew up with a fairly polarised view of sport. For some, like me, it's been part of my life since childhood. I spent every weekend at the Iver Heath Tennis Club with my mum or Denham United Football Club with my dad. I've never known it any other way. And yet I took part in enough PE lessons at school to know that for many, sport was a far less compelling prospect. Getting into sport in the 1980s was a less forgiving process – cross country in February was what it was, take it or, well, hide in the woods until the end of the lesson.

My experience is that these preconceptions from our teenage years stayed with my generation until well into our thirties, and then something interesting started to happen. I started to notice on Facebook that some of my school friends from the PE refusenik brigade were starting to wear trainers. And they seemed to be – wait for it – going running.

When I asked them about it, the answers were strikingly similar: 'It's the only time I can get away.' 'It takes me some-where the kids can't find me.' 'It gives me the same buzz I used to get from clubbing.' (I tend not to ask too many questions about that one.) 'It's a chance for a proper gossip with my running buddy – you never know who's listening at the school gate.'

Whatever the specific motivation for this new sporty incarnation of Generation X, the broad theme is strikingly similar – it's sport for mental health at a crazily busy time in their lives, during the peak of family and working responsibilities. Despite having competed throughout my life, I, too, find that the mental break sport gives me is more important than anything else to me at this time of my life. I wrote most of this book after dawn runs (as did my co-author and fellow Gen X-er Kerry) because I find I can't focus otherwise.

One woman who has harnessed Generation X's new favourite hobby and, well, run with it is Mel Bound, founder of This Mum Runs (TMR). As a stressed, time-pressed mother of young children, she launched her running community in her hometown of Bristol in 2015. It began with a tentative Facebook post in a local mums' group asking if anyone wanted to come for a run with her. They sure did. Now TMR is a worldwide movement – both online and in person – of 100,000 mums, mainly aged between 36–55. 'Sport had been a huge part of my life – I was very active and worked in sports marketing,' says Mel. 'But I'd had an accident while out running off-road with my daughter in her pushchair, and slipped a disc. I needed surgery, which led to me becoming inactive for three years and losing all my confidence to exercise. This experience gave me a deep empathy for how so many women feel. I thought, *If I – someone really sporty – feel like it's really hard to take the first steps back to becoming active, how on earth must it be for other mums?*' When TMR members go running together there's an unwritten rule: 'We don't talk about our kids. It's about escape and headspace. It's about saying, "Actually I'm worthy of a couple of hours a week just for me."'

INSIDER INSIGHT: **MEL BOUND**

Despite being sporty from a young age and having a career in sports marketing, Bristol-based Mel had been inactive for three years when she had the idea for running community This Mum Runs. In 2014, while recovering from spinal surgery and juggling the demands of raising a young family, she tentatively set up a local running group via Facebook, unsure whether anyone would respond. Six years on, she heads up the world's largest running community for mums.

Your aim is to 'change how women feel about exercise'. Why does it need changing?

Before launch I spent several months looking at the barriers to exercise for women. The main one for inactive women is fear. The sorts of carrots dangled to be active are 'lose weight' or 'enter a race and get a personal best'. They're very goal-driven. For some women having those goals are a reason for starting but if they don't reach those goals they become the reason for stopping. We realised that if we could flip a switch to make women feel like they had permission to exercise simply because it made them feel a bit better, that was profoundly powerful. This is because firstly women find it difficult to give themselves permission to do anything that's just for themselves and secondly that aim felt achievable and sustainable. It's about long-term behaviour change around exercise. It's about how we can take a woman who's been inactive for decades and change that mindset so she's active for the rest of her life. The only way you can do that is if you change how you feel about it.

What do women typically say to you about This Mum Runs?

Community is the key thing. That's a powerful driver for women, particularly the women who are able to connect offline and meet in real life too. Being able to forge those connections with local women is everything. I've had countless messages from people saying it's literally transformed their life. They'd done no exercise since school because they'd been scarred by PE.

So many people have those PE horror stories – does something need to change in how PE is taught in schools?

Yes, I think so. I'm chronically asthmatic and when I was a child the doctor told me that being more active would help. So I fell into being sporty. But I did feel it was profoundly unfair that the kids who weren't good were excluded or the ones who tried really hard didn't get any recognition. When I left my secondary school, I left a trophy to be awarded to whoever had tried the hardest. The way PE was taught was putting girls off sport. It's got even worse, even less inclusive. The curriculum pressures on schools are so huge there's no time to give value to sport. Then there are the stereotypes around what sports girls 'should' do, boys telling them they can't do it and so on.

Have you considered launching This Dad Runs?

We bought the URL for This Dad Runs and we own the trademark. The intention is there to do something but I think it'll look different. That need for social connection and willingness to be an active part of a community is not something that comes that easily to men. The proposition is about carving out time for yourself and I don't think men need that in the same way. It's a bit of a stereotype but I don't think there are the same pressures on dads as mums.

What's next for This Mum Runs?

We've launched an app to try to reach those women who are currently inactive and support them to take that first step. We need to work on how we reach younger mums. We're also quite middle class so how do we go into more socially deprived areas? What are the needs of those women and how do we best support them? And we've been working with mums all over the world – India, Singapore, Canada, New Zealand and various parts of Europe. Their attitudes to exercise and the barriers are the same. It's pretty universal.

Your predictions – and hopes – for the future of sport?

So much has been thrown up in the air by the pandemic. I think there will be a surge in participation in accessible sports, like cycling and running, driven by people who didn't think they could participate before. Brands will be interested in working with organisations that are helping support people with their physical and mental health coming out of a crisis. Rather than those big-ticket things, like sponsoring Premiership football, brands will start to look at organisations that make a genuine difference at grassroots level. The pandemic has shown us all that community is everything, and that human connections are powerful and can drive change.

Then we come to the millennial group and sport. Rather than search for existing sports that fit the realities of their working lives, as Generation X have done, they've simply tried whatever activity takes their fancy and had little care for definitions and structure. Take the explosion in gym memberships in the UK we noted earlier, driven principally by the millennial demographic, for whom it offered an alternative – and more preferable – form of social interaction to the pub. For many it was an either/or choice given the tightness of their finances, and the treadmill and smoothie bar won. According to a global survey by fitness-industry brand Les Mills, millennials and Generation Z represent more than 80 per cent of global gym memberships.[13]

People-watching in gyms is fascinating. Generation X turn up ready to go; head to a class or a treadmill, earphones in, and disappear as quickly as they arrived. Millennials and Generation Z take time both sides of their class or session, chat along the way and tend to round off the trip with a green juice or coffee in the café afterwards. Neither is better, they're just different. Baby boomers take time to exercise properly and look like they get the best workout of all.

It's not just playing sport and keeping fit that still works for all demographics – it's true of watching the action also. Not only has the number of people attending sports events continued to rise after London 2012, according to research by Two Circles (the sports agency that my wife Claire and I co-founded) it's made Britain the only country in the world for whom total sporting attendance each year is bigger than its actual population, which means many people are attending multiple events.[14]

The trends are most revealing when you look at the growth areas for this love of live action. Two Circles research shows that the percentage of tickets bought by 16- to 24-year-olds has leaped from 15 to 23 per cent in the years since the London

Olympics. Sports like cricket have done a terrific job of repackaging their product to be more appealing to millennials' desire for experiences over physical possessions, offering a balance of opportunities to watch women as well as men in action. For example, the sold-out Women's Cricket World Cup final at Lord's in 2017 contained 65 per cent of match-goers who were new to cricket, and a 45 per cent female audience.[15]

It's simplistic (but not too far from the truth) to say millennials and Generation Z prefer an experience to owning things, baby boomers have the cash and time to be able to do both, and Generation X will dip in when they can, in search of escapism, assuming that kids' tickets or a babysitter are readily available. Sport can meet all of these needs, sometimes even simultaneously. parkrun, with its free Saturday morning group 5k runs (or walks) that have seen phenomenal growth in public parks across Britain and now overseas, is a great example. Boomers run, jog, volunteer and use their coffee loyalty cards at the café afterwards. Generation X either turn up with the dog and kids or leave the world at home, but, either way, are back home by ten o'clock. Millennials take part and then head off with friends for a lazy brunch. Generation Z, meanwhile, grew up with parkrun as an option for an active start to the weekend and are far more likely than their elders to be able to make a nine o'clock Saturday start without a hangover . . .

What came across loud and clear from the teens and early twentysomethings we spoke to while researching this book is that Generation Z are even more relaxed about definitions and boundaries around sport than millennials. Ellie Peart, a 21-year-old graduate and daughter of ultra-runner Sonny Peart, who'll we meet later, is typical of her cohort. 'Oh, I'm not sporty,' she says breezily, before revealing that, having danced since the age of five, she competed for her university in Latin and ballroom dancing. 'I just see it as a hobby, a social activity. The fitness side is a bonus,' she shrugs. Cordi Mahony, an 18-year-old rower who competes at national level and took part in our Generation Z panel debate below, suggests the best way to bring more young people into sport is to 'make it enjoyable without making it seem like sport. Put the emphasis on being active. Doing laser tag, for example, gets you moving but it doesn't feel like you are doing a sport.' Pushy parents, take note.

INSIDER INSIGHT:
GENERATION Z PANEL

Alfie Beckett, Lucy Denly and Cordi Mahony are all sport-loving members of Generation Z. Alfie, 18, has played rugby since the age of six, going on to represent Oxfordshire, Wasps Academy and latterly Ealing Trailfinders Academy. He's currently studying at Brunel University. Lucy, 21, played netball, athletics, basketball and rounders for her school, plus tennis and hockey at county level. She studies at Oxford University where she has captained the blues tennis team. She's recently taken up climbing. Cordi, 18, has been rowing for six years during which time she's won three national gold medals and was hoping to be selected for the 2020 World Junior Championships (which were cancelled due to COVID-19). Next stop: studying at Princeton University on a sports scholarship.

What was it about playing sport that hooked you?

Alfie: The friendship that comes with it. I wouldn't have kept going if it wasn't so fun.

Cordi: Having a very sporty family, it was just always something that I did. Also playing team sports gave me that sense of community. And it's taught me a lot in terms of life lessons. Having the desire to perform in sport has massively helped me academically but at the same time it's given me something separate to my academic stuff.

Lucy: I got into it because my family is very sporty, too, but I also liked the challenge of trying something new. I like that feeling of doing something quite challenging but getting a lot from it in return.

What is an elite athlete's role today? Do they have a duty to be a role model or activist?

Alfie: Being an elite athlete is a job more than it used to be and I think their role is to inspire others. It's not necessarily their role to share their views – they obviously can if they want to but it's not essential – but they should definitely be a role model in their own field, so maintain excellent discipline and things like that.

Lucy: Lots of athletes use their platforms to campaign now. In the sports I'm involved in, particularly tennis, you get athletes who do a lot of that – like how Serena Williams is a big supporter of women's and Black people's rights – and athletes who don't do any of it, and those athletes who do campaign are respected a lot more. Role models have always been important to me, especially when I'm getting into a sport. Now I'm doing some rock climbing and just looking at the Instagram of someone like Shauna Coxsey makes me want to get into it.

What is your personal definition of sport?

Alfie: A physical activity that allows you to have fun and express yourself in different ways.

Lucy: I'd say it's a physical, mental and emotional challenge.

Cordi: A physical activity that involves mental and emotional challenge.

Some people say that skateboarding or breakdancing aren't sports, yet both are soon to be included in the Olympics. Thoughts?

Alfie: They are sports, but they're not conventional sports. They both require a huge amount of skill and attention to detail.

Lucy: They are sports and they have the right to be in the Olympics. There's a lot of discussion now about online sports like gaming – I'm not sure where I stand on that, because I don't see that as much of a physical challenge but equally it could be conceived as a sport because of its competitive nature.

Cordi: The thing about sport is to be the best at what you do requires a lot of hours to go into it, so you can't dismiss something that someone has put hours of practice into just because it's not in the Olympics.

How can we engage young people who aren't traditionally sporty?

Alfie: Introduce more variety to schools because everyone follows pretty much the same curriculum, so give people more opportunity to try new sports. Then I'd supplement that with grassroots-level stuff – focus on getting kids into sports clubs.

Lucy: Taking away the competitive aspect could be a good thing, because lots of kids view themselves as not sporty because of PE lessons, so they box themselves into that group. But if we take out the competitive element, that would hopefully stop people from ranking themselves within their own peer groups. The competitive aspect can come in from when you're five years old, which leads to parents getting pushy. That can take away from the enjoyment and cause a big dropout rate.

What do you think older generations get wrong about sport?

Cordi: You see pushy parents trying to live their failed sporting dreams through their children. And sometimes people let competition take over from the real reasons people started playing sport in the first place. Too much of a focus on winning or losing, rather than the athlete's journey as a whole, can be made so much worse by the media.

Generation Z seem very aware of the mental health benefits of sport. Discuss ...

Cordi: Mental health in sport isn't spoken about enough, especially for young athletes. It's difficult to find a balance between wanting to perform and massively obsessing over it in an unhealthy way. With rowing, if you are struggling mentally, it's difficult to voice those worries because you don't want to come across as weak to coaches. This is something that needs to change. It's definitely spoken about more, with teams having more psychologists now. I've seen a psychologist for the past year and that's helped me so much, performance-wise, but still I get questions from people who don't understand why I do this.

What are your predictions – and hopes – for the future of sport?

Cordi: There's a movement away from sports that increase inequalities. For example, rowing is such an expensive sport that there's a very narrow demographic who take part. In the future we're likely to see sports like that being removed from the Olympics to make a more level playing field. I also think sport is becoming more creative – like skateboarding being in the Olympics – so there will be more respect for sports like skateboarding, as they increase in popularity.

Lucy: I'd like it to be more inclusive. One of the main debates in sport going forward will be what happens with transgender and intersex athletes, as we gain more information on the physical and biological side of it. At the moment, lots of intersex and transgender people are put off from playing sport because there's such a stigma. Sports like tennis and hockey, which are predominantly regarded as 'private school sports', also should become more inclusive. It'd be nice to see a lot more diversity in who plays what.

And so we return to our timeline, and the highs and lows of the teenage years of the twenty-first century. We saw all the thrilling potential swagger of a joined-up Olympic Britain but then, as the decade progressed, looked on helplessly as it fractured, along social, generational and political fault lines (and we've not even mentioned race yet). But, crucially, it did not break entirely, not even as the decade hurtled to a chaotic end in 2019. Ours is a challenged nation, no doubt. But it is also one where our thirst for live sport continues to grow and our participation ticks gently upwards, despite it being trickier for many of us to get involved. We almost broke as a nation, but we didn't – and that's partly because of sport. We agree on very little but with sport we find community and common ground – in gold medals, a jog with a friend or even just a wander outdoors. The future powerhouse generations – millennials and Generation Z – are far more attuned to their health than their elders, preferring to lift weights than down pints, even if they have to fork out to do so. Which is music to the ears of our cash-strapped NHS.

As the balance of power changes – both in life and sport – our future will no longer be defined by generations who have grown up in an era where professional athletes were put on a pedestal, where school PE was polarising, where 'sport' had to have rules and teams, and was still rife with gender stereotyping. New generations will live life in a healthier, more inclusive way. They will be more challenging of class and gender divides, and more flexible in how they view the role of sport. They'll also be more interested in going to a game than buying clothes. While generational change has caused some material schisms in society, the passing of time should be the catalyst to delivering on sport's true potential.

We exited the century's difficult teenage years with the best of times yet to come.

CHAPTER 3 / Athlete Activism and the New Recipe for Changing the Game

Boston is the world's oldest marathon, having started with 15 runners in 1897. In running circles, it is what Wimbledon is to tennis – both an iconic part of running's history, but also a key influence to this day. The difference with the Boston Marathon is that keen amateurs like me get to take part alongside the best in the world.

After the events of 2013, however, I wasn't sure that it was my place to be on that starting line in 2014. Maybe, I thought, it was best to leave the city to heal itself after the bombings and, to use the language adopted by the locals, 'reclaim the finish line'. On the other hand, perhaps 2014's race was an important part of the process of getting back to business as usual. In the end, I decided to go and give it everything I had, to run bravely and have no regrets that I'd given anything other than my very best effort.

I wasn't alone in that conclusion. The running community's collective response to Boston was to run down fear, with the race receiving four times the number of entries it had previously.

The build-up to the race – picking up my number, getting up at the crack of dawn to head over to the start – felt very similar to other big-city marathons I have done. However, in the hour before the race, as the organisers paid a tribute to those who had been impacted by the bombing the year before, the daunting significance of this year's run really started to hit home. I stood shoulder to shoulder, in silence, with runners of all nationalities, reflecting on the previous year's race. After the national anthem at the start, tears were silently running down everyone's cheeks. On that sunny spring morning, it was clear to everyone present that Boston 2014 would be both appropriately different, but also defiantly the same.

I set off exactly as I planned. Boston is notoriously tough to pace as the first half is predominantly downhill, with a sting in the tail towards the end in the shape of a series of challenging hills. I was a touch quicker than I should have been through the first half; only 45 seconds to a minute but that's enough to make a difference. As a result, things got tough towards the end as those hills kicked in but this meant I would deliver on my promise to myself to leave not a trace of energy out on the course. As I left the seemingly endless inclines and slowed to pick up water at an aid station, I heard volunteers saying Meb Keflezighi had just crossed the finish line to become the first American man to win the Boston Marathon since 1983.[16]

Meb Keflezighi wasn't just any American winner of the Boston Marathon as he tore through the streets in front of me. Behind the historical nature of his victory, his journey told the story of America's struggles to come to terms with its changing identity. He was born in war-torn Eritrea and made the move to the United States as an immigrant, aged 12. When he won the New York City marathon in 2009, there was some debate over whether he was 'really' American. But in an interview with *Time* magazine, Keflezighi said he might not have become a runner had he not become a US citizen. 'I ran my first mile here,' he said. 'I didn't know the sport was an option in Eritrea.' His victory was the perfect riposte to the terrorism of 2013 that was haunting, and yet driving the 2014 race forward.

Despite the extra security and my own weariness, the final miles felt like one long celebration among the crowds lining the streets. As I finished, I was confronted by a bear of a steward who spotted the Union Jack depicting my nationality on my running number. I could hardly focus on anything by that point, but I remember vividly the look in his eyes. He gave me a massive hug (I think the expression 'bear hug' was created for him) and said, 'Thanks for coming this year, it means so much to our city.'[17]

Boston had experienced the worst of times but during my trip to Boston I had experienced the best of them. That race will stay with me forever. There are few things in life that can beat sport's ability to unexpectedly bring us together when we are most likely to be torn apart. This magic touch was much needed across the Atlantic, too, as Britain unravelled in the years that followed.

Back with a bump to Britain in December 2019. A world in which the problems of the preceding decade were worsening rather than improving. But despite the gloominess and for all the wrangles in the divorce courts of the EU, something more positive was brewing. Sport had started, just started, to respond.

The changes that were afoot weren't the stuff of news reports and column inches – good news stories that take a bit of piecing together rarely are, not least when there is enough bleak stuff to fill a paper several times over every day.

Rather than tackling public debt, a divided nation and changing tastes in how people view and participate head-on, sport had started to work around these obstacles. There wasn't any grand, coordinated plan but a series of small organic changes taking place across the country, in different realms.

They might have been easy to miss but the signs were there. Evolving values, new sports, a fresh understanding of the impact sport can have on broader society and a clutch of innovative ideas popping up to solve specific problems. These were addressing issues that weren't only affecting sport itself, but were also impacting on related areas – health, widening access, social change, even climate change.

Many of these ideas involved doing things very differently and thinking creatively to make a difference in a world where money was very often too tight to mention. They meant building new models and relationships between the private and public sector, entrepreneurs and volunteers, to create a new recipe for success.

With my ear to the ground, I started to sense that some creative people across the country were slowly – perhaps even unwittingly – starting to build a very effective antidote for many of Britain's biggest problems, with tools in the form of social media at their disposal to make change happen.

NEW VALUES

Meb Keflezighi's influence in the United States endures through his leadership of a foundation promoting health, education and fitness for youngsters.

A foundation of this nature would have been bigger news in 2014. Nowadays it's increasingly common in a new breed of athletes who, empowered by social media, see the opportunity to make a material difference to society. This hasn't always been straightforward – at the same time as Keflezighi was retiring from running in late 2016, a storm was brewing in his adopted country. Before a game, American football player Colin Kaepernick, knelt during the national anthem to protest at what he perceived as systemic racism and violence in American society against people of colour, echoing the protests of Smith and Carlos at the Mexico Olympic Games. As with his historical counterparts, Kaepernick's gesture initially led to rejection – he was ostracised from the National Football League and criticised by Donald Trump, the president at the time. But his time would come.

By contrast, over in Britain the trickle of athletes seeing it as their role to express their views as explicitly as Kaepernick was becoming a torrent. England footballer Raheem Sterling subverted his bad-boy image and gained positive front- and back-page coverage for his proactive stance against systemic racism here in the UK; his influence reaching as far as the *Financial Times*, who dubbed him a 'fleet-footed freedom fighter' in 2019.

As the newspaper put it, Sterling 'triggered a national discussion about how Black sporting success is portrayed in the media'. The coverage of Sterling in the tabloid press has been noticeably more positive ever since. Emboldened, the footballer has continued to make more public interventions, such as calling for points deductions against teams whose supporters engage in racist chanting. The debate continues among fans, players, coaches and officials. Sterling has made the issue of racism in football impossible to ignore. 'If I don't do it, if the one after me doesn't do it, it will just keep going,' he says. 'When football is finished, will I live off what I did on the field? No. I want to be able to help people be the best they can be.'[18]

Born in Jamaica, Sterling moved to central London at the age of five with his mother.[19] He progressed quickly in his sport and was the subject of big-money transfers to teams in the north of England; a move approved by his mum who was concerned about the potential impact of gang culture on her young son in the capital. Accusations on that theme later surfaced, ahead of the FIFA 2018 World Cup, with controversy about his tattoo of an M16 assault rifle. However, a post on his Instagram account told a different story. 'When I was two my father died from being gunned down to death,' he wrote. 'I made a promise to myself I would never touch a gun in my lifetime. I shoot with my right foot so it has a deeper meaning.' What was striking was not only the candour with which Sterling defended himself, but also that social media enabled him to do so directly.

Sterling's influence continues as one of seven sportspeople named in the Powerlist 2020, a list of the 100 most influential people of African or African Caribbean heritage in the United Kingdom.[20] He belongs to a generation far less willing to keep their heads down and 'just' play football. Instead, they're prepared to use their influence to fight injustice. Sterling was the start of that wave.

We'll look in detail at how the pandemic shook up sport in the next chapter but it's remiss to write about the rise of the sports star as social activist without mentioning Marcus Rashford. The then 22-year-old Manchester United forward became a national hero in 2020, thanks to his efforts to ensure disadvantaged children, for whom their free hot school lunch might be their only proper meal of the day, were fed during the holidays. He used his influence to consistently pressure the government over its free school meals voucher scheme, which was put in place when the COVID-19 lockdown began. It was initially due to close at the end of the summer term of 2020, leaving 1.3 million children from the poorest families in the UK, many of whom particularly hard hit by the pandemic's impact on jobs and personal finances, without a guaranteed meal during the six-week school holidays. Rashford wrote an eloquent open letter to the country's 650 MPs, detailing his own childhood experiences, which he deftly leveraged to draw support for his cause, and making the government look wildly out of touch with the harsh realities of many people's lives in the process. His mother Melanie, a single parent, struggled to feed her five children. 'The system was not built for families like mine to succeed, regardless of how hard my mum worked,' he said. 'As a family, we relied on breakfast clubs, free school meals, and the kind actions of neighbours and coaches.' The government duly made a U-turn and extended the scheme. Combating food poverty had been in Rashford's sights for a while – he'd already raised £20 million to feed 3 million children per week through his championing of charity FareShare. Before the year was out, he was honoured with an MBE for his efforts.

Digital technology, of course, is a very powerful tool with regard to athlete activism. There is a perfect storm here in that fans increasingly demand to see behind the scenes; to observe how sports stars live their lives off, as well as on, the pitch. Nearly 10 million people follow Marcus Rashford on Instagram, while 7.5 million follow Raheem Sterling. It's a fanbase the latter in particular uses to good effect, blending insight into his daily life with social comment and interviews from other sportspeople, including Megan Rapinoe, star of the US women's soccer team and advocate for several LGBT organisations. Social media channels offer sports stars the chance to champion their causes, break down the stereotypes about them, and share their viewpoints directly, in ways that often challenge the prevailing mood of the day.

Around the turn of the decade, Britain was starting to see new, successful role models, many of whom had moved on from tough upbringings, emerge across the sporting landscape. British Olympic gold medallist and world heavyweight boxing champion Anthony Joshua had brushes with the law. 'To me what boxing meant was a way to better myself. It helped me as a person and changed my outlook on life,' he says.[21] Sport helped Joshua rehabilitate himself but also it is the platform from which he can now advocate a better route to others.

As the end of the decade approached, a close friend of Joshua, a star from the music world who had performed the boxer's ring-entry music, was equally instrumental in encouraging young Black Britons to call out injustice and make themselves heard. One of the headline acts of Glastonbury Festival in 2019 was grime artist Stormzy, the British rapper, singer and songwriter – and, like Joshua, a man with a hard-knock London upbringing. Only the second rap act to headline the festival, he has a history of political activism, including calling out the prime minister for a lack of action over the Grenfell Tower fire of 2017.

In the past, high-profile musicians have typically been more adept than sportspeople at calling for social change. Sportspeople have historically had to play by the rules – not only of their game, but also their teams. Their identity (and commercial opportunity) is derived from their place within a football team, or on a golf leaderboard. Musicians, on the other hand, are more likely to control their own destinies. They write their own lyrics and music, and commercial opportunity often comes from being a totally different proposition to the rest. And if they're a solo star, they don't have any bandmates to worry about.

Stormzy has taken political activism in music to a new level. He appeared at Glastonbury wearing a bulletproof vest, with a Union Jack design. He is passionate about the importance of education, but that view does not come with a resentment of traditional academic routes, rather a desire to enable access for all. He has put his money where his mouth is, partnering with Cambridge University to fund the Stormzy Scholarship for

Black British students. Even as a music artist, he sees the role that sport, as well as music, can play in supporting young Black Britons, and has visited local boxing clubs on several occasions to support their rehabilitative role.[22]

The music industry has shown the world of sport how to find its voice in recent years. The boundaries between the two industries have blurred – Rashford is expertly managed by Roc Nation, US rapper Jay-Z's management agency that now has a flourishing sports arm in the UK.

If sport's biggest stars had been playing catch-up with music's new socially conscious vanguard – had taken longer to find their voices and the confidence to use them – 2019 was certainly the tipping point. Two weeks after the US women's soccer team led by Megan Rapinoe won the FIFA World Cup, she was still goading President Trump. In reference to the President's admiration for 'sportspeople, winners, Team America', she said, 'We are everything he loves – with the exception that we're powerful, strong women.'[23] Suddenly female sportspeople were not only deserving of equal representation but demanding of them.

It wasn't only that athletes, Generation Z or millennials conditioned to wear their hearts on their sleeves were prepared to stand up for their beliefs, but also that they were met by large tranches of society not only willing and (thanks to digital) able to listen, but actively looking for an antidote to a political class and institution that they don't identify with, let alone trust. As Rapinoe told the *Guardian*: 'How can you see all the shit that's happening and not say anything? Everyone has the responsibility to do their part – I just happen to be naturally very confident, and it seems that people listen to me.'

Where eyeballs go, businesses follow. Sports brands were quick to pick up on the change in public sentiment. Nike launched a campaign in support of Colin Kaepernick in 2018 with the strapline: 'Believe in something. Even if it means sacrificing everything.' In taking this line, the brand risked the wrath of the NFL, a long-time partner – and the White House. 'Nike is getting absolutely killed with anger and boycotts,' retorted President Trump. In fact, Nike's sales increased steadily by over 30 per cent in the aftermath and it claimed $6 billion of additional brand value from the campaign.

As the decade came to an end, we hadn't just learnt that athletes were coming out of the shadows, but also that digital and demography combined were providing an audience receptive to their messages. Social media advocacy – essentially the voice of younger generations – was ultimately more important to Nike than that of the US President in driving their agenda forward.[24]

A streetwise brand like Nike wasn't the only business to play a role in righting former wrongs in terms of racial inequality in the United States. Strange as it may seem, breakfast cereals also played a role in showing how far the country had come. In this case, they provided a level of vindication for Tommie Smith, who as we mentioned earlier was thrown out of the American team at the Mexico 1968 Olympics. In 2020, Smith received the ultimate symbol of national recognition for a sportsperson in the Unites States. Over 50 years after being banished by his team, he joined the likes of Michael Jordan, Andre Agassi and Serena Williams and was featured on the front of the pack of Wheaties, America's favourite breakfast cereal; a tradition that stretches back to the early 1930s. By extending the invitation, Middle America was finally recognising and celebrating the importance of Smith's gesture – albeit far too late. Wheaties owner General Mills said, 'We're celebrating one of the original activist athletes who defined a movement by raising his fist in protest of racial inequality.' Even in America the debate on race inequality was changing fast, with sport very much to the fore.

It was not only on issues of politics and race that athletes were speaking out. The year 2019 also saw significant improvements in understanding how sportspeople's lives on the pitch impacted on their mental health – and a far greater willingness to discuss it. The Professional Footballers' Association and the charity Sporting Chance reported a six-fold increase in professional footballers seeking mental health support since 2013.[25] Football has traditionally been unwilling or unable to open up to these realities. Former Chelsea Football Club star player and manager Frank Lampard told a BBC documentary, created in partnership with Prince William's organisation Heads Together: 'During my playing days we were stuck in the stone age in many ways. I was certainly at fault for it. Now I look back and go: "I wish there was a bit more maturity."'[26]

What's more, fans were given far greater insight into the challenges of competition. Japanese double Grand Slam tennis champion Naomi Osaka overtook Serena Williams as the best-paid women's athlete in a single year, with $37 million in earnings. Osaka's appeal stems from her on-court performance at an early age, her multicultural background (she has a Japanese mother and a Haitian American father) and her frank personality. Born in 1997, she looks set to become a force of nature in sport beyond tennis in the coming years – she recently became co-owner of a US women's football team, North Carolina Courage, inspired in part by the national team's battle for equal pay. She is loud and proud about being an activist and role model, declaring: 'As athletes we have a voice and I won't back down from using mine.'

She is also candid in the way she talks about mental health and her struggles to be the best player she can be. On Twitter, for example, she talked of 'the worst months of my life', admitting that she 'hadn't had fun playing tennis' in a good while. Osaka doesn't airbrush her emotional ups and downs; she lays them out there.

Women's tennis began advocating a more open approach, with the WTA Women's Tour putting microphones into conversations between players and coaches at the change of ends. While this insight into tennis tactics has been fascinating for hardcore tennis fans like me, the more general sports fan has been given an insight into quite how tormenting elite sport competition can be. 'I could hit 100 balls right,' Osaka said at a press conference, 'and the one ball that I hit wrong is the thing that I think about the entire time.'

This kind of openness has a two-fold benefit. Not only does it enable sporting authorities to understand the duty of care they have to their athletes, but also it encourages fans of those athletes to be similarly candid about their own tough times.

As the decade drew to a close, there was a growing understanding of just how pivotal a role sport could play in helping to manage the emerging mental health epidemic in the UK. Our understanding of the impact of sport on physical health was well documented, but until now knowledge of its effect on mental health had lagged behind. While not yet headline news, pilot GP surgeries were prescribing exercise to address mental as well as physical illness. Stormbreak, a small, pioneering charity in Poole, Dorset, which I support, offers children tools to develop mental coping skills through movement and exercise. As 2019 came to a close, it was beginning to receive some hugely exciting results from its pilot primary schools. We'll delve deeper into Stormbreak and other initiatives later. It's clear that 2019 was a year of sowing the seeds rather than reaping the results, but early signs were hugely promising.

WE CAN BE HEROES (AND NOT JUST FOR ONE DAY)

In *The Last Dance*, the wildly successful 2020 Netflix documentary series about Michael Jordan's career, the basketball megastar, who was idolised by millions across the globe, talks about how he didn't consider himself to be a role model or activist during his 1980s and 1990s imperial phase, despite being, arguably, the most famous – and potentially influential – sportsperson in the world at that time. He reflects on the criticism he received in 1990 when he was called on to endorse Black Democrat Harvey Gantt, former mayor of Charlotte in North Carolina, the state where Jordan grew up. Gantt was in a Senate race against Republican Jesse Helms, a man frequently accused of racism. Jordan, to the surprise of some, refused to back Gantt. 'Republicans buy sneakers too,' he said at the time, referring to his lucrative Nike endorsement deal. Thirty years later, the documentary finds Jordan in a less flippant, more reflective mood regarding his role off the court. 'I do commend Muhammad Ali for standing up for what he believed in but I never thought of myself as an activist,' he says. 'I thought of myself as a basketball player. I wasn't a politician when I was playing my sport. I was focused on my craft. Was that selfish? Probably. But that was my energy. That's where my energy was.' He continues: 'The way I go about my life is I set examples. If it inspires you? Great, I will continue to do that. If it doesn't? Then maybe I'm not the person you should be following.'

Through a 2020 lens, it's striking to hear an elite superstar athlete unwilling to engage with, let alone harness, his power and influence beyond the game. But for many years, sports stars weren't expected to be role models at all. Simon Oliveira, who has worked as an agent with celebrities including David Beckham, Andy Murray, Lewis Hamilton and One

Direction's Liam Payne, told the Unofficial Partner podcast: 'If you go back to the 1940s and 1950s there was an unofficial pact between celebrities and journalists where, for access to celebrities, it was agreed a private life stayed private. Then in the 1960s and 1970s counterculture period, it was important to have an edge and an opinion. To a degree, this is where we are now once again.'

During George Best's 1970s heyday and throughout the 1980s, however, tabloid culture dominated. In response, celebrities hired PR firms to protect their private lives. There's no doubt that this period created a culture of mutual distrust. High-profile sportspeople were shielded from the tabloids by their PR reps so the tabloids would up their efforts to land scoops, finding the action off the pitch fertile ground. During the 1990s, Premier League footballers became public enemy number one thanks to their sky-rocketing salaries in tandem with the louche behaviour of a significant minority. In truth, that louche behaviour was probably not surprising: if at that time you gave any group of 1,000 men between the ages of 18 and 35 – men who had skipped large parts of their education – a role that involved travel, a pressurised working environment and significant free time, and paid them tens of thousands of pounds a week, you'd see very similar problems. However, football is big news in Britain and with that comes responsibility. The tabloids brought a regular supply of very dirty linen into the public domain with the likes of Ryan Giggs, Adrian Mutu, John Terry and many more besides accused of disgraceful behaviour. The public was shocked at the ways in which they had allegedly misused their influence. And, as is always the case, the alleged behaviour of a few colours the perception of the entire group. Things went from bad to worse as even the players' wives and girlfriends (christened WAGs by the press) became headline news during

England's near-miss at the FIFA 2006 World Cup in Germany. Whether their partying distracted the players or not during the competition is open to some debate but it undoubtedly gave the public reason to believe the players' minds weren't totally on the job.

'I used to be embarrassed to say I was a professional footballer,' recalls Steve Gregory, who played in midfield for Bournemouth, AFC Wimbledon and Wycombe Wanderers between 2005–12. 'If I went for a haircut and the barber asked me what I did for a living, I'd lie. There was such a stigma – people used to hate footballers. Now there's definitely a much better relationship between footballers and the general public and I tell people about my playing career with pride rather than shame.' Steve's right – things are very different now. Part of it is a generational shift: younger millennial and Generation Z elite sportsmen and women are a more serious-minded and socially conscious bunch than previous cohorts, as are their non-sporting peers of the same age. This makes sense – we're living in far more serious, straitened and sober (in all senses) times.

INSIDER INSIGHT: STEVE GREGORY

Ex-professional footballer Steve played in midfield for Bournemouth, AFC Wimbledon and Wycombe Wanderers between 2005 and 2012. Now 33, he is co-founder of FitLife gym in rural Buckinghamshire; an inclusive, much-loved community hub.

How has professional football culture changed since you were playing?

The biggest change has been social media. Now sportspeople have a platform to communicate with a much bigger audience and can speak out on topics beyond their sport, which can be very positive – look at Marcus Rashford. On the flipside, as you become more famous, you get more abuse. I wasn't a high-profile Premiership footballer but I ended up deleting my Twitter account. I got fed up with getting messages telling me I'd had a crap game. I took the decision for my own performance and mental wellbeing.

But as a footballer you must be used to blokes in the stands shouting at you?

Yes and I was fine with that. When I stepped onto a pitch in front of thousands, I was thick-skinned. But I struggled when it was me sitting alone at home and an abusive message would ping on my phone. I wanted to draw a line between work and my personal life.

What's your take on the stereotype of the badly behaved footballer?

When I stepped up a level and signed to Bournemouth, I noticed that behaviour more – the higher up you play, the more you'll find individuals who live in their own bubble. Playing football every day and getting paid a lot of money really isn't the real world. But you are very young and you think it is, because it's all you know. Everything is done for you – your washing is done by the kitman, if you move to a new club you're found a new home so you don't have to interact with estate agents. Because I came up from lower leagues, I was doing all that myself already but there are players who'll go through young adult life and not even know what a council tax bill is because the club sorted it. So with that comes childish behaviour, spending too much time in nightclubs, not having inhibitions and making the wrong decisions.

There was a period when footballers were very unpopular.

Yes, and it's only now, with some distance, I tell people I used to be a professional footballer with pride rather than shame. I think today's footballers have learnt from that period 10–15 years ago. There's definitely a better relationship between them and the public.

Are the new generation more serious-minded?

It's more professional now. It comes down to there being more money from sponsors and TV so there has to be more professionalism, more discipline. Even ten years ago you could get away with bad behaviour, not having a great diet or missing training sessions.

They seem more comfortable with talking about their feelings now too.

Yes, footballers are more willing to be vulnerable, which is fantastic. I played with a guy who committed suicide at 23 – his wife had been unfaithful and he didn't talk about it. My dad passed away while I was playing and although my club were fantastic with me and my team wore black armbands for my first match afterwards, I didn't speak about it once with those players. Hopefully those things are behind us now as people are so much more open.

As a gym owner, how has the pandemic changed things?

It's put health at the forefront of everyone's mind – everything else is irrelevant if you don't have your health. People have now realised health is the number-one priority and have been willing to take care of themselves. As for the fitness industry itself, short term we'll struggle because we couldn't operate normally for months. But long term we'll benefit.

You're very inclusive at FitLife – you champion your whole community not just the ones with six-packs.

I thought the fitness industry was failing by aligning itself only with beautiful-looking people – that pushes the people who need the industry the most further away because they feel like they don't belong. On our social media, we showcase all the people who are benefitting from what we do, rather than those who just look great. So that could be an 80-year-old member. Our gym is for everyone and we make sure we portray that in the images we use.

Your predictions for the future of sport and fitness?

People are talking a lot about the Joe Wicks effect and whether fitness will go primarily online but I truly believe we are social beings. We've forgotten what it feels like to be in a dynamic group environment in a class, to chat face to face with a trainer. It won't all be virtual classes, people will still go to physical spaces for fitness.

INSIDER INSIGHT: STEVE GREGORY

As part of that transition Steve mentions, fans are able to make their own minds up about which players they want to get to know on a personal level and how players are living their lives. As Simon Oliveira says, 'I think we're now seeing a new generation come through. Because they own their own channels, you'll start to see these individuals and stars be more honest in what they're saying. Lewis Hamilton has set himself a challenge now – where he sees injustice he is going to call that out.'

The increasingly large sums of money involved in elite sport also come into play. Clubs are painstakingly performing their due diligence before they bring out their chequebooks. Sports agent Clifford Bloxham, senior vice president at Octagon, says: 'The clubs now focus on how players behave off the field. If it's a big signing, before the club commits they will send someone to watch them in social environments, to check out what they get up to at weekends. If you're investing £100 million in a player, you want to know what they're really like. That player will be intrinsically linked to the club's brand and that brand is becoming increasingly valuable. You don't want some Charlie devaluing it by behaving appallingly.'

INSIDER INSIGHT: CLIFFORD BLOXHAM

An industry veteran, Clifford is the senior vice president at Octagon sports agency, where for 35 years he's worked with top athletes, including ballerina Dame Darcey Bussell, Olympic swimming legend Michael Phelps and Britain's most successful tennis player Andy Murray.

You've been an agent for 35 years so you've presumably seen it all?

Oh yes. The most surreal time was when [footballer] Daniel Sturridge's dog was kidnapped in LA. We got him on US TV shows so he could appeal for its return. It worked! If you are going to be a good agent you need to be ready to do anything and everything. We do lots of little things that aren't rocket science but we have to do them unbelievably well because, for a sports personality, little things can be a massive deal. It's not hard to fill out a competition entry form but what happens if you forget to fill in your tennis player's form for Wimbledon?

What have you learnt along the way?

That you can never say no. Top athletes set incredibly high standards and believe everything is achievable – when you come back with a 'no', it's not in their vocabulary or mindset. And that's not because they're spoilt but they always find a way to get where they want to get to. We're looking to work with the best of the best. We started working with Michael Phelps from the age of 15 and Andy Murray when he was 11. You don't know how far the athlete you start working with will go but you have to treat them all as if they'll become the best. You can't treat them as average and think, 'I'll just do an average job.' We sign on the basis that they may become the best ever. You can adjust backwards, come up with a Plan B, if they don't.

How has the landscape changed over the years?

The rise of social media has changed things hugely. Our job is to help the athletes understand it, to use it to grow their career and reach their goals. We start with the premise that everything you do is part of that journey – the way you behave, the way you act, the way you treat the media. You can't become the best without being aware of all those things. If they understand how it can help them, it's a very valuable tool. The ones who come unstuck are the ones who have a split personality – what they do on social media doesn't reflect what they're like in real life. That eventually ends in heartache.

Are top sportspeople better behaved these days?

That stuff still goes on but they're more discreet. But there is less of it – it's a minority. Generally they're more professional than they were – they aren't drinking so much, they usually don't smoke. It's hard to generalise though – there's guys who are happy to be average and others who only want to be the best. Thirty years ago, most top sportsmen wouldn't be getting smashed down the pub. But now no sportsperson at all can afford to get smashed down the pub because of social media.

The athlete as activist – where are we going with this?

Athletes increasingly realise their responsibility and influence beyond sport. You'll see more sportspeople go into politics in the future. One of the biggest challenges with team sports stars is for their club because the relationship between athlete and club can be transient. Marcus Rashford may not be at Manchester United in two years' time so it's harder for the club to manage their relationship with him as a role model.

Looking ahead, what are the sports industry's responsibilities and challenges?

Take the obesity epidemic – the industry should help solve that. It has thousands of role models – how can they help? I do think the government will embrace sport to help overcome obesity, given Boris Johnson's experience with COVID-19. And sport needs to do more to reach those who aren't currently participating. People are staying healthier for longer – let's reach out to the older generation, those who are still buying tennis racquets and football boots much later in life.

Your predictions – and hopes – for the future of sport?

You'll see more performance-related renumeration in team sport, especially in football, maybe up to 50 per cent of players' salaries. Clubs can't afford to keep paying these high salaries. The superstar who is a game changer should be renumerated, but average guys have done very well with salary inflation. Generally, I feel positive more than ever about sport – it's the most powerful passion-driver around, covering physical, mental and social health. Sport is a uniting force – it can bring us back together in these divided times.

In the wake of the protests following the murder of George Floyd by US police in the summer of 2020, Coco Gauff, the then 16-year-old American tennis hotshot, declared, 'I promise to always use my platform to spread vital information and spread awareness.' British footballers, 35 per cent of whom in the Premier League are Black, threw their weight behind the Black Lives Matter movement, taking the knee before each game. This was a surprising denouement to the story of Colin Kaepernick, the American NFL player who, as we've seen, had popularised taking the knee during the pre-game national anthem, as part of his protest against racial injustice. Following the outcry around George Floyd's death, the NFL's commissioner Roger Goodell said: 'We were wrong for not listening to NFL players earlier and encourage all to speak out and peacefully protest. We believe Black lives matter. I will be reaching out to players who have raised their voices and others on how we can improve.'

This was a breathtaking volte-face and a stark admission – and not just because it attracted the ire of US President, Donald Trump. The NFL was also risking the wrath of hometown America, traditionally their core viewer base. America's biggest sports league was making its own values-based judgement, choosing their players and the attitude of the future rather than the prejudice of the past and present.

The NFL may have lost the President but it belatedly caught the prevailing mood of generations intent on change. For years, sport had been a laggard in recognising the world was evolving but the NFL's statement showed that it wasn't just individual athletes now willing to speak up. The leaders of the biggest sports were now prepared to initiate change rather than merely react to it.

The uniting role that athletes can play has been noted in the corridors of power. The generation coming through now have a real social conscience. They are more aware of the world around them than we ever were because their world is more global,' says Sally Munday, the chief executive of UK Sport, the body responsible for investing in Olympic and Paralympic sport. We want to unleash our athletes to be social citizens and to be advocates of social impact. They're not all going to have an interest in the same thing – so it could be Marcus Rashford on school meals or our synchronised swimmers doing a display in a pool full of plastic bottles to make the point about plastic waste. Whatever their cause, we want to enable them to use their platform.'

INSIDER INSIGHT: **SALLY MUNDAY**

Since 2019 Sally has been the CEO of UK Sport, the government agency that distributes funding to Olympic and Paralympic sports. Previously, she was CEO of GB Hockey for a decade, overseeing a golden era of the sport. Highlights included the Team GB women securing their first-ever Olympic hockey gold at the Rio 2016 Games and a huge increase in participation in the sport following London 2012.

The sports star as campaigner and activist: what's the opportunity for Olympic and Paralympic athletes here?

We are focused on three ambitions: performance success, a system that works more collaboratively and is more diverse, and the third area is about engagement and impact. The aim is to help performance sport to have a greater impact on society. We're embarking on creating 'the greatest decade of sporting moments'. That's not just about when somebody crosses the line or scores the winning goal. It's about when your son goes to school and an Olympian turns up with their medal and the look on the boy's face when he puts the medal in his hand. Or when one of our boxers goes into an old people's home and brings to life eight oldies suffering from dementia by telling them stories. That has a social impact.

Do you see an increased desire to do this with the current crop of athletes?

Definitely. People talk a lot about winning and we're really clear that we want to keep winning. But we want to win because it gives us a platform to have a positive impact on society. For example, we have a collective ambition to make our system more diverse and stamp out racism and inequality. We want that for sport but also believe that if sport can become the beacon of how society can be more equal, the impact we can have on our communities up and down the nation could be incredible. Sport has the power to shift things in society like almost nothing else.

During your GB hockey days, how did you use London 2012 to grow participation in the sport?

We wanted to increase club numbers and we knew that 80 per cent of the Games' ticket holders who'd come to watch the hockey were not hockey players. So we had all our staff with iPads chatting to people saying, 'There's a session tomorrow close to your house – why don't you take the kids down?' After that we saw a massive surge in regular club players – from 80,000 to 129,000.

Post-pandemic, do you think the government's commitment to sport will change?

Yes and COVID-19 has helped with that. Throughout lockdown we could go running or out on our bikes and they've been very clear in recognising the health and wellbeing benefits of that. I also think the government are seeing now the role that sport can play in global Britain – the idea of Britain being open for business.

Should we believe in sport? Won't there always be cheating?

In society there are bad people, and sport will get its fair share of those willing to go beyond what's in the rules. Whether it's drugs or other forms of cheating, all of us who believe in the simplicity of sport have to try to stay one step ahead of those who want to cheat. But we are naive if we think that people like that won't come into sport. The purity and integrity of sport is a big part of its attraction.

What are your predictions – and hopes – for the future of sport?

I think it will be more inclusive, from boardroom to coaches to participants, and so better reflect society. We will utilise our sporting success in a way that has a much more obvious impact on society. Finally, we will continue to win medals and give people those moments they love. I'm a rugby fan and I start thinking about Six Nations weekend matches on a Wednesday. I start thinking about how the day is going to pan out ahead of the five o'clock kick-off and who's coming round to watch with me. On the day, the excitement and joy just builds and builds. We talk a lot about making people feel happy and more connected. Sport can do that.

Where we are today feels a long way from Michael Jordan flogging his snazzy Nike Air Jordan trainers but refusing to engage with the issues of the day. While it is promising progress, we should remember that these are very young women and men who are in the full glare of the public spotlight by virtue of being brilliant at their sport, so we shouldn't ask too much of them or too often. Their fame is a by-product of their career success rather than the entire point (unlike, for example, reality TV contestants) and the choppy waters that fame brings can be tricky to navigate, especially when your key focus is on your game. As Stormzy puts it (well, he borrowed it from Shakespeare, to be precise): heavy is the head that wears the crown.

If the job spec of the sports star now requires activism as a desirable trait, if not non-negotiable, then emerging stars must be able to juggle the twin responsibilities of being the best in their sport *and* using their influence wisely, all while being constantly scrutinised.

NEW GENERATIONS, NEW SPORTS

As 2020 approached, not only had Britain's athletes been emboldened to influence a society changing at pace, but also sports themselves had begun to reflect those societal changes. As we have seen, sport has always changed to meet the times. Football and rugby, for example, changed beyond all measure at the end of the nineteenth century as industrial Britain took shape. A completely new sport was born in rugby league, which enabled talented rugby players in northern towns to play the game they loved for renumeration. New sports don't develop by chance – they happen because a groundswell of people, who don't feel catered for by what is currently on offer, invent something new. The same is true this time around. Enabling those new sports to thrive is fundamental. If a restaurant isn't catering to its customers, it needs to change the menu or shut up shop – and sport is no different.

Our new sports are being driven by a confluence of digitisation and generational shift. You can't put genies such as Generation Z, Instagram and Raheem Sterling back into their bottles, and evidence of sport shape-shifting is everywhere.

Change has happened fast, and new sports have forced their way on to the top table very quickly. We saw this in the British athletes vying for spots to compete for Team GB at the Tokyo Olympics. The difference this time around was that athletes were also trying to qualify in the new Olympic disciplines of skateboarding, surfing and climbing. In Paris 2024 those sports will be joined by breaking (or breakdancing, as it is known to those of us of a certain vintage).

These new sports have grown up as sub-cultures outside traditional structures. They haven't belonged to anyone, apart from those who take part. These vibrant cultures, entirely youth-driven, are in many ways more important for their athletes than the actual competition. This tension is not new. Snowboarding was similar in its evolution into the Winter Games, as traditionally the focus for the sport is tricks over times. And not every elite triathlete wanted their sport to become an Olympic one at Sydney 2000. The challenge here for any organically developing sport is to use the exposure and financial support that a trip to the Olympic Games provides to grow activity at the grassroots, but without losing its soul. Snowboarding and triathlon, for example, have both managed this transition largely intact.

One of the underground successes in Britain in recent years has been parkour – a no-holds-barred discipline in which you run, jump, and generally throw yourself around the urban skyline with efficiency of effort and great athleticism. It makes for compelling TV – and therein lies the challenge, as many of the 100,000 people Sport England estimates take part tend to prefer it to remain a secret. It's a little like the Banksy of British sport, revelling in its subversion. A row broke out in 2018 with the *Guardian* reporting that the parkour community felt the International Gymnastics Federation was trying to take control of their sport, saying they did not want to be part of a bigger, Olympic sport.[27] The parkour community campaigned against this with the hashtag #weareNOTgymnastics. Nobody wins in that scenario – this is an era where sport needs to reflect society in order to thrive, not aim to constrain it. The truth is it doesn't matter what people are playing, as long as they're active.

Things are less combative in the world of skateboarding, thanks to the thoughtful leadership of James Hope-Gill, head of its governing body, Skateboard GB. 'We are not going to compromise skateboarding's integrity,' he says. 'It is not seen as a sport by the vast majority of skateboarders. It's a lifestyle and a culture, and it's wrapped up with who you are as an individual. They're quite uncomfortable with it being treated as and labelled as a sport. They're sceptical of outsiders coming in and trying to make money or influence it. Our job is to be an organisation that'll make sure that decisions are made by skateboarders, so they control its destiny as it grows.'

INSIDER INSIGHT: JAMES HOPE-GILL

Chief executive at Skateboard GB, James was appointed in 2014 to set up a governing body for the sport. Previously, he spent 20 years working in football, latterly as chief executive of Sheffield & Hallamshire County FA.

Why did the skateboarding community decide they wanted a governing body?

Brands were starting to impose their commercial clout and some skateboarders were saying, 'We're not really comfortable with that.' Skateboarding was being used as a marketing tool, not as a sport, because the brands saw they could get this phenomenal imagery. So the idea is we are the custodians. The way we talk to government funders like UK Sport is very different to how we talk to skateboarders. Never the twain shall meet!

There's the perception of skateboarding as being countercultural – with a governing body and inclusion in the Olympics, is it now growing up?

I don't know. I do know the UK was one of the last countries to have a governing body. We're trying to create something that's absolutely relevant to the culture of skateboarding. An example: as a governing body, we're supposed to have a membership. You're judged on that if you want funding. But the vast majority of skateboarders are kids on the street or at the skate park.

What right do we have to say, 'Hello, we're the governing body, you need to become a member and pay us money'? That's never going to work. So we're looking for ways to engage with the community so at some point, if there are tangible benefits, they might want to support it financially, pay a few quid a year. We can't do what other sports do and just have a financial transaction with our members because skateboarding is a lifestyle.

You're not a skater are you? Is that ever a problem?

No, I'm too old and decrepit! Certainly at the beginning there was a lot of suspicion and I was called 'The Football Guy'. People would say on social media, 'Do an Ollie – you can't even do that!' I'd think, *I've been asked to come here, with a certain skillset, to help you as a community. I'm not trying to pretend I'm a skateboarder. I want to help you become more robust so your destiny is in your hands.* I think that message is out there now. I hope I'm trusted now.

What do you hope to achieve?

We want to provide sport for change – how can skateboarding impact individuals and communities for good? Instead of just chasing the numbers in terms of participation and facilities. For example, skateboarders want to be involved in skateboarding all the time so they might want to work in it. How can we help these people reach that potential? It might be setting up franchises, apprenticeships, asking underrepresented communities, 'What are your needs? How can we help you?'

Skateboarding is included in the 2021 Tokyo Olympics. How did that come about?

The International Olympic Committee [IOC] have opened their eyes to new possibilities. The criteria for choosing new sports are youth engagement, accessibility and legacy – and skateboarding hits all of those. And with my cynical head on, I'll point out that the average age of the Olympics TV audience is currently high, mid-to-late fifties, and Coca-Cola sells to a 14-year-old, not a fiftysomething.

Is everyone happy about skateboarding being in the Olympics?

There are 750,000 skateboarders in the UK but only a couple of hundred who want to compete. So when it's thrust into the Olympics, that's changing the emphasis for some. There's a lot of opposition. People want to retain the culture. But if we get it right in terms of competition structure, how we coach, how we deliver for people at the top end without compromising the integrity, it won't affect anyone else. But it will increase profile and participation, which should increase the funding, which means we can get better facilities in the right places.

What lies ahead for women's skateboarding?

The potential is enormous. We know that when girls first get on a skateboard they're very self-conscious. If there are boys present it puts them off. There's a skate park in Manchester that has a girls' development officer who put girls-only sessions on. It's been a huge hit. And Sky Brown [the Anglo-Japanese skater who became the world's youngest pro at 12] is an amazing role model so that helps.

What's next for skateboarding?

We've seen a lot of people in their thirties, forties and fifties coming back to it. Their kids have asked for a board so they've bought one for themselves too. We'd love skateboarding to become part of active travel. I'd like to see the skateboarding equivalent of the cycling proficiency test to teach children basic skills.

Your predictions – and hopes – for the future of sport?

Choice is key. Ten or 20 years ago, you'd play football and you'd pay the FA membership fees and they'd think they own you. Now people do multiple sports all the time. Governing bodies have to adapt to meet those needs and not be precious about people coming in and out of their sport. And they need to understand that we can't just deliver sport for sport's sake – what are our obligations to society?

INSIDER INSIGHT: JAMES HOPE-GILL

While new sports that tend to prioritise culture over medals are developing, so this mindset has started to seep into other sports. For example, two British 'freestyle footballers' Billy Wingrove and Jeremy Lynch, collectively known as the F2, have built a social media following of 30 million across different platforms since they launched a YouTube channel in 2011 showcasing football skills and tricks. Calling themselves 'the #1 global football influencers', they build campaigns for brands looking to target the Generation Z audience, and earn more from YouTube advertising each month (a cool $719,000 a month in 2019) than any Premier League club.[28]

What this shows is that how we think about sport is evolving. The F2 are excellent sportsmen, hugely talented and practised at what they do. But according to the *Oxford English Dictionary* definition, they are not taking part in sport at all, because they are not competing. It describes sport as 'an activity involving physical exertion and skill in which an individual or team competes against another or others for entertainment'. My 13-year-old son Conor would ask why competition matters if it is fun, and I find it hard to argue with him. Competitive football needs acts like the F2 to broaden the experience for kids who are used to a culture of cool tricks and video clips, but equally the F2 needs competitive football, as it's still a packed stadium that the kids most dream of competing in.

So are acts like the F2 a good thing? I think so – because it shows that sport is starting to listen to younger generations, whose engagement it relies on for survival. If we believe that playing is good for kids, we need to relax and let them shape that play.

The key point here is not to be drawn into semantics but to recognise that our definition of competition is outdated. If heartrate increase is the principal barometer of physical exertion then Conor playing a tense game of *Fortnite* against his mates, all sitting on their respective sofas, is closer to our current definition of sport than the F2 juggling a football against the crossbar. But none of this actually matters. Ultimately, it's all 'play'.

Faced with this crossover of tastes and challenge to what sport even means, the guardians of our games have had to be brave. The year 2019 was the point at which they stood up to the plate. Just like in politics, making a decision based on what the future might hold in ten years' time is never easy, but leadership rarely is in any walk of life.

One of the best examples of brave decision-making as the decade came to an end was a new professional cricket competition called the Hundred, launched by the the England and Wales Cricket Board (ECB). The competition was designed to attract new audiences to the game, building on the work the Women's World Cup had done in 2017. The competition involved some new rules to make the game faster (each innings was to be only 100 balls in length, hence the name) and more in-stadium entertainment woven into the show. This was backed up with a new TV contract with the BBC so all could watch, the equal billing of the women's tournament, cheap tickets for kids and the integration of a raft of overseas stars to complement domestic talent, all of which was intended to attract new audiences to the game. Despite this, the move was unpopular among many of the cricketing hardcore who were principally uncomfortable with the move away from teams competing as counties, and the changes to the structure of the game's rules.

Newspapers griped and critiqued at the launch of the Hundred, but the truth is we'd seen it all before. The ECB generated the same reaction with the launch of the most recent new format in England in 2003, Twenty20 cricket. In 2003 shortening the game to only 20 overs (or 120 balls) per team was widely derided as detracting from the whole ethos of the game as a (minimum) day's entertainment. In actual fact, the financial injection from Twenty20 saved the sport in this country and expanded its reach worldwide. Ticket sales remain extremely healthy nearly 20 years on, with around a million tickets sold for the event in England and Wales in 2019 alone.[29]

Twenty20 has developed a new hardcore fan base. While the ECB could rest on its laurels and take the plaudits, the Hundred is a brave attempt to take the sport to newer audiences. Let's not forget that the cricket economy has been a perilous one since the gambling era of its early years. The book *Cricket 2.0* by Tim Wigmore and Freddie Wilde explains that before Twenty20 was created (still less than 20 years ago, let's remember), only 10 per cent of the income of the sport came from domestic cricket, with the remainder from the international version of the game. But that's not healthy for any game hoping to develop local clubs, talent and heroes – it's impossible to sustain a whole sporting economy through a national team. Compare cricket's challenge to football, where 80 per cent of the wealth at the same time was in the club game. Twenty20 has played a significant role in starting to develop a locally healthy game, and the Hundred needs to keep moving in the same direction. Lo and behold, when tickets went on sale for the (ultimately cancelled) summer 2020 inaugural competition, they flew. Several matches were close to sell-out five months before the tournament and 20,000 tickets had been purchased for under 16s, each at just £5. The Hundred is a risky step, for sure, but it's also a brave and necessary one.

Innovation should always be embraced and we should be grateful to those willing to try it – after all, it would have been far simpler for those at the top of English cricket to sit back, feet up on the desk and enjoy the easy life. England were world champions, attendances were robust, all was rosy. But instead they chose to push things forward with the Hundred. As Tom Harrison, the ECB's chief executive, told the *Financial Times*, 'I'll be judged in 10 years' time, long after I've left this job. I'm terrified I'll wake up and say, "God, we had an opportunity to do something exceptional and we didn't take it."'[30] If you truly love a sport, it seems obvious that ensuring its survival for future generations is both your priority and your duty.

Sport matters to us all in the format we knew as children, but we cannot live in the past. Nostalgia should not prevent progress. Just as there were those who railed against the All England Club at Wimbledon allowing professional players into an event in 1967 – ditto the FA letting football clubs in English towns become professional 100 years previously – we cannot hold back innovation intended to safeguard the future of the sport. Let's linger for a moment on the subject of those £5 kids' tickets at the Hundred. Over the last few years, sport at the top level has received a lot of criticism for the escalating prices of tickets. While it is true that the best seats in the house for top sporting events have reached premium levels, clubs would argue that is purely a function of demand and if they didn't charge significant amounts for big games then ticket touts would be making the money instead.

While that's essentially just solving one societal problem by creating another one, clubs have in truth generally become much more sensitive to fan lobbying around balancing commercial intent with their responsibilities to their fans. For example, Liverpool Football Club's new Main Stand hospital-ity area was controversial when it launched due to the prices being charged for access, but general entrance ticket prices at Anfield have been frozen for four consecutive years. This is despite the fact the stadium would sell out at all levels several times over for each game.

Having worked in the industry for many years, I know most clubs are faced with a tough balancing act. Professional football clubs are, as they always have been, businesses. They have to balance the long-term loyalty of their supporters (or customers, as they occasionally dare to call them) with the short-term need to balance the books. They are often criticised for becoming 'too commercial' yet are expected to fund a team that can win trophies. When you look closely, you notice it is often those fans complaining most about ticket prices who are the same ones complaining about a lack of trophies or big-name signings. At which point you just have to put your hands up and realise that sometimes sports' leaders just can't win. Two Circles data shows that attendances at live sporting events continued to rise right into 2019, which points to demand and supply being pretty healthily matched.

That's not to say that all prices should be rising. Increasingly we are seeing fans' groups lobby against prices when they become too high, which creates an important and healthy tension in the relationship to ensure clubs do not become too complacent. No business can afford to price swathes of its customers out of the market, and the trick for commercial sport will be to find ways to meet both objectives – a wider range of pricing options to enable the whole of society to watch the action, just as we see in the Hundred. In practice, this means the higher priced tickets subsidising the cheaper ones. There is no point building new sporting concepts to attract younger generations, only to then price them out of the experience. If we want sport to play a key role in our future, it has to be attractive, accessible and also financially sustainable.

THE SPORTING RECIPE

While a big day out to watch professional sport has proven itself largely recession-proof to date, the provision of public sport facilities has sadly not been. It's perhaps no coincidence that the new Olympic sports, which have been picked specifically because they are compelling to younger generations, require very little equipment. Surfing and climbing rely principally on mother nature; skateboarding and breaking, just some flat ground. As for parkour, that doesn't even need any ground.

It's been a challenging time in Britain, as we've seen. We've had to learn a new alphabet: Austerity, Brexit, COVID-19. That means we need sport – for escapism, for mental and physical health. However, the problem of this new alphabet is that after A, B and C has come an inescapable D. Debt. To grow sport during austerity times in Britain, sport needs to find ways to develop that don't rely on public coffers, while recognising that private purse strings are also likely to have tightened. Attempting to build *anything* game-changing and thrilling in our modern, often cynical, world is fraught with risk.

So what is it that makes some things in life capture the hearts and minds of the British public? Writing in the *Financial Times* about the Industrial Revolution, chief economist of the Bank of England, Andy Haldane, attributed its success in permanently changing society for the better to a trinity of factors:

> The private sector provided the innovative spark, the state provided insurance to the incomes, jobs and health of citizens, and the social sector provided the support network to cope with disruption to lives and livelihoods[31]

I believe there is a similar set of three requirements to create positive change in Britain through sport. A 'Sporting Recipe', if you will, cooked up for a country where social support networks are stretched to the max and public debt levels are bigger than the entire economy. For sport to work its magic for today's troubled nation, it needs a liberal helping of the following three ingredients, which in combination alchemise into a truly special movement. Sport today needs to be:

- *Popular* – Any movement needs to be compelling enough that it naturally draws people to it. A carrot rather than a stick in a cynical age, essentially.
- *Accessible* – That movement needs also to be accessed easily by everyone, not just a small percentage of the population.
- *Paid for* – It's important that the movement can be enabled at least in part by the commercial sector as it grows, so that the government/public purse doesn't need to foot the bill.

Look at the London 2012 Olympics through that lens, you can see this Sporting Recipe come to life:

- *Popular* – As the Games drew near, the public supported them in droves even if the media was sceptical. By April 2011, organisers had received applications for 20 million tickets when there were only 6.6 million available.
- *Accessible* – For those lucky enough to be able to make it to London, the Games had offered around 20 per cent of total tickets on a 'pay your age' scheme for under 16s. Plus 120,000 were free to London schoolchildren, while 90 per cent of the public tickets were £100 or less, 66 per cent at £50 or less and 2.5 million cost £20 or less. Millions crowded the routes to watch road cycling, marathons and

triathlons for free, basking in the summer sun. Even for those unable to take in the action in person, tuning in was easy. Unlike many home broadcasters for Olympic Games, big moments were not interspersed with adverts or hidden on pay TV. There were 17 days of pure sport on the BBC.

- *Paid for* – Commercial sponsors and ticket sales covered all the costs. Public funds were spent only on regeneration and facilities that would be available long after the Games had left town. For example, £1 billion of the cost of the Games were spent on cleaning the soil in the now Olympic Park. Without that investment, the subsequent creation of a new, vibrant area of London would have been impossible as decades of pollution made much of the local area an unusable, toxic rubbish dump.

Now brimming with new housing, schools and hospitals, universities, great transport links and revitalised wildlife, the Queen Elizabeth Olympic Park in Stratford is a shining light of modern Britain, reachable via a decent public transport network. None of this would have been achievable without the impetus and investment of London 2012. The Sporting Recipe provided the underlying principles for it; however, as we will see, the challenge going forward is to replicate projects like this when public money is even tighter.

parkrun – the free, weekly Saturday morning 5k running event that takes place in public parks across the land (and many other lands now too) – is another enduring example:

- *Popular* – parkrun provides a regular weekly meeting point for families and friends to be active without pressure, or to volunteer to help others be so. By late 2019, parkrun had notched up 6 million sign-ups.

- *Accessible* – There is no drain on the public purses to put on the events; in fact, parking fees and park café sales contribute to council coffers at an otherwise quiet time of the day. This mean the parks don't charge parkrun, which in turn means there is no fee to take part, so no barrier to entry for potential runners.
- *Paid for* – parkrun's software keeps the cost of delivery down as it doesn't need to pay a big technology company to do it for it. Add in the contribution of commercial partners and new clothing line venture, Contra (we'll come on to this later), and this means parkrun can be free for all, forever.

The key thing in the Sporting Recipe is the need for all three components. Take one ingredient of the recipe away, and the taste just wouldn't be right. If parkrun had more outgoings, then the runs could not be free. If the runs were not free, then numbers would reduce. If numbers reduced, in all likelihood only the more affluent, keener runners would remain. Which would in turn reduce the social impact parkrun can have now, let alone when the full potential of GPs 'prescribing' parkrun to patients is realised by the cash-strapped NHS.

parkrun is just one of an increasing number of initiatives in the sports world that picked up the impetus and didn't rail against the realities of austerity Britain. Rather, it worked around them.

THE SPORTING RECIPE CREATES SOCIAL CHANGE

So what does this tell us about the prospects of the other areas of sport we have covered in this chapter, and how or why they succeed?

Let's look at the Hundred again. In truth, the event is a lot more than a cricket tournament. It's the principal means the

ECB has to try to reach new communities up and down the country. It's a not-for-profit organisation, which means that every pound it makes goes back into growing the game and can only sow what it reaps. But what that means is if the ECB has new things it wants to do, it has to either find new sources of funding or drop something it is already doing.

While the success of the England women's and men's teams and the 20-over county format is terrific, that alone won't support every ambition the ECB has for the game. So if the game doesn't grow commercially, the ECB can't cover the costs of new plans it has to take the sport into every state school in the country or step up its use of sport as a bridge to engage ethnic minorities in inner cities (cricket, of course, is huge in India, Pakistan and the Caribbean islands). It won't be able to extend the development of AstroTurf wickets in clubs to enable the sport to continue in a soggy British summer, or create a step change of support in the women's game. At least, it wouldn't be able to do these things without stopping its work in other areas. So innovation is a financial necessity.

The challenge for the Hundred is twofold. Firstly, it has to create a spark of excitement among new audiences, which coaches in schools, for example, can then build on. Secondly, it also has to make a decent profit through sponsors, TV companies and the more premium ticket sales, which will then fund the ECB's bold plans to grow the game. Creating popularity and commercial income simultaneously is a massive challenge, the ultimate Sporting Recipe in some ways. However, the prize of a healthier game that plays a major role in extending the social inclusion of the game has to be a risk worth taking.

On the subject of social inclusion, the model also provides some clues as to how Rashford, Sterling, Rapinoe and Osaka – just like Stormzy – have been able to cut through. Social media provides the opportunity for them to share their views, using their popularity to raise issues close to home. They also have the financial means to turn words into action; Raheem Sterling not only talked about racism and privilege, in October 2020 he invested his own money to launch a foundation to help disadvantaged youngsters, providing a rumoured seven-figure sum, but also the personal drive to persuade his club and sponsors to join.[32] The foundation offers work experience and university scholarship opportunities. This follows the Sporting Recipe perfectly – he's a popular figure, whose personal funding offsets the need for the initiative to pull on the public purse. It also potentially breaks down the barriers around kids asking for support – after all, it's potentially easier to go to a professional footballer's organisation to ask for support than a more conventional-looking charity.

But how sustainable is this really? After all, there are only so many multi-millionaire sportspeople in Britain ... and even Raheem Sterling's pockets won't stretch to supporting all those who need it. Can the Sporting Recipe offer any clues to that discussion?

Let's look at Rashford's focus on the school meals campaign to see if that offers any clues. Just like Sterling, social media provided him with a platform to take his opinions to mass audiences, without needing the immediate support of TV stations or the newspapers. The mainstream media came around, but only once he had a groundswell of grassroots support. Interestingly, the government originally resisted his campaigns to extend free school meals, so Rashford took it upon himself to campaign for local cafés and businesses to provide free meals to kids. In doing so, he took away the burden from the public purse and found commercial partners who would support him, with a torrent of support up and down the country; he had created a pop-up social enterprise.

It was only at that point that the government relented – seemingly taking the view that feeding citizens was too fundamental a role to outsource. With the support of his followers, Rashford had built his own Sporting Recipe to work around the challenges of the day. As he tweeted: 'I don't even know what to say. Just look at what we can do when we come together, THIS is England in 2020.'

In this way, affluent and influential professional sportspeople have started to understand how to use the Sporting Recipe as a means of becoming social entrepreneurs. However, they need the support of industry or the public purse to help them scale their ideas. That means the government needs to see proof of the long-term benefit of the social enterprises our athletes are building; to see proof that proper nutrition and exercise for kids early in life saves the NHS a fortune down the road; to be persuaded of the benefits of social mobility in creating a stable, tolerant nation, as well as helping Britain redefine its role in a post-Brexit world. Sport can be the impetus, and the Sporting Recipe shows us how. As we will see in the chapters to come, the penny is slowly dropping in the corridors of power too.

THE DECADE'S END

New Year's Eve 2019. To me, the country seemed in a mess, increasingly divided politically thanks to the ongoing wrangles around our withdrawal from the EU and the polarising nature of domestic politics. Like many others, I sought solace in sport, noting that London was to host men's Euro 2020 football finals the following summer. As 'Three Lions (Football's Coming

Home)' (England's enduring anthem from Euro '96) rang out during the televised New Year's Eve celebrations, I felt that, despite the gloom, maybe sport's punchier, more open, more radical new look could play a role in regenerating our nation. We were out of Europe and yet we were very much still in it. Worst of times, best of times.

Sport has spent 150 years adjusting to the social and economic climate within which it operates so I figured it was simply doing so again. I'd seen enough clues throughout the year to feel confident that sport would play an important role in helping to get Britain back on its feet. My sporting resolution for the new decade was of brave leadership, new sporting models and a different kind of thinking to drive change, enabled by social media and new generations less prepared to accept the way things had traditionally been done.

How quickly things change. Little did anyone know how much further we had to fall first. Football was indeed coming home – but actually, we all were. And we weren't going anywhere any time soon.

CHAPTER 4 / Pandemic Stops Play ...
But Sport Rises to the Challenge

Wimbledon! Euro 2020! The Tokyo Olympics! Summer 2020 was shaping up to be a bumper summer of sport for even the most casual of fans. Until suddenly, it wasn't. Time out. Game over.

When the UK first went into lockdown in March 2020, bracing itself for the COVID-19 pandemic, sport, like almost all other industries, suffered an almighty seizure. Arenas, pitches, courts, pools and stadiums were shuttered, gyms pulled the plug on their treadmills, and every single sports club across the land immediately cancelled all training and fixtures for the foreseeable future. Kids were cut adrift without their Saturday-morning kickabout; ditto their parents, bereft of their small window to get active themselves or have a gossip on the touch-line. Never mind the physical and mental benefits of exercise, what about all that community bonding, all those cherished rituals that punctuate our lives, gone in a flash? Things looked grim – and there was a limit to how many TikTok dance routines, cooked up by bored footballers in their marble designer kitch-ens, that we could stomach in one day.

But of course where there's a will, there's a way. And sport is too tightly woven into the fabric of our lives for that thread to be easily unpicked and discarded. We may not have been happy with our new normal but we swiftly adapted to it. Creative thinking was key. And with it came ideas with legs beyond the pandemic, new ways of thinking about old habits that we might *just* be able to carry into the future, whatever that may hold. It was challenging to talk about silver linings when death stalked all around us but they were there, peppered amid the bleakness, twinkling gently, waiting patiently.

Within a week of our first lockdown beginning, my children, frustrated at the closure of their beloved cricket club, had persuaded us to rid our long, narrow driveway of its pesky cars and install DIY netting so they could bowl and thwack balls to their hearts' content. My co-author Kerry's 11-year-old elite-gymnast daughter took the cancellation of her 18 hours of weekly training in her stride, leaping straight on to the tatty trampoline in the garden, where she perfected her backflips day in, day out, for months on end.

Others went further. Sabian Kulczynski, a then 18-year-old junior triathlete champion, found himself unable to practise his front crawl when the swimming pools closed. So he bought a supersized paddling pool, used a strap to attach himself to the side of his parents' County Clare bungalow and swam on the spot. Think watery treadmill. 'It has to be the most boring thing ever,' he noted. It did the job though.

The All England Lawn Tennis and Croquet Club, hosts of the Wimbledon Championships, found a way to harness this kind of ingenuity, while also keeping its community engaged, with its #WimbledonRecreated campaign. Tennis fans were encouraged to create a DIY championship vibe at home, be it marking out lines in the garden with toilet roll or deploying their trusty Swingball.

Meanwhile, the postponement of April 2020's London Marathon didn't stop its runners from hitting the pavements – hordes took part in the 2.6 Challenge, running 2.6 miles each during the week it should have taken place in a digital relay, raising money for charity while they did so.

I embarked upon my own alternative, spontaneous version of the London Marathon in the early weeks of the first lockdown. Like everyone else, I was unsettled by how swiftly and terrifyingly life had been turned on its head and what the future might hold. I've always found escape from life's problems in running – and it seemed a problem of this magnitude required a really big run. One morning, without giving it much thought, I got up, pulled on my trainers and somehow ran 28 miles, looping across fields, down country lanes and through the surrounding villages. Toward the end of my four-hour odyssey, I passed by my house, collecting my son Conor to join me for 2.6 miles to complete his own charity challenge, before depositing him home and taking my daughter Niamh for the final stretch to do the same. She went for a sprint finish, which was a little cruel as I was a bit the worse for wear by then. While I am an experienced marathon runner, this is not something I would ever normally do on a whim, without first following a carefully calibrated training programme. In hindsight, I was lucky to escape injury – but it was worth it. I'm still not entirely sure what compelled me to become Forrest Gump for a day but it certainly did the trick. I ran away ... but then ran home again, and I felt reset. My mind was serene even though my feet were epically blistered.

Joining the dots between exercise and mental health, which had until now largely been the preserve of a few candid sports stars, their Generation Z fans and the hardcore exercise brigade, became a mainstream coping mechanism for swathes of the nation during the darkest days of the pandemic. When Prime Minister Boris Johnson first announced on 23 March 2020 that people in England should only leave the house for very limited reasons, one of which being to exercise once per day, many saw this literal get-out clause as mental salvation. There were very few lockdown-approved activities: you could take your pick from walking, running or cycling; all of which could be undertaken outside and without going near anyone else or sharing equipment. Fortuitously for a nation in the midst of a collective once-in-a-lifetime trauma, these activities have another shared quality: they're the best kind of exercise for reducing stress.

'Neuroscience has shown that some of the neurotransmitters in our brains that help us to problem solve, think creatively and so on, seem to be helped by aerobic exercise, specifically the kind of hypnotic, repetitive exercise where you go into a trance and zone out,' says Simon Marshall, sports psychologist, professor of mental toughness (great job title, right?) at the University of San Diego and author of *The Brave Athlete*, which he co-wrote with his wife, world champion triathlete Lesley Paterson.

> There are two methods of managing stress. Problem-focused coping means taking action to reduce the source of your stress. So if the problem is you've got too much work, the solution might be to work harder to get it done. Then you've got emotion-focused coping. This method doesn't change the source of stress but it changes the filter you use internally to view it. So meditation fits the bill, or a more destructive example is drinking to numb your feelings. The unique thing about aerobic,

endurance, repetitive exercise like running or cycling is it's one of the few things that hits both methods. Most of us are aware of how a run can help change our emotional outlook – we'll often talk about heading out to blow off steam. But lots of people don't realise that their run is a problem-focusing coping mechanism too – we regu-larly come back home having thought about problems in different ways and found solutions.

INSIDER INSIGHT: DR SIMON MARSHALL

An expert in sports psychology, Simon is a professor of mental toughness at the University of California in San Diego. He's also author of Brave Athlete: Calm the F*ck Down and Rise to the Occasion, *a straight-talking brain-training guide, written with his wife Lesley Paterson, a world champion triathlete.*

People found sport and exercise comforting during the pandemic. Why?

We're social primates – our brains are wired to interact with one another in a group. History shows that people tend to survive longer when they're in a group than when they go it alone. So there are evolutionary mechanisms that drive us to find our tribe. Tribal identity is really important for much of sport – it represents a sense of belonging. You bond with your fellow tribe members and develop trusting relationships in moments of vulnerability and weakness, not in moments of strength. So when you suffer together or do something discomfiting together, that bond becomes stronger. It's no wonder that many sports have evolved to become as socially and culturally significant as they have. It isn't just about kicking, running or jumping as high as you can.

The pandemic saw the government encouraging the nation to get fitter, to stand the best chance of fighting off COVID-19. But how can they reach exercise refuseniks?

Getting fitter is a laudable goal but if a motive is forced on us – someone nags us or we feel pressured to lose weight before our summer holiday, for example – we don't have a good track record. The motivation needs to come from within. So we need to establish someone's motivational readiness to change. We talk about pre-contemplators – they're not even thinking about doing more exercise; the proud couch-potato type. The pre-contemplators are the biggest swathe in society and they're hard to find. We use stealth health methods with them. One of the biggest barriers to exercise given by British women, for example, is 'I'm not the sporty type.' It ties into identity. So marketing techniques that suggest people will want to emulate an elite athlete won't work for these people. The other reason is 'I don't have time.' But we know that when we remove time as a barrier, they still don't exercise. It's an excuse. So we start with tiny amounts and encourage a new habit for a minute or two each day.

People are increasingly joining the dots between exercise and mental health, it seems.

Yes, our physical and mental health are intimately connected and this is something scientists have learnt over the last 25 or 30 years. We're not just talking about the obvious thing here – the brain, which is running on electrical and chemical impulses – but things like our gut health and how its microbiome affects our moods.

How has psychology's role in sport evolved?

One of the founding fathers was Norman Triplett in the late 1800s. He studied social facilitation – the idea that we perform better in the presence of others. He found this in analysing cyclists' time trials. That started off the field of study that considers mindset in sport, asking the question: how does what I think/feel affect what I do physically? Elite sport is now focused on this. Athletes started to learn about techniques in the 1950s and 1960s and universities started to offer sport psychology programmes from the late 1980s.

So the athlete's brain is as important as their body?

Absolutely. But many coaches and parents don't know how to coach mindset. There's no one way to improve. The metaphor we often use for success in sport is 'it's a cargo net, not a ladder'. Look at those who are role models in sport – trying to be like them mentally might not be the best option for you. There's more than one way to develop the skills needed to perform at a high level. You have to find a mindset that works for you.

This must have a broader application beyond sport?

Yes, most of my work is no longer in elite sport. Sports psychologists have pivoted – they talk about themselves as performance psychologists now. When you step out onto a stage, or into a boardroom, or into your boss's office to ask for a pay rise, the stakes are high. What you do will be judged. It's the same as stepping out into a sports environment.

Your predictions – and hopes – for the future of sport?

We're increasingly using our heads to earn a living while sitting at desks and the price we pay for that is we feel physically unfulfilled. We're hunter-gatherers by nature but we've engineered physical discomfort out of our lives. So we'll increasingly look for physical experiences that involve endurance – Tough Mudders, obstacle races and so on. We're paying for the opportunity to run through mud, jump into pits and be electrocuted because we're desperate for physical, sensory experiences that take us out of our knowledge-work environment. We'll also further recognise the role of exercise as a mental health adjunct, rather than just as a supporter of physical health. We're getting people to see exercise as therapy. What used to be sports science departments at universities are now exercise and health departments. We know the role of movement has a much stronger role to play than simply helping us not die from physical conditions.

It was striking how many of us took the government's guidance on exercise as a direct order. It was – and sorry to deploy the most overused adjective of the pandemic – an unprecedented moment for sport and fitness. The prime minister live on TV telling us we must go for a bike ride! The NHS had been advising the public for nine years to take 150 minutes of exercise per week but 34 per cent of men and 42 per cent of women weren't hitting that target. Now, overnight, the paths, tracks and spookily silent roads were filled with newbie joggers and families of wobbly cyclists. When you're only allowed out of the house to exercise, suddenly exercise seemed strangely alluring to former refuseniks. In a similar vein, Kerry told me stories of friends of hers taking joy in shedding the #workingfromhome sweatpants and dressing up in their most glamorous outfits to go stand in a queue outside the supermarket once a week. As she explained to me, you've got to get your kicks where you can in desperate times.

A Nuffield Health survey found that 76 per cent of Brits took up at least one new form of exercise during the lockdown of 2020, while Sports Direct reported a 218 per cent increase in trainer sales during that period compared to the same period the previous year. Fitness app Strava, meanwhile, saw its users increase threefold, ditto its data usage. Smartwatch manufacturer Garmin, a firm favourite of those who track their runs and rides, shared combined data from their users for the month of April, the height of lockdown restrictions. This showed that while total worldwide steps decreased by 12 per cent in April 2020, total steps from just workout activities increased by 24 per cent.[33] Those with Garmin devices were moving around less in total (as you would expect – they were hardly allowed out of their homes) but had increased their levels of exercise to offset this as best they could. Runners were getting out more frequently – even if lockdown meant that they were unable to run for more than an hour each time. Individual pursuits – running, cycling and the like – were also picking up the slack from team pursuits, which were paused at the time.

Brits also dusted off the dumbbells and exercise bikes in their garages and started to use them again out of necessity, more so than any other nation. Incredibly, Garmin's survey showed that Britain saw the world's biggest increase in fitness equipment usage in April 2020, compared to the same month in 2019, despite the fact that Britain's 10 million gym members could not access their facilities. In fact, Sport England reported that overall activity only reduced by 5.4 per cent in women and 8.9 per cent in men during the March–May 2020 period – a relatively minor reduction in the context of a full lockdown and the removal of pools, pitches and teammates from the equation nationwide.[34]

In total 1.3 million Brits bought a bike during lockdown (normally about 3 million bikes are sold in Britain in an entire year). The amount of cycling taking place in Britain was up 70 per cent according to the Department of Transport. Campaigners tried for years with limited success to persuade town planners to consider decent cycle-lane networks and councils to install them. But the pandemic bestowed a new urgency and relevance on to that call to action – when the prime minister tells people to avoid using public transport, the viable alternatives have to finally be taken seriously. The government announced a £2 billion investment in cycling and walking, with Transport for London pledging £22.2 million to create or improve cycle routes across the capital. Our collective response to normal life coming to an abrupt standstill was to try to move regardless.

Not everyone though. A Sport England survey didn't paint an entirely rosy picture: 'Overall, activity levels held up relatively well throughout – with a third of adults doing 30 minutes or more of physical activity (at a level that raised their breathing rate) on five or more days a week. However, below the surface, we see familiar inequalities replicated, even exacerbated,' it reported. 'The whole population has been affected, but not affected equally. The wider public health, social and economic impact of coronavirus is likely to have a greater negative impact on the capability, opportunity and motivation to be physically active for some groups over others. We see this reflected in people's behaviour. A person's gender, affluence, ethnicity, disability, age and family status all have an impact on their like-lihood to be active, and the demographic groups and audiences we were focusing on prior to the pandemic are still finding it harder to be active.' The most hard-up areas of Britain were hit hardest by COVID-19, and exercise was part of that. Online home workouts were a great idea for those with sufficient space to work out in, a decent wi-fi signal and the digital skills to get stuck in – but not everyone has access to those three things.

Many of the traditional sports, of course, were stopped in their tracks. They were almost immediately deprived of every ingredient of our Sporting Recipe – no visibility to share activ-ities (because no sport was in the media), no funds (no sport meant no revenue) and fewer staff (because no funds meant furlough for coaches and administrators up and down the country). Public funds understandably had other immediate priorities. So those of us who were used to structured sport were left to our own devices as our regular sporting pursuits were put on ice. I was lucky, living near fields to run in. Others much less so.

Of course, this wasn't merely a physical health challenge. Inactivity compounded the feelings of stress and anxiety many felt on isolation. Small things like the doorstep clapping for the NHS on Thursday evenings created communal anchors in people's days that exercise classes and the like had previously catered for, but even the most lively applause did not quite manage to get the heart racing in quite the same way, let alone enable the social interactions that are so key to our love of sport. The government seemed to acknowledge this so that when lockdown returned to Britain later in 2020 and then again in the harrowing winter at the start of 2021, outdoor exercise was again encouraged. This time, however, the government went a step further and allowed a meeting with another person. As BBC sports editor Dan Roan noted, 'there seemed to be a new appreciation for its importance as an essential service – a means of delivering the physical and mental health that society now desperately needs to recover from the pandemic, but also to help tackle a range of social challenges the crisis it will leave in its wake.'[35]

GO JOE

It's impossible to talk about how the pandemic impacted on the lives and sporting habits of Brits without noting the ascendance of Joe Wicks, personal trainer, diet-plan author and social media star, to national treasure status. The Body Coach – forgive me if this sounds glib – had a very good pandemic. As schools closed down in March, he announced he would be live-streaming a daily 9am PE lesson on his YouTube channel. Parents, desperate for *anything* to create structure for their families in a world that suddenly had none, spread the word and, on the first Monday of lockdown, Wicks bounced into his living room – and mine – like a puppy in Lycra, and clocked up almost 1 million streams of his 30-minute, child-friendly workout. And so began a new sporting ritual (undertaken in

119

fancy dress on Fridays, sometimes gate-crashed by his young children), with families around the world doing squats, lunges and press-ups together, including, according to the comments on Wicks's social media feeds, many who had never exercised before. My ten-year-old daughter, denied her usual cricket training, was a regular. She had one screen with Joe strutting his stuff, and then another with a Skype video call running with her mates, who were also taking part. The workouts kept her active but were also a conduit for the social contact she craved. Within ten days, Wicks's videos had clocked up 28 million views. He donated all the advertising revenue he earned to NHS charities, a figure that stood at £580,000 by the time he did his last session of the first lockdown, four months on, on 22 July 2020. Little did he know at that point that he would be back again six months later. After Prime Minister Boris Johnson announced the closure of schools once again in January 2021, within days Wicks returned to the nation's front rooms. As Boris Johnson concluded his speech, England footballer-turned-broadcaster Peter Crouch tweeted, 'I hope Joe Wicks has stretched off.'

Wicks's story is another example of the Sporting Recipe in action. He picked up on the vacuum of a population devoid of their Jazzercise, five-a-side or school PE, and quickly brought exercise into the front room. He didn't need armies of people or a budget to do so, just a decent profile, a good idea and a laptop. He made exercise accessible to most (although not all) through his use of YouTube, engaging and inclusive (the hysteria when my daughter's friend received a live shoutout lasted for days) and financially sustainable through the proceeds from YouTube advertising. Not only did he not cost the public purse any money, he saved it some through the NHS donation. When my co-author Kerry interviewed Wicks in January 2021 for the *Evening Standard* he said: 'I am the only person in the UK who can do this on a massive scale, I'm the only person who can inspire these kids to get moving.'

Elsewhere, with all gyms closed, virtual classes also helped members who didn't have dumbbells lurking in the garage stay fit and stay connected. Forward-thinking gym owners were quick to pivot to Zoom or Facebook Live workouts to keep their communities engaged. Within days of lockdown Steve Gregory, ex-professional footballer and owner of the FitLife boutique gym in Buckinghamshire, created an extensive schedule of livestreamed workouts that were, crucially, free to all, not just members. 'I said to my staff on the day we had to close the gym, "This is a chance for us to show that we care about people and our community, we're not just doing this as a business." Obviously it's been an awful time and far too many people have died but it's made everyone more conscious of their health. Everything is irrelevant if you don't have your health so you must prioritise it, which is what we in the fitness industry have been telling people for a really long time. I could see that in the short term it'd be hard for the industry but in the long term we'd benefit.'

While Wicks provided free exercise classes for children, Marcus Rashford, of course, helped out with free food. He wasn't the only footballer who raised his game off the pitch during the pandemic – a fact that left the government with egg on its face on several occasions. Early on in lockdown, Health Secretary Matt Hancock declared top players should 'take a pay cut and play their part' during the pandemic: 'the first thing Premier League footballers can do is make a contribution,' he said. Many people would now argue that, during those dark days of 2020, Britain's football clubs and their players made a far more meaningful contribution to their communities than many of our elected officials.

In an absence of strong, humane authority figures and leadership, sports stars like Rashford filled the vacuum. Working-class players (and football is, of course, historically and still today a working-class sport) showed themselves to be far more in touch with the people than the government. Ditto Joe Wicks. He told Kerry that after a troubled upbringing in a cramped council flat in Surrey, he was fully aware that many people had limited space in which to work out. 'I've lived in flats where you can't swing a cat. That's why my workouts are designed so you can do them within a space the size of a yoga mat,' he said.

Rashford's England teammate Harry Kane boosted the coffers of his old team Leyton Orient by sponsoring their front of shirt for the 2020/21. He resisted the temptation to have his name emblazoned on the players' chests, instead championing three causes. The home shirt featured a note of thanks to frontline workers, the away one was dedicated to Haven House Children's Hospice and a third one was for Mind, the mental health charity.

England's women's captain Steph Houghton was also very visible during lockdown, taking part in and rallying support for the '100k in May' running and walking challenge, which raised over £200,000 for the Darby Rimmer Motor Neurone Disease (MND) Foundation – a charity set up by her husband Stephen Darby, himself a former professional footballer, who was diagnosed with MND at just 29.

Ten or 15 years ago, professional footballers were generally regarded as overpaid and poorly behaved and having a penchant for silly sports cars. The new generation, as we discussed in the previous chapter, are a different breed, who, during 2020, truly found their voices and became comfortable with standing up for their beliefs.

It wasn't just the voices of a few superstar footballers driving change. There was a broader shift occurring during the pandemic, as football started to become newly confident in understanding how its working-class background could help it be an authentic and credible voice as a driver of change, in a way that's more challenging for some of the traditionally more upper-class sports. This grounded approach came from the top. The new CEO of the FA, Mark Bullingham, who was appointed in 2019, is a family man and dedicated kids' football coach – a world away from the stereotype many still hold of a grasping football official. Like millions of others, he also spends his Sunday mornings putting out cones for kids' sessions. During the pandemic, Bullingham led from the front at the start of lockdown, announcing that all FA employees earning more than £50,000 per year would take a temporary pay cut of 7.5 per cent, rising to 30 per cent for the organisation's highest earners.

England men's team manager, Gareth Southgate, widely respected as a class act and superlative leader, wrote an open letter to England supporters, as it became clear that all sport was cancelled indefinitely, including the much-anticipated European Championship. Sounding thoroughly statesmanlike, he wrote:

> We are conscious of the economic uncertainty affecting so many businesses and, consequently, virtually every family. Coupled with the unique challenges of self-isolation, the loss of routine to normal working and social life, we face real challenges to our mental wellbeing. Our children may feel anxious with uncertainty. It's not normal for any of us and it's going to challenge us all. Look out for each other. Please don't suffer alone,

and remember that our great country has come through these enormous challenges before – and, together, we will do so again.

The pandemic seemed to embolden the FA. When it launched its new strategy in 2021, its words showed real intent to use this newly held confidence to make its influence count. It wrote:

Football is a game for all. Where anyone can change the world. That might seem a bold claim, but we know it is true. Just look at how football steps up when times are tough. It provides education and empowerment, escapism and enjoyment. Promoting health and wellbeing, and the power of teamwork.

This might have felt a little over the top before the era of Sterling, Rashford and Co, but they were now pointing to previous success. In a fragmented nation beset by class divide, the cohesion and ambition were a breath of fresh air. It all felt a very long way from Gazza's 1990s dentist's chair antics

THE GREAT OUTDOORS

As the pandemic progressed and more information emerged about COVID-19, it became clear that there was a link between obesity-related conditions, such as diabetes and heart disease, and an increased risk of severe symptoms and death. One NHS study found obese people who caught COVID-19 were twice as likely to die than people who were of normal weight, while another study of critically ill patients in UK intensive care units showed that only 26 per cent had a healthy BMI, with the rest overweight or obese.[36]

As a result, many people started reconsidering their lifestyles. Sales of organic food and drink rose sharply.[37] In March 2020 the sales of vitamins jumped by nearly 20 per cent, with the sales of multivitamins aimed at the 50+ age-group leaping 93 per cent.[38] Friends who had only ever run to the bar at last orders started peppering their social media feeds with keen-bean 'Couch to 5k' updates. This NHS-endorsed app, a nine-week running programme designed for complete beginners, saw an incredible 92 per cent increase in downloads between March and June 2020, compared with the same period the previous year.[39] The best part of a million Brits – 858,000 to be precise – gave it a whirl, enticed by the promise of physical and mental benefits. And quite possibly because there wasn't much else to do. 'Because of the lockdown I couldn't go to the pub,' said one convert, a 36-year-old Bristolian. 'I just wanted to do something that got me out.'

If we weren't running during the pandemic, it seems we were watching TV about other people being active. A slew of sports documentaries kept us gripped, the biggest hit being Netflix's *The Last Dance*, the story of iconic basketballer Michael Jordan's final season at the Chicago Bulls in 1998, which was watched by 23.8 million households worldwide, not including the US, within a month of release. Zero interest in shooting hoops was required to get lost in this often-poignant exploration of friendship, teamwork and epic ambition. We may not have been able to watch any live sport but we could still revel in its stories and live every high and low of its rollercoaster narratives. Other winners for the sofa-based sports fan during lockdown were Netflix's *Cheer*, about the journey of a Texan college cheerleading squad, *Losers*, which looked at the psychology of defeat in sport, and Amazon Prime's *All or Nothing* series, which followed the fortunes of professional sports teams around the world. Our family was glued to *The Test* – a behind-the-scenes glimpse of the Australian cricket team in 2018 and 2019. It required no real understanding of cricket to follow the story of a squad of young men on the edge of elite performance.

When professional sport was initially halted in its tracks, it was still possible to get a live-sport fix of sorts – if you didn't mind a trip down memory lane. Revelling in nostalgia is a useful psychological coping mechanism during tough times, as the millions who enjoyed archive sports TV footage during lockdown will testify. The BBC called it 'uniting the nation with great sporting moments' as it re-broadcasted classic Wimbledon matches, key Euro 96 games and highlights of the 2012 Olympics. The fans were very much still there, even if the sport itself wasn't.

Hundreds of thousands listened to the epic 2019 five-day Ashes Test Match on the radio, with the action also live tweeted – despite everyone, obviously, knowing that England won, against the odds, courtesy of a Ben Stokes masterclass that has gone down in history. Sky, meanwhile, offered the previous year's Cricket World Cup in 'watch-athon' form, with the team's key players reflecting on the matches in real time, while the BBC's *Test Match Special* simultaneously replayed the radio commentary. Unprecedented times indeed – even sports broadcasters, normally fiercely competitive, learnt to collaborate.

Similarly, the world of darts deployed some lateral think-ing, with the Professional Darts Corporation (PDC) running a 32-night competition, streamed on its subscription channel, with players taking part virtually in their own homes. When social distancing was required, darts had one major advantage over almost all other sports – it can be played by people who aren't in the same room as each other. And so we got a peek inside the living rooms of the sport's biggest stars, who wrestled with dodgy wi-fi connections and unpredictable tech, just like the rest of us.

Even in the more elevated world of Grand Slam tennis, the world's biggest names were able to let down their guard during the downtime and came across as fun, fully rounded human beings. This is unusual for tennis players. Their game requires ferocious levels of concentration due to the highly combative one-on-one nature of the sport, which often means its top stars are seen as lacking personality. But we got to see Andy Murray and his wife Kim, and Novak and Jelena Djokovic, rallying in their gardens for the '100-Volley Challenge'. Then Murray and Roger Federer joined Rafa Nadal for an Instagram live chat, with the latter struggling with the technical challenge of adding Federer to the chat. 'This is brilliant – he can win 52 French Opens, but not work Instagram,' grinned Murray. These displays of easy, warm friendship may have surprised many tennis fans who assumed the players clustered at the top of the rankings would be simmering with resentment at their nemeses.

Not everyone hit the right note though – Djokovic's lockdown side-project hit the headlines for all the wrong reasons. When his home country of Croatia began easing lockdown measures, the star organised an independent tournament, the Adria Tour, to help boost the profiles of players from his region and raise money for charities. Four thousand fans attended the first leg and the players were pictured dancing in close proximity to each other in a Belgrade nightclub. Within days, Djokovic, his wife Jelena and players Grigor Dimitrov, Borna Ćorić and Viktor Troicki all tested positive for COVID-19, and the world number one cancelled the rest of the tour and apologised profusely. But the damage was done – he looked arrogant and out of touch with the sacrifices normal people had been forced to make during the pandemic. Declaring himself an anti-vaxxer as vaccines brought hope to the world didn't exactly help on that front either, nor did his complaints about having to self-isolate on travelling to the Australian Open in early 2021. His attitude seemed to echo an era of privilege that had disappeared without trace in a very short amount of time.

Federer, as usual, aced it. He used the unexpected breather in his schedule to call for the merger of the Association of Tennis Professionals (ATP), for men, and the Women's Tennis Association (WTA) tours. Although tennis is the most gender-balanced of major sports, the two bodies operate separately, competing for broadcast and sponsorship deals. 'Am I the only one thinking that now is the time for men's and women's tennis to be united and come together as one?' he tweeted. This was a massive statement coming from such an icon of the game – his vast influence as a solo sports star, as opposed to, say, one sole player from a football team – means that people finally listened to an argument that some women in tennis (Billie Jean King, for one) have been making for years. At the time of writing, it remains to be seen if this bold change will eventually be made. What is clear, though, is that one benefit of the pandemic pressing pause on our lives and our sport was that we had the time and headspace to reassess, question and unpick how we do things, to look at the normal order of play with fresh eyes.

The sports industry also did its best to help where it could, with the focus on goodwill rather than good PR. Formula One teams used their engineering prowess to make CPAP breathing aids for intensive care units. My team, Chelsea, was one of many football clubs to offer up its facilities (two London hotels for NHS staff to stay in) and financial aid (15,000 meals delivered weekly to five different hospitals) in a slew of community-led initiatives. Sports facilities also came to the fore as vaccination centres up and down the country. Tottenham was one of several clubs to volunteer its stadium as an NHS vaccination centre, having also handed it over to the NHS during the first lockdown for use as an antenatal centre in a relatively deprived area of central London. It felt like the concept of the football club had come full circle, returning to its late nineteenth-century roots when northern industrialists set up teams to gel working-class communities together.

This signalled a significant increase in social contribution from some of the world's biggest teams. To their credit, they stepped up. The post-pandemic, Generation X-driven world is one where social contribution is simply expected of any large organisation, and there is an increasing number of stories where professional sports organisations are stepping up to support their local communities. Their budgets, facilities and expertise can often transform what is otherwise possible. For example, approximately a third of the early mass-vaccination sites opened in the UK were in professional-grade sports facilities. Perhaps Camilla Cavendish put it best in the *Financial Times*, writing:

> Cycling past Lord's Cricket Ground in London this week, I did a double-take. It was as if Covid had been a bad dream and cricket had resumed: white-haired men were queuing at the gates, chatting expectantly. They were waiting to be vaccinated.[40]

It wasn't only the large professional teams who lent a hand. On a more modest scale, British mass trail-running events business Maverick, which uses the marketing strapline

'The Outdoors Awaits', sold bespoke T-shirts during lockdown entitled 'The Outdoors Will Wait', with all proceeds going to the NHS. Online running community This Mum Runs' Bristol contingent came up with a novel way of both getting their runner's high and enjoying the warm glow of doing something for others. When pharmacies were overwhelmed with prescription orders at the start of lockdown, an army of runners whizzed around the city delivering medicine to the elderly and others who were shielding. And although PR wasn't the primary objective in any of these cases, every little helps. Businesses, in sport and beyond, will be judged on how they behaved in the crisis at the beginning of this decade. These days it's not enough for brands to simply create a brilliant product or experience. They must behave responsibly and ethically. And that's got to be progress.

Sport was one of the first things to be taken away from us when the pandemic hit, and rightly so. But in a brave new world with our beloved rituals – be it a Tuesday-evening Zumba class or going to the match on Saturday afternoon – stripped away, we started to ponder those things we once took for granted. The luckier among us were able to find the means to re-engage with them. The pandemic did not change sport and fitness's direction of travel but it did condense what otherwise might have been 20 years' worth of change into a much tighter time frame. A game changer? You bet.

CHAPTER 5 / How Sport Will Bring Society Together (When Everything Else is Tearing Us Apart)

IN IT TOGETHER

Even though all my usual running races were cancelled during the 2020 lockdown, I still found a way to compete. My club, Metros, based in west London, got creative when it came to its Summer League fixtures, which are usually dotted through the warmer months. Club members ran 10k individually, around their local areas, and inputted their times to win points for their clubs. Traditionally the Summer League races finish with a short inter-club relay, and this time round this fun (but painful) 400m went virtual, which saw me handing over an imaginary baton to another member at the end of my sprint. My mum also joined in, 20 miles away at her home, as did my young nephews Finn and Kane in the junior race. You could take part at any point during the weekend, so people's times and photos popped up on our family WhatsApp group, as well as on our club's Facebook page.

A fun diversion, yes, although not a patch on the real deal. We runners often revel in the solitude and peace our sport offers. But equally we relish a calendar punctuated with races, when you're one among a pack and all you can hear is the rhythmic, hypnotic thud, thud, thud of thousands of feet hitting the road. Training for these events incentivises us to go that bit further or faster – or even just get out of the house at all – on a cold February evening when Netflix and the sofa seem devilishly alluring. Securing a spot in a sold-out London Marathon is the runner's version of nailing a gold-dust Glastonbury ticket. And although it wasn't quite the same, Metros' Summer League was at least *something*. It gave purpose to the early morning runs and reconnected us with our clubmates.

Sport, at its best, has always been about community and it turns out nothing hammers home the importance of our local connections more than a global pandemic. In some cases, the hastily cooked-up methods of maintaining that togetherness were charmingly low-key. When professional football matches resumed without fans allowed back into the grounds, clubs improvised by offering cardboard cut-outs of supporters, dotted around the stands, so fans still got to take their seat. But it was rather more advanced technology that saved the day in many cases. We may have tired of endless Zoom calls while working in the back bedroom but it's indisputable that digital tech helped sports aficionados come together in spirit if not in person – parkrun kept its community tightly gelled with, in a similar vein to Summer League, its (not)parkrun initiative. Participants were asked to run a solo 5k – *not* at 9am on a Saturday morning at their usual parkrun venue, though, in order to avoid gatherings – and to log it. parkrun also offered a weekly video-call quiz, with members joining from around the world.

Another brand that strongly champions its community, Peloton, the purveyors of the connected stationary bicycles beloved by urban millennials, saw so many people stuck in their living rooms wanting to ride with others also stuck in their living rooms that they doubled production to meet demand. The bikes swiftly became the new status symbol to have stashed in the living room on a work video call, an adjunct to everyone's suspiciously impressive bookshelves. The implicit message – 'I'm never too far from my next workout' – showed how integrated into a working day sport has become. The days of physical activity being something that only happens outside the office and the hours of nine-to-five were gone for good. I'd hazard a guess that during lockdown there were more conference calls conducted in Lycra than in a well-pressed shirt. I was invited to speak on Zoom for the Sports Industry Awards in South Africa, where the dress code was 'Business Attire on Top, Sports Gear at the Bottom'!

BUT IS IT SPORT (AND DOES IT MATTER ANYWAY)?

It wasn't quite as much fun as being there in person, but the technology let us interact a little, and create a virtual community even though I couldn't physically be in South Africa. For many, gaming enables that sense of community, even if it can create parental tension.

Eighteenth of June 2020 was a momentous day in our house. The Premier League was roaring back into action after being halted in March due to lockdown restrictions. I couldn't have been more excited. My 13-year-old son Conor was equally excited because a new season of the online video game *Fortnite* launched that day. So began an epic dad vs son battle for control of the primary screen, the main TV in the lounge. Dad lost. As I observed Conor interacting on his headset with his friends as the action unfolded on the screen in front of him, I was relegated to watching Aston Villa vs Sheffield United on my diddy laptop screen. While top-flight football and an esport (like it or not, that's what competitive multiplayer video games are called) such as *Fortnite* seem poles apart – markers of the wildly different leisure tastes of different generations – I was struck by how traditional sport was attempting to create a similar type of engagement in football stadiums devoid of fans. Where *Fortnite* went first, football was following suit. Sky launched a 'Watch Together' stream so fans could watch separately from their sofas but chat as the action progressed. Amazon Prime went one step further and streamed its live games on its gaming platform Twitch, which meant a constant stream of live conversation among viewers. Football was plundering from the gaming world and it seemed to be working.

You may not have heard the term esport before. My co-author Kerry hadn't – although her children play esports most days, conducting *Roblox* play-a-long Zoom calls with their friends. So, you may be surprised to discover what huge business they are. Globally, 45 million people played EA Games' FIFA esports franchise in 2019 – that's only slightly fewer than the number of actual registered footballers in the whole of Europe. The UK is the world's fifth-biggest gaming market, trailing China and the USA (where more than 50 colleges now have varsity esports programmes). Gaming is often seen (by worried parents) as detrimental to children's education and health but now we're starting to understand how and where it fits alongside and complements traditional forms of sport.

There are 6.5 million Brits who watch organised esport competitions. Older generations may not understand the appeal of watching other people playing computer games but younger ones certainly do – it is part and parcel of how many of them consume and play sport. And how they define it too – many will question whether an esport is actually a sport. But that distinction between digital and physical activity doesn't exist in the minds of Generation Z.

Drone Racing League (DRL), a sport born just five years ago in the United States, is taking the country by storm. It has several forms. There is a simulator game that wannabe pilots can practise on, with the very best selected to race real drones in locations around the world as professionals. These shows are broadcast on regular TV networks in the US and, as you would expect, also through social media channels, as are some simulator races. The digital and physical worlds are completely fused – and the audience loves it.

Having worked in professional sports for 20 years at the US National Basketball Association (NBA), Rachel Jacobson, president of the Drone Racing League, found the move to the DRL refreshing. 'As a new event we can be really agile to break all the rules I had to abide by at the NBA. "Can we move the date of this race?" Yes of course we can!' she says. 'I try to see the world through the eyes of my ten-year-old twins. Children are growing up in a world that we didn't know. Screens for our kids are primary ways to consume the sports they love. If you're not seeing drones in an arena, we will bring it to you – what you want, where you want, how you want it.'

Setting aside the fact that it won't add to your daily step count, there is money to be made and there are jobs to be created in the esports sector. Global esports revenues were estimated to hit $1.1 billion in 2020, up from $950.6 million in the previous year. And in 2020, $822.4 million in revenue – three-quarters of the total market – is predicted to come from media rights and sponsorship.

The British Esports Association, formed in 2016, takes a softly-softly approach to naysayers. 'We are not pushing esports as a rival to traditional sport,' it says, perhaps to reassure parents fearful that their child would play *Minecraft* for eight hours straight if left to their own devices, 'but as a credible activity in its own right, which can have positive cognitive and other benefits when done in moderation. Esports promotes teamwork and communication, develops communities and provides jobs.' It may not be the kind of community that the sports traditionalist cares much for but it's there nonetheless. And as long as esports are played in combination with activities that *do* boost your fitness, they certainly have their place.

One of the main advantages of the Drone Racing League is how tantalisingly close you can feel to being a professional. As Jacobson says, 'If you learn to use our simulator, you can then go straight outside and successfully fly a real drone – it's so similar. Whereas you can't play *NBA Live* and then go outside and immediately become Lebron James.' This brings the professional game within reach for the amateurs watching them compete, which is a recipe for success in a world where digital has broken down the barriers between amateur and elite.

This isn't the only barrier that esports break down. Watching kids play esports, I'm always fascinated by their ability to be totally transfixed by the action, and yet also have a laptop at their sides with a professional playing live on YouTube on a second screen. I'm never sure whether that's a good thing or not, but as a minimum it should ensure that my son will become far better at multitasking than I am.

INSIDER INSIGHT: **RACHEL JACOBSON**

The newly minted sport of professional drone racing launched just five years ago but already has a huge following in the United States and, increasingly, the UK. Billing itself as 'the sport of the future', it straddles the line between esport and sport in the traditional sense. As president of the Drone Racing League (DRL) in the US, Rachel leads global partnerships and media rights deals, and heads up the marketing and business development teams. Previously she spent 21 years at the NBA. Named one of Sport Business Journal's *40 Under 40 high achievers, she joined DRL from Landit, a platform aimed at helping women progress in their careers.*

First things first: what exactly is drone racing?

It's the most exhilarating sport where pilots fly first-person-view drones through aerial courses, at the fastest speeds. It started out as an underground hobby that our founder, Nicholas Horbaczewski, discovered in 2015 and transformed into a professional, internationally broadcast sport. At DRL, we take the best drone pilots in the world, custom-build 90mph-flying racing drones, and design spectacular live and virtual drone-racing events around the world. As a mum, I love how inclusive drone racing is – it brings people of all backgrounds together to compete at the highest level – and the fact that the sport is built on science and technology, authentically offering opportunities for STEM education. The UK, where we air on Sky Sports, is one of our biggest international markets, with such an incredible fanbase there and ever-growing drone pilot community. We recently launched our DRL game on console for players everywhere to learn to fly like the pros.

What kind of people does the DRL attract as both viewers and participants?

We reach young, innovative, tech-obsessed, adventure-seeking sports fans. Three-quarters of our fans are younger than 35, 70 per cent of them don't follow or engage with the 'big five' sports in the US [American football, basketball, baseball, hockey, soccer] and they're four times more likely than the general population to be passionate about gaming. So for companies looking to reach that next-generation sports fan, DRL brings this incredible audience that's on the pulse of technology and new entertainment trends.

Do pilots use the simulator game to progress to competing in your live events?

Yes, pilots can absolutely qualify for the live championship series through the simulator. Our 2019 champion came from a grassroots event where he qualified. We identify the best talent from all over the world. One big priority for us is gender diversity. When I joined, I looked at our pilot pool and said, 'Where are all the women?' We know there are female pilots out there, there's no reason why women can't compete with the men.

It can be challenging to encourage women to work in and participate in sport.

Here we're doing a great job of gender diversity on the business side. Women comprise more than half our organisation and our senior team is now majority women. We'll keep focusing on the pilots. We know the most innovative thinking comes from all types of diversity around the table, and we can improve in areas beyond gender, as everyone can. We have also built up a STEM curriculum that looks to inspire a next generation of scientists and engineers – because if you don't have access to the right thinking and technology at eight, nine, ten years old then it will never be a career to which you aspire. We want to inspire a generation of kids not only to become pilots, but to work in our sport and other technology-driven companies. And we're focused on getting to girls at a really early age so they grow up feeling they have exactly the same opportunities as the boys.

Your predictions – and hopes – for the future of sport?

As sports evolve into more tech-led competitions, brand partnerships will evolve too. Just like how DRL can integrate technology straight into our drones and competitions, we'll see major tech companies literally powering the future of sport to showcase the next evolution of technological breakthroughs – whether that's AI, 5G, AR and anything that we haven't even thought of yet! And I cannot wait to unveil our first female drone pilot. The push for gender parity, diversity and inclusion across the sports and tech industries is so vital.

FACE TO FACE

Much as esports do have benefits (and more than we might often give them credit for), even for my kids interacting with their mates on Zoom isn't the same as being face-to-face with them. The best sports clubs, global brands and volunteer-run local ones alike understand their key purpose as community hubs, not just open to all, but welcoming to all. While digital tools picked up the slack and kept us connected during the lockdown, that strange period gave us a deeper appreciation of the power of in-person interaction in our sporting endeavours.

As a trustee of Halton Tennis Club in Buckinghamshire, I found it interesting to watch members come streaming back on-site after the first lockdown ended and we were allowed to reopen the courts. Initially the club's buildings remained shuttered – the club house, the café – with members asked to head straight to their court, which they had to book online, with slots limited to one hour. There were no handshakes and players had to change ends via different sides of the court to ensure social distancing. While the members who play to a high level were happy as Larry to be back hitting balls, the less regular players' feedback seemed a little lukewarm somehow. While they were grateful the club had reopened and their game was fine, the experience just wasn't the same. A highly efficient, protocol-following, social interaction-free, truncated game of tennis didn't quite do it for them. It wasn't how they got their kicks. This is because the sport alone isn't enough for most players. Once you strip out the incidental stuff – having a beer with your doubles partner afterwards, bumping into your coach and having a chat on the way in, bringing your children down to hang out with their pals – the experience is reduced to its bare essentials, the nuts and bolts. It's playing tennis, yes, and it's better than not playing, but it's not the experience we know and love. Sports clubs help us feel like we're part of something and, at their best, they're third spaces; an appealing alternative to home or work. At Halton, the bustling café is always busy but, as is so often the case with cafés, it's no money-spinner. Its value is social rather than monetary – it's the glue that binds the club's community together, that makes members feel part of something bigger than themselves. They may not play for the first team but they still belong; they're still part of the gang.

For all the helpful advances in technology, digitisation shouldn't be allowed to eliminate this togetherness. The organisers of parkrun understand the importance of this: while registration is automated and it's easy to find a race and track your progress online, you're still encouraged to have a chat with the volunteers on-site. This is because parts of the process that could be automated, such as the new-joiner briefing or entry of results into the system – are deliberately left as manual tasks, which encourages teamwork and creates conversations between volunteers who would not otherwise have to get to know each other.

My tennis club's approach is similar to the kinds of sports clubs that exist in parts of Europe, in particular the Netherlands. According to a University of Sheffield report published in 2017, Dutch sports clubs are, on average, the biggest in Europe, with an average of 270 members per club compared to just 112 in England. Dutch sports clubs play a fundamental role in local communities. While 27 per cent of the Dutch take part in sport at a local club, only 11 per cent do the same in England.[41]

So what is it that makes sports clubs in the Netherlands so successful? Firstly, the Dutch government is forward-thinking in the ways in which it uses sport. It sees it as a powerful lever to achieve social objectives such as increasing social participation, social integration, healthy lifestyles and creating safe neigh-bourhoods. The government matches each of these objec-tives with funds for specific activities, which take place at local clubs. Secondly, legislation in the Netherlands allows volun-teers in sports clubs to receive payment for time committed and expenses, up to a maximum of 1,500 euros, tax free. Nearly a fifth of the Dutch population (18 per cent) volunteers in sports clubs, compared to 11 per cent of English people. Finally, Dutch clubs are adept at creating a sense of social community – build-ing an environment where it's not simply about playing the game. Their bars and cafés look and feel like the ones at Halton, albeit with more Heineken and less gin.

Our leisure culture is changing. The days of the menfolk spending all day in the pub at the weekend while the women look after the kids at home are largely over – and rightly so. Pubs are closing, a process hastened by the pandemic and, in part, the lack of demand is because modern families need community hubs that work for all members of the family and their lifestyles. The rise of the coffee shop is a good example and sports clubs fit the bill here too. Now that five pubs in my local area have shut, the local cricket club – which doesn't need to turn a specific profit like a commercial pub does – has a flow of volunteers behind the bar, so they're increasingly able to offer a service to their local community and keep the doors of the club open for as much of the year as possible.

What's more, with our increasingly busy lives, a trip to the pub can seem like an indulgence – who has the time to while away an afternoon or an evening propping up a bar these days? We now look to add value to our downtime, to multitask even when we're in repose – so we may still enjoy that glass of wine but it might be an add-on when we take the children to football training or after our yoga class. And, in light of those generational demographics that show rising levels of teetotalism among younger people, when those football- or hockey-playing children come of drinking age, they'll be far less likely than previous generations to immediately run to the nearest bar and down a yard of ale. So is the sports club or fitness studio the new pub? It might just be – and I'll raise a glass to that.

REPRESENTING ALL VOICES

Of course, in order to be powerful social hubs, sports also need to be open and welcoming to the whole community. Although times are changing, the reality can still be starkly different, despite the efforts of activist athletes to drive change from the top down. Tanya Joseph, the brains behind the 'This Girl Can' campaign who we met earlier, is forthright about the challenges sport faces around structural racism. 'Sport is extraordinarily racist,' she says. 'People in sport have used the N-word in front of me in meetings with national governing bodies on more than one occasion. And it's the narratives: the tendency to think that all Black youths are on the verge of criminality so we should give them basketballs to stop them being drug dealers. The belief that all Asian boys are going to be good at cricket. There's a real lack of understanding. Just look at who's employed in sport. The under-representation of ethnic minorities is quite extraordinary. Lots of these organisations are based in London so there's absolutely no reason for them not to employ people from diverse backgrounds.'

Sport England independent board member Chris Grant, one of the most senior Black administrators in sport, told the BBC: 'problems have grown up quietly over decades. I salute [footballers] Raheem Sterling, Eni Aluko and Alice Dearing, who will be our first Black swimmer at [the Olympic Games in] Tokyo, for speaking out. At the same time, it is not their job to fix this. Right now there are lots of initiatives across many sports, but we are looking at systemic issues. You can't fix a system by dealing with things one at a time.'

When it comes to be listened to, athletes stand in a privileged position in the context of significant public mistrust of politicians and other establishment figures. To that extent, they can play a major role in pushing awareness of societal challenges. But they don't have the political power to change things in and of themselves.

The return of the Black Lives Matter cause to the front pages drove a broader discussion around the experience of minority groups' access to sport. Clearly the racial debate crosses boundaries here with other factors, not least geography and demography. Ethnic minority communities are more likely to live in urban environments, where sporting facilities are more likely to be expensive and over-subscribed.

Ultra-running – for those for whom 26.2 miles isn't enough – is booming. It's technically any race that's longer than a standard marathon, although many events are 50 miles, 100 miles or more (there's no upper limit). At the turn of the millennium, only a few hundred would complete a race in the UK; 20 years on, it's more like 20,000. But while the sport may not have a popularity problem, it does have a diversity one. 'I did a race at the weekend and was the only Black runner out of 240 starters,' says Harrow-based ultra-runner Sonny Peart, who recently co-founded Black Trail Runners, a campaigning and community group. There's a variety of factors for this, says Peart: as mentioned, the fact that most people of colour live in cities can make access to rural trails tricky. 'It's not just a physical constraint, it's a psychological one too,' he says. 'If discrimination has been part of your life experience you'd naturally want to spend your time in places you're not going to experience that, where you're not going to be challenged, where you don't have to explain your presence. As someone who spends a lot of time out in the trails, my experience is almost entirely enjoyable. But unless you've been there and done that you don't know that.' Cost is also a barrier: you can't just pull on your trainers and run, there's a certain amount of kit needed to last those kind of distances, not to mention the price of travel, support crews and race fees. Black Trail Runners' first steps were to ask race organisers to start collating ethnicity data and to ensure a diverse mix of runners are represented in their marketing materials. It's a start.

INSIDER INSIGHT: SONNY PEART

Sonny is an ultra-runner and co-founder of Black Trail Runners, a community and campaigning group. When he's not running insane distances, he's a lecturer in business management at King's College London.

How did Black Trail Runners come about?

After the resurgence of the Black Lives Matter movement, I was contacted by James Elson, race director at Centurion Running, which organises 50- and 100-mile races. He wanted me to come on his podcast because he said he could count the Black runners in his races on one hand and knew the name of every single one. He wanted to talk about why this was and what could be done. Black Trail Runners grew from there. It's a running group that has three main objectives: to increase participation, to increase representation and to increase inclusion. And inclusion is a word that gets misused a lot. People will often say, 'We're very inclusive,' but what they actually mean is 'we're tolerant' – 'we didn't invite you to the party but now you're here, you can stay.' That's not going to work because people will not come to the party.

There doesn't seem to be many women in ultra-running either. Is the amount of time involved a barrier?

Definitely. Even a low-mileage ultra-runner is going to spend several hours a week running and not everyone can afford to do that. I've had a few conversations with female runners recently who've felt guilty about taking that time out to run. There's no question that it is a predominantly white middle-aged male sport. The race results are all categorised by age group and I'm 52, and during races I think, *I must be doing well in the age 50+ group*. But there are always dozens and dozens of other men in their fifties ahead of me! Men of that age have got time, they've got disposable income – and that sense of obsession. The gender split is changing though. A lot of organisers have tried hard to get more women involved. Physically and temperamentally, it's a sport that's suited to women – they are good at extreme endurance. While a top female runner is never going to beat a top male runner in a road marathon, women beat men in ultras sometimes. When you're running up to 250 miles through difficult conditions, other things beyond physicality come into play. It's a psychological battle. My female pacer has a theory that men's egos get in the way. Men go too fast and beyond their capability, while women will say, 'I'm not worried about beating you in the first 20 miles because I'll still be there at 90 miles.'

How can the sports industry more broadly reach the kind of people who are traditionally hard to reach?

That's something bigger than sport. The pandemic made it harder for a lot of people to be active. Sport can't fix the fact that people have to do two or three jobs and manage childcare. They have insecure jobs so they can't afford to be ill, they can't afford to take time off, they don't have disposable income. That's a societal problem. There's a large proportion of society who live an economically precarious existence. Sport is not top of their agenda, it's about making ends meet. We know if they were active, they would be healthier. But they haven't got the time or money to be healthy. It's a catch-22.

Your predictions – and hopes – for the future of sport?

Sport needs different people to get involved, not just participating and watching but in governing sport. It's about power. The stats on this make fairly depressing reading: look at the number of Black professional footballers and then look at the number of Black managers, let alone Black owners. Look at the number of governing bodies in the UK that have any people of colour in their senior echelons. It's not many. Until that changes, we won't see major structural change. Yes, there's clearly been an upswing in diverse people participating. But there are certain people in sport who think enough has been done – they'll say, 'What's the problem? Look at that football team, it's diverse.' But we know that diversity comes in many shapes and forms. We still have a major gender issue in sport and then you have things like sexuality – how we are still in a position in 2020 where we imagine there are no gay professional footballers? On a positive note, I see a greater range and variety of sports that are considered to be acceptable to take part in. Years ago if you didn't do one of the 'big' sports, what were you going to do? I think this change is down to social media – you can have a community around a particular activity that wasn't possible before. There are lots of sports where you don't need anyone in your street or town to do the same activity because you can connect with people all around the world.

UNDER THE INFLUENCE

Sonny's story shows that you don't need to be an elite athlete on the field to be an influence beyond it. This is certainly the case for the new breed of sports and fitness social media influencers, who often make a virtue of their ordinariness and accessibility, which helps them command huge audiences on Instagram, Facebook and YouTube. They're part of the influencer marketing industry, which is only around a decade old yet set to be worth $15 billion by 2022.[42] Joe Wicks is the highest profile example in the UK: having started out in 2012 offering £5 bootcamps in a London park that would attract precisely zero attendees on some days, he was quick to understand the power of social media in growing his audience and duly crossed over from his niche into mainstream culture and international fame. Although you'll find countless parents forever grateful for Wicks's lockdown kids' PE sessions, you'll also find naysayers who view him as a shameless self-publicist. The rise of the fitness influencer has been a controversial one. Instagram teems with selfies of perfect (digitally altered?) sixpacks and biceps, following in Wicks's slipstream, alongside workouts offered by self-styled experts. Just follow their programme, they imply, and your body will look just like that too. But will it *really*? And has your gorgeous new guru actually *got* any expertise?

Tally Rye is a qualified personal trainer who's worked in London gyms since 2014 and is the author of *Train Happy: An Intuitive Exercise Plan for Every Body*. She describes herself as an 'anti-diet, weight-inclusive PT'. Having been part of Instagram's fitness influencer community since the platform's infancy ten years ago (she currently has 111,000 followers), she's seen it all over the years. 'A lot of fitness influencing is pitched as being aspirational and that's where we get the objectification of bodies – here are the abs you should be striving for,' she says. 'It's about posing for fitness rather than actually *doing* the fitness. But fitness isn't about what your body looks like, it's about what your body can do.' Some influencers sell online workout plans, despite having never actually trained anyone in real life. And, as Tally points out, everyone is different so a one-size-fits-all programme can only improve your fitness so far. What's more, PT qualifications can be very easy to come by. 'You can just do a six-week course,' says Tally. 'Lots of influencers are gifted PT courses so they don't even pay for it but use it as a box-ticking exercise, as a springboard into their fitness career. People have come on to Instagram, thinking, *Oh I can make some money here*.' And then there are the ones who don't even do the course at all – there's nothing to stop you setting yourself up as a fitness expert because you went to a gym once.

Not only can their advice be untrustworthy, some of the content produced can be problematic for young women who have issues with self-esteem, their bodies and eating disorders. A 2015 study by Australian psychologists gathered 130 female Instagram users and showed one group 'fitspiration' images and the other group a control set of travel images.[43] The former group reported more negative moods, body-image dissatisfaction and decreasing self-esteem than the latter. Of course, fitness influencing is a relatively new phenomenon so there aren't many of these kind of studies but the few carried out have seen similar results. As Kerry points out from personal experience, if a confident, fit, healthy woman in her forties, with decades of life experience under her belt, can feel demoralised and demotivated after browsing images of impossibly lithe fitness influencers, the potential impact on younger, more impressionable minds is worrying. We are hardwired to compare ourselves to others, even though we know it's a fool's errand.

All that said, when you look beyond the unhelpful #fitspo selfies – and that's certainly not Tally Rye's all-inclusive style – there are many positives. Influencers have democratised fitness for participants – you don't need an expensive gym or studio membership or all the gear to join in, just grab your phone. And many of these figureheads, airbrushed abs aside, feel more relatable, accessible and, well, human than superstar elite athletes – there's a closer connection, a greater intimacy there. Joe Wicks will tell you what he's had for breakfast, along with how well he's slept and if he's in a bad mood. Self-obsessed maybe (and your view on this tends to depend on your generation) but at least he's honest.

You also don't need to be a ripped millennial to get in on the act these days. Joan MacDonald is a somewhat unlikely online fitness guru but the charming septuagenarian American has 1.1 million followers on Instagram, where she posts OAP-friendly workouts, which her personal trainer daughter helps devise. Her bio reads: 'You can't turn back the clock but you can wind it up again.' Influencers, says Tally Rye, have opened up fitness to everyone, whatever their age, body size, fitness level, ethnicity, lifestyle or preferences: 'There's so much fitness content out there now that people are trying out new ways to exercise which they might never have had access to before,' she says. 'Once you might have bought one fitness DVD but now you can try all these different things, for free. Those tasters get people excited and help them find the activity that works for them.' She continues, 'I think social media has made fitness cool. A few years ago, if a high-street brand launched activewear, it was really exciting, now every high street brand offers it. That's a huge transformation.'

Tally also makes an important distinction between sport and fitness: 'I had zero interest in PE or sport at school but I've now found a way of exercising that I enjoy. That's where social media came in – it showcased what fitness can be and lots of people who weren't 'sporty' thought, *Oh, I can actually do that*.' A significant minority of interviewees for this book – all of whom you would consider to be 'sporty' – make similar points, recalling humiliating experiences in PE lessons that have echoed down the decades. Often (and especially so with women) these unhappy formative memories – being forced to run cross country in torrential rain as a punishment, say – put people off embracing an active lifestyle. If social media can help mitigate this by showcasing a diverse range of people enjoying a broad range of fitness options, then we should applaud it.

INSIDER INSIGHT: TALLY RYE

The author of Train Happy: An Intuitive Exercise Plan for Every Body, *Tally has been a personal trainer since 2014, working in various London gyms. She's also one of the first wave of Instagram's fitness influencers (current follower count: 111,000) and has worked with brands such as adidas and with the 'This Girl Can' campaign.*

How did you get into fitness influencing?

It was just a hobby at first. Instagram wasn't monetised in the early days; for me it was more about finding a community and sharing my fitness journey. In 2014, I graduated from drama school and had become very interested in fitness while I was studying, in terms of how it related to being a healthy performer. I qualified as a personal trainer and was quite obsessive about what I ate and how I exercised. The clear message I found on social media was that health and fitness was something you did to lose weight and look good.

What changed?

As I became more educated, I felt like I couldn't approach fitness constantly feeling like I wasn't not doing it well enough, that I didn't look right, that I didn't weigh the right amount. There was too much pressure so I took a step back from that. I discovered a weight-inclusive approach to fitness – the anti-diet movement. It's about promoting fitness as a health-promoting behaviour that makes you feel good. So self-care rather than punishment. That resonated with me personally, it helped me feel relaxed around my food and my body. And professionally it heavily influenced what I do now. My followers have grown since I stripped out the weight loss and aesthetics stuff, which I find very encouraging.

Your Instagram feed is more inclusive and non-intimidating than people might expect from a fitness influencer.

I'm focused on inclusivity and I'm passionate about celebrating fitness that comes in all shapes and sizes. I wanted to show less of me on my feed – my goal is not to sell my body. I don't want people to exercise to try to look like me so I often ask other women to demonstrate my workouts. When I post a plus-size woman exercising that gets the most engagement. Women say, 'I relate to that. I've finally seen someone who looks like me do that so I think I can do it too.'

How can we address the problem of unrealistic fitness images on social media? They make so many women feel terrible.

Don't follow people, or mute them if they make you feel bad. A lot of the content I look at isn't selfies, it's workout videos or educational information. It's up to you how you choose to engage with social media. I know there are problems with fitness on social media, especially the tendency to compare yourself to other women, but you need to have an awareness of how certain content makes you feel. Choose brilliant people to follow. And, of course, take time away from being online.

On a positive note, social media stars like Joe Wicks are making fitness much easier to access.

Yes, there's a plethora of fitness content now on YouTube and there are so many people now doing these workouts who never had access to fitness before. They might have previously bought one fitness DVD, but now they can try loads of things online for free. That taster has got people excited to try out other classes and activities.

What kind of feedback do you get from women who listen to your Radio 5 Live *Fit & Fearless* podcast?

Women often say, 'I actually just enjoyed my workout for the first time. I stopped putting pressure on myself and I started enjoying it.' It's about having a good relationship with exercise. Whether you had a traumatic experience with PE at school or have only ever associated exercise with dieting before your holiday, you can make it something you enjoy.

Your predictions – and hopes – for the future of sport and fitness?

I hope we'll continue to increasingly see fitness in a more holistic way, as something that makes us feel good and brings benefits like reducing the risk of breast cancer or hip fractures – things that are so unglamorous but vital to our health. And there are a lot of people in the UK who don't have the time and energy to think about fitness in the way that middle-class people do. One of the biggest health markers is postcode – we need to invest in fitness that's accessible for poorer communities and work out how can we use fitness to help people manage their wellbeing in those areas.

ENDORPHINS AS AN AGENT FOR CHANGE

Most of us know that the happy hormones released when we exercise are good for our minds, bodies and souls. But can they be good for our wider communities and social cohesion too? Increasing numbers of forward-thinkers are creating sports projects with a social conscience. GoodGym, founded by Ivo Gormley, aims to get people off treadmills and into their communities. The idea came when Gormley offered to deliver supplies to a housebound elderly man who lived a mile down the road from him. A twice-weekly newspaper was requested and Gormley would run down with it and have a chat with his new pal. And so began a scheme that now operates in 58 areas across the UK, in collaboration with Age UK. Runners visit elderly people to help them with jobs and chores, or just keep them company, as well as helping with community projects. Think a workout with a double whammy of feelgood factor. StreetGames, meanwhile, is a charity that works with disadvantaged children, providing sports programmes for families who might not normally be able to afford this kind of structured activity. The charity has found that encouraging children to become more active increases social cohesion as well as boosting the participants' broader ambitions. With 3.5 million children currently living in poverty in England, never has this kind of work been more needed.

It's not just new ventures putting community first. We're increasingly seeing fresh thinking within existing organisations. One excellent example can be found in south-west London, in Wandsworth, a borough of contradictions. While there are areas of extreme affluence and beautiful green space takes up one-fifth of the footprint of the borough, one in three children lives in an income-deprived household. Around 30 per cent of residents are from ethnic minorities. In this context, sport has to be local, affordable and bridge divides rather than reinforce them.

Hockey might not sound like the obvious answer. It's a challenging sport to access. AstroTurf pitches are often impossible for state schools to offer and the sport often comes with a price tag that is prohibitive for stretched parents. The hugely successful Spencer Hockey Club noticed that its junior membership did not reflect the diverse community in which it was located. To address this, the club set up a specific organisation in 2019 – Spencer Lynx Hockey – to provide free access to the sport for a cohort of ten state schools in Wandsworth and Lambeth, the majority being children from ethnic minority backgrounds. Registered as a charity and funded by the sport's governing body, England Hockey, Surrey Hockey and charitable fundraising, it delivers sessions in schools and provides free Sunday-morning hockey to children who have enjoyed those taster sessions. The aim is to encourage those children to find a sport for life in hockey, with the financial support in the form of bursaries to enable this.

This kind of proactive action is exactly the way forward for broadening access for minority groups to sport – providing specific efforts to reach new communities, breaking down initial barriers of price, perception and access, and then allowing new generations to explore the sport at their own pace. Spencer Lynx also follows the Sporting Recipe – popular/accessible/paid for – essential for forging change that we covered in Chapter 3. The social imperative creates a wave of volunteers from the club to make it happen; public bodies fund where they can, with sponsors providing the kit and a private school the pitch facilities. It is early days but the signs are very positive.

Then we come on to the blossoming of volunteer culture. The meaning of the word has been subtly redefined since the

London 2012 Olympics. Before the Games, volunteering still carried some sense of making a sacrifice for the good of others, having originally been used as a military term for soldiers prepared to fight for a cause. London 2012 changed this by calling its volunteer army the 'Games Makers'. This phrasing made it clear this was no peripheral, low-skilled effort but rather the individuals London 2012 was recruiting were going to make the difference. They did exactly that, with 70,000 Games Makers turning the Olympics and Paralympics from an event into an experience. When the flame of the Paralympic Games finally disappeared at the closing ceremony, the cheers for those Games Makers were deafeningly loud. The appreciation was mutual. The Games Makers themselves were open about how much they'd relished their roles and their smiles were infectious.

The Games Makers were a tipping point for volunteering in Britain. It continued apace inside and outside sport, with the nation increasingly reliant on volunteering as a means to get things done. During times of austerity, we've needed volunteers to take on huge responsibilities, running libraries, staffing hospitals and pulling pints at ailing pubs that have been taken on by local communities. To their great credit, the baby-boomer generation has taken a significant role. While they may have left the paid workforce, they continue to contribute in so many ways. The key to unlocking volunteering across the generations, as London 2012 did, has been to repackage opportunities as ways for individuals to use their skills in new settings with payback in terms of learning and community engagement.

parkrun, which has had over 300,000 helpers contribute to date, has a clear stance on volunteering – it's just as rewarding (and often more so) than running. It is also noticeable how many younger children volunteer alongside parents, which has normalised the process for future generations.

The sports industry has at times been accused of being glitzy, grasping and overly focused on its elite superstars. As ever there are two sides to the story. Dig just beneath the surface and you'll find all manner of clever, successful community-based projects and people giving back, making a difference to the hearts and minds of young and old alike. It's quite the buzz.

OPENING DOORS TO ALL

One of the areas that has changed beyond all measure in Britain – kickstarted by the build-up and delivery of the London 2012 Olympics – is the access and integration to opportunities provided to disability athletes. But while facilities have improved markedly, disability sport charity WheelPower CEO Martin McElhatton points out that sport, too, needs a shift in mindset.

It's every child's right to have access to sport and physical activity – whether that's a sports wheelchair, whether it's a blade for an amputee, whether it's a piece of equipment for children to be able to play with their friends,' he says. 'And there needs to be greater awareness and training for PE teachers – disabled children need to be included more at school.' Martin continues: 'I would like to see an effort in terms of making facilities more accessible and welcoming.

And that not only being in the physical nature of buildings but in the training of staff and coaches within the facilities.

So that positive experience for disabled people starts from the minute they go into a facility. There should be a disabled toilet and it shouldn't be full of chairs and mops! Gyms are not going to buy specialised kit, it's too expensive. But they need to understand that disabled people live in their communities and they don't want to get in a car and drive 30 mins to a gym. They want to go to the one down the road.

I am privileged to have worked (and played sport) with several disabled athletes, elite and otherwise, and it is extraordinary to see the challenges they still encounter. On one occasion I was due to attend a meeting with a Paralympian. Fifteen minutes before our slot, she called me from a supermarket car park to explain that she was running late as she was unable to get into her car. Although she was parked in a disabled bay, she was stuck because a member of the public had parked their vehicle too close to her driver's side. She sounded weary and resigned rather than angry, a sign that this kind of thoughtlessness is a daily occurrence. Since the 2012 Games, we may now enthusiastically cheer on our Paralympic athletes with as much gusto as our Olympic heroes but, on a quotidian level, there's still a lot of work to be done to achieve true equality.

INSIDER INSIGHT: MARTIN MCELHATTON

The CEO of the charity WheelPower, Martin was awarded an OBE for services to disability sport in the 2020 New Year Honours. He's lived with a spinal injury for almost 40 years and competed in wheelchair basketball for Great Britain in the 1984 Paralympic Games at Stoke Mandeville. Martin is passionate about providing young and newly disabled people opportunities to play sport.

The Paralympic Games were a huge hit at London 2012 – what happened next? What was their legacy?

The games did an amazing job in raising the profile in the UK of elite athletes. We went from having a couple of household names to a whole host of well-known faces. The 'Meet the Super-humans' campaign [Channel 4's award-winning film to promote its 2012 Paralympics coverage] was such a revolutionary way of looking at disabled people. It changed attitudes. That said, it wasn't all positive. Some disabled people said, 'We're not all superhuman'. Or, 'Just because I get up and go and do my job doesn't mean I'm an inspiration'. Not all disabled people feel represented by elite athletes. The Paralympians push that bar up too far for some people – we need to have other bars people can easily reach at every level in sport.

How do the Paralympics help grassroots disability sport?

They increase understanding and that gives us a framework to have conversations with sponsors, schools, and charitable funding that supports grassroots disability sport – and you don't have to explain what it is because people know. We say, 'You know about the Paralympics but think about the other end – how do we get young people with disabilities to do PE at school? How do we get people who become disabled later in life to do activity that helps their physical and mental wellbeing?'

Are that second group harder to reach?

Yes. Like in broader society, not everyone who's disabled is interested in sport. So how do you pitch it in a way that attracts them and makes them feel welcome? That's where the other benefit of the 2012 Games comes in – the improvements in access and in attitude. Someone disabled going into a leisure centre would hopefully feel there's a greater reception and understanding. But we need to educate more coaches and work with governing bodies so their programmes are more inclusive. There's a lot more work to do. Geography and finances can be challenges. If you live in a good area, you have access to good facilities – that's the same for everyone, including disabled people. But if you're disabled and poor you're going to have even less chance.

You look at sport's mental benefits as well as physical, don't you?

For disabled people, sport isn't always the number-one priority – if you're the parent of a disabled child you're thinking about their medical needs, their physio, their education. But by pushing sport up the agenda, it gives people joy and builds their self-esteem and confidence.

What other barriers do disabled people face?

They might be scared of losing benefits if they do sport. They don't want people to say, 'You can play basketball, so why can't you get a job?' Inclusion and accessibility can be problematic. parkrun is fantastic but I've heard instances where someone's gone along in a wheelchair and, because it's on grass, they've felt they can't do it. Or they've felt they're seen as a danger to the other runners. Participation events should be accessible for everyone. If someone rocks up in a wheelchair or they're deaf or they have a learning disability, we should have the capability to adapt the environment to make them feel welcome. Because if we don't, they're not going to come back. That happens to a lot of disabled people. Their first experience of sport is a poor one and then we don't see them again.

What challenges has the pandemic posed for disability sport?

We want to ensure that it isn't an afterthought as we rebuild society. We need to ensure that disabled people aren't forgotten and that we don't lose all the gains we've made in the last 20 years, and since 2012 especially. A lot of disabled people were and still are shielding – they are still scared to go out to their local park, let alone go to a gym. It's going to be about giving people confidence and giving them a route back into normal life.

INSIDER INSIGHT: MARTIN MCELHATTON

Your predictions – and hopes for – the future of sport?

I would like to see a further effort in making facilities more accessible and welcoming for disabled people. That's not only in the physical nature of buildings but in the training of staff and coaches within the facilities. On another note, I worry that, post-pandemic, people might not want to come back to volunteer in sport. People have had a reset, they've enjoyed the time away. But one of the positives of the pandemic is that we had to adapt – we've used Zoom cafés, online resources, promoting new ways of doing things at home. We've reached out to new people and new organisations who wouldn't have engaged with us normally. We will continue to build on this new connectivity with people in their own homes.

THE SOLE REMAINING WATERCOOLER CHAT?

An interesting news story cropped up in early 2020 about sports-themed banter in offices. Ann Francke, head of the Chartered Management Institute, told BBC Radio 4's *Today* programme that bosses should discourage wisecracks about topics such as video assistance referees (VAR) in football as they can exclude women from the conversation and foster a culture of sexist, laddish behaviour. A heated debate followed – many pointed out that calling for this in the first place is sexist because it incorrectly assumes that women aren't interested in sport. It was pleasingly meta that for a few days the nation's watercooler chat was about water-cooler chat. Regardless of your view (and it seems only right to defer to Kerry here, who has worked in many female-dominated offices and happily chatted with colleagues about Wimbledon, David Beckham's haircuts and everything in between, and never heard an instance of another woman feeling excluded), the story illustrates the ongoing power of sport as a conversational topic to engage communities. Chewing the fat about sport as a diversion from work is a shared ritual, a comfort, a way to bond, even if you're arguing about your respective football teams' prowess.

Sport has always offered a respite from the harsher realities of life, for both viewers and participants. When you dive into your local lido or settle on the sofa to watch a match, your worries, responsibilities and mental to-do lists recede for a brief period. You are truly in the moment and, given that modern lifestyles allow very few opportunities to focus simply on the here and now, this is a precious thing. We come back to this idea of social glue – small talk about sport before you settle down in front of your computer screen or into a meeting's agenda both binds us together and punctuates our working day with moments of levity.

There's also a very prosaic reason why sport endures as a watercooler moment. The way we watch TV has changed. Now we dare not discuss *Game of Thrones*, *Fleabag*, *Bridgerton* or any other show that grips the nation in case the person we're talking to hasn't caught up. Giving away spoilers is a lapse of modern social etiquette so it's usually best to say nothing at all. But sport is nearly always watched live rather than on demand. After all, who would risk those spoilers by putting off watching a World Cup match for a few hours? Unless you instigate a full media blackout, close your eyes and stick your fingers in your ears, it's a pointless exercise. So major sports fixtures are the one thing we all still watch together, cheering or groaning in unison.

There's also no evidence that the working-from-home culture created by the pandemic killed off the office sports chat. In fact, the need for the idle five minutes of small talk is greater when you're glued to a Zoom meeting diary and don't have all the other stimuli within an office to use as a conversational icebreaker. I can't currently make my colleagues a coffee but I can still ask them if they saw the game last night.

It's an obvious point but one that bears repeating: community is everything – and sport is at the centre of so many of our communities. The industry still has serious work to do around inclusion and diversity, as do many other industries. However, even the most traditional, conservative of sports are starting to open up their doors; some enthusiastically throwing them wide, some nudging them a chink but keeping the chain on for now. We should remember that sport is not owned by its governing bodies, participants or audience. Like the arts or fashion, sport is a platform with which everyone is entitled to interact and enjoy in any way they choose. Everyone likes to feel part of something. And everyone should be welcome.

CHAPTER 6 / How We Need to Stay in the Park (and Out of the Hospital)

Looking back, I can see that the trouble started when I found myself strapping on a head torch every morning at 5.30am to go running in the dark. I'd trudge the deserted pavements, feeling pleased with myself for eking out an hour of my day to exercise. But I was tired. Very tired. The kind of bone-tired that a few early nights and a quiet weekend couldn't solve. Not that weekends were ever quiet any more; in fact, life couldn't get any busier. I was heading towards 40 and, like many people around my age, felt like I was juggling so many responsibilities I needed octopus arms. I didn't have enough hours in the day to do everything I felt I should be doing – parenting our two young children, then aged four and seven, with their burgeoning schedule of after-school activities, sports clubs and matches; leading a fast-growing firm; being a good husband to my equally busy wife and co-founder, Claire.

I knew I still needed my sport, though. I knew I was a better dad, husband, son and business leader when I could carve out enough time to run or hit balls on a daily basis. That said, even though it was meant to be an escape, it involved yet more pressure – entirely self-inflicted – as I pushed myself to perform at a high level. Sacrificing an hour of sleep each day seemed the best option to shoehorn it in. I would fall out of the door to go running, having woken less than five minutes beforehand. Once I ran a few steps before realising I didn't even have any shoes on.

I tried my best to manage my body through the physical tiredness because I valued the mental release so highly. I knew the names of all the vegetable smoothies in Pret A Manger off by heart, relegated craft beer to the 'treat' category and offset my coffee habit with the odd peppermint tea. It wasn't enough though.

In hindsight, there were warning signs. If the kids caught a sniffle through school, I would always pick it up too. Bugs would linger for weeks and I'd be frustrated, grumpy and, unable to train, I'd be thus unable to find any headspace. I'd always fall ill the minute I downed tools for Christmas or summer holidays.

The winter of 2015 was the low point. Claire and I were heading up a deal that would see our business invested in by advertising company WPP. For six long months, at least one of us was always working, seven days a week. Fifteen-hour days were the norm. And at the crack of dawn most days, I was trudging along the dark, dank roads and trails of Oxfordshire, in preparation for my crack at the Boston Marathon; a race I'd spent five years trying to run quickly enough to qualify for. We just about held on, got the deal done and breathed a sigh of relief. But I knew that something had to change. The business was a roaring success – we couldn't move for plaudits, new clients and awards – but there was just too much collateral damage in areas of my life that ultimately I cared more about.

It wasn't really a case of reassessing my priorities, more working out how I could deliver on them more effectively. Family was, and had always been, a non-negotiable number one. And I simply wasn't willing to give up on sport. So the only thing I could change was my work. Nine months later I stepped back from day-to-day leadership of the business for an executive chairman role with a longer term, more external focus. I felt relieved to be more in control of my time again.

But as my mind relaxed, my body decided to go on strike. I had a couple of bouts of skin cancer treatment; my fair, Irish complexion was ravaged from decades of playing tennis under sunny skies. I continued to pick up every illness going, and in December 2016 (despite my more sustainable career trajectory) I started the Christmas break with man flu for the fourth year in a row.

Desperate to work out what was going on, I enlisted the help of Dr Tamsin Lewis, founder of Wellgevity, a medical wellness service. Tamsin, a former professional triathlete and Ironman UK champion turned doctor, specialises in helping people who want to be more proactive in looking after themselves; often people accustomed to burning the candle at both ends in work and play. She conducted a series of blood and hormone tests that showed that my immunity was very low, principally because of poor gut health. It wasn't immediate cause for alarm, but it could cause more serious health problems later down the line. My body was struggling to regulate cortisol, the fight-or-flight hormone, caused by a stressful lifestyle. My blood-sugar levels were too high and I was borderline diabetic. It was all a little hard to swallow for someone who's always quietly considered himself to be super fit and healthy ... although not as hard as some of the horrendous live bacteria potions Tamsin made me take to soothe my gut. I also had to significantly increase my consumption of vitamin D, as caking my body with suntan cream to keep my skin safe was stopping me from picking it up naturally. By using a specific mix of vitamin supplements and thinking more creatively about my diet, I have been able to fight back in these areas. Five years on,

I still do intermittent blood tests to check I am moving things in the right direction.

Tamsin's support helped me pin down and quantify what I instinctively knew, and make the corresponding changes to my lifestyle. But this kind of data-driven, bespoke, preventative treatment doesn't come cheap. It can cost the best part of £1,000 to dig yourself out of the kind of hole I was in. A lucrative market in premium-priced preventative healthcare has sprung up in recent years, following in the slipstream of the rise of wellbeing as an aspirational lifestyle choice. Case in point: Goop, the wellness site created by Hollywood actor turned health guru Gwyneth Paltrow. It may be widely mocked and criticised for promoting ideas and flogging products with zero scientific credibility but the business, launched in 2008, is now worth £250 million. So, *someone* is buying the £27 'psychic vampire repellent spray', which you apparently spritz 'around your aura to protect from emotional harm'.

Warding off the psychic vampires may not be a must-buy for most, but we are starting to see a trickle-down effect, with the wider population increasingly engaged with finessing and future-proofing its health. COVID-19 has played a role in this too, reminding us not only that we are all mortal, but specifically that the choices we make every day can impact our longevity for good and for bad. Many are taking a holistic approach, recognising diet, sport and exercise and mental wellbeing as intertwined elements; all pieces of a bigger puzzle. We don't tend to be engaged with one aspect in isolation – it's rare to find a gym bunny who spins at 6am every day but then retires to the local caff for a full fry-up before a day spent scoffing doughnuts. And if you've got a penchant for green juice and quinoa, you may well have an equally keen interest in yoga and meditation. Nowadays many of us are adopting what previously would have been seen as an elite athlete's lifestyle and mindset: we fine-tune our health and fitness to have the energy and stamina to deal with what life throws at us. The previous generation's no-nonsense approach of 'eat less, move more' has been superseded by a far more nuanced, deeper understanding of nutrition and exercise in sustaining physical and mental health.

With this has come the rise of the fitness tracker, now so ubiquitously wrapped around the wrists of the nation that traditional watchmakers must be despairing. My tracker of choice – and that of the Duke and Duchess of Sussex too, apparently – is a ring rather than a watch. The Oura is a tiny metal band that packs a mighty punch, measuring your core body temperature, heartrate variability, steps, movement and so on. Investing in one was a key aspect of my midlife health drive. It's helped me tune in more fully to what my body is trying to tell me, flagging up when I'm going to get a cold a few days before it hits by analysing my body's temperature changes and both sleep quality and patterns. This early warning system means I can adjust my behaviour accordingly, which might mean having a few early nights, upping my vitamin C intake and scaling back on long runs. On average, I think it helps me to avoid – or at the least lessen the symptoms of – two to three illnesses per year.

But fitness trackers' potential applications are far greater than just keeping me free of man flu. They are evolving to become a healthcare tool from which everyone can benefit on a collective basis. US academics used Ouras to track COVID-19 symptoms to help them better understand the disease, while the Sands Hotel in Las Vegas used them as digital PPE, giving them to employees to track any worrying body-temperature increases when they reopened after lockdown. Indeed, prior to the pandemic, some companies were already giving Ouras to their employees, as part of their corporate wellbeing programmes, in order to see off work-related stress and burnout at the pass. There are rightly questions being raised around privacy once employers become involved – for example, would you like your line manager to know what time you go to bed? Is what you do in your free time any of your boss's business? On balance, however, assuming they aren't compulsory, I feel the health pros outweigh the cons.

What's more, with the technology behind the sensors in these gadgets ever advancing, we are heading to a point where your tracker might start to vibrate not simply because you've hit your daily step target but because it can tell from your breath that you're dehydrated. Or because your doctor is concerned that a sensor has flagged your blood pressure as too high. Or to warn you that the air around you is so polluted it could set off your asthma. Obviously, this heath utopia of the future relies not just on the capability to create this data, but the individual – and their health practitioners – having the time and expertise to interpret it. But given that, during the pandemic, GPs swiftly pivoted their service so that 97 per cent of consultations took place over the phone or via video call, we can be hopeful that their role in the future will include remote data-monitoring of this nature.

I am fully aware how lucky I was to be able to pay for Tamsin's support. But things are changing fast in this space too with bespoke services becoming increasingly affordable. Thriva, for example, provide blood tests for around £80 that check your levels of certain vitamins, minerals and hormones, as well as assessing things such as liver function. The tests are chosen based upon information you provide when you fill out an initial questionnaire, thus allowing customers to be more proactive in managing their health. This kind of approach is still by no means within reach of all but what is currently a privilege is well on its way to being democratised to the point where it becomes NHS policy.

A government consultation, 'Advancing Our Health Prevention in the 2020s', published shortly before the pandemic hit, heralded a new dawn of intelligent public health. 'The 2020s will be the decade of proactive, predictive, and personalised prevention,' it said. 'This means targeted support, tailored lifestyle advice, personalised care, greater protection against future threats.' (That last one reads somewhat ominously given what happened next, doesn't it?) It continues:

> In the 2020s, people will not be passive recipients of care. They will be co-creators of their own health. The challenge is to equip them with the skills, knowledge and confidence they need to help themselves. When our health is good, we take it for granted. When it's bad, we expect the NHS to do their best to fix it. We need to view health as an asset to invest in throughout our lives, and not just a problem to fix when it goes wrong.[44]

Prevention is not just always better than cure but it's usually far cheaper too. This is where sport comes in.

SPORT AS MEDICINE

The UK Chief Medical Officer's current guidelines advise adults to engage in at least 150 minutes (2.5 hours) of moderate intensity physical activity (such as brisk walking) or 75 minutes of vigorous intensity activity (such as running) per week. Doing this, we're told, will benefit our health, improve our sleep, help us maintain a healthy weight, manage stress and improve our quality of life. It will also reduce our chance of contracting type

2 diabetes by 40 per cent, cardiovascular disease by 35 per cent, joint and back pain by 25 per cent, and colon and breast cancer by 20 per cent. 'If physical activity were a drug, we would refer to it as a miracle cure, due to the great many illnesses it can prevent and help treat,' said Professor Dame Sally Davies in 2017, during her tenure as Chief Medical Officer.

So it's a no brainer, right? Quick, grab your trainers and let's go. Well, not exactly. Only one-third of British adults actually hit this target. A quarter of women and a fifth of men in England are physically inactive, i.e. doing less than 30 minutes of moderate physical activity per week. A combination of poor diet plus inactivity means 64 per cent of UK adults are overweight and 29 per cent are obese. When it comes to children, one in ten are obese when they start primary school, rising to one in five by the time they leave. We are the third most obese nation in Europe, after Turkey and Malta.[45]

The government's activity recommendations on their own aren't enough. Something is going badly wrong. We know the theory: preventative healthcare, of which sport and activity are a key component, will help keep us in the park and out of the hospital, and cost us less as a nation. But in practice, it's not working, at least not yet.

For a start, not everyone does know the theory – or has the time, headspace or money to prioritise it. Dr Sally Lewis is a GP in West Berkshire who prescribes exercise to her patients to help them manage health conditions. For example, she may refer someone showing early signs of a chronic disease such as arthritis to a local leisure centre to try subsidised fitness classes. From a position of middle-class, well-educated, Oura ring-wearing privilege, it's easy to be flabbergasted by the notion of a doctor spending her time explaining to people that exercise is a good thing for their health. But it's not quite that simple for everyone. 'For many the idea of them just popping out for a run is impossible,' says Sally. 'A frequent thing I see is disadvantaged families where the husband might work a 12-hour night-shift so he gets home at eight o'clock and sleeps all day, while the mum has three young kids at home. There's no way she can do anything with all of them and she can't afford to pay for any kit or clubs. So through no fault of their own, there's no parental role model there to encourage the kids to be active – these are not the kind of people who can take their children to football training three times a week. Plus, the children might not have the right brand or colour or style of trainers so they're too embarrassed to do sport – kids really care about that kind of thing.'

Sally is also passionate about the role of exercise in treating some mental health issues. Government guidelines state that hitting the weekly recommending activity levels can reduce the risk of depression by 30 per cent. 'I explain to patients that management of depression is like a jigsaw. Medication might be one piece of that jigsaw, talking therapies another. But another piece is lifestyle. I ask people, "What's stopping you being active? How can you build some activity into your life once a week?" And it might be something as simple as going for a walk with your family at the weekend, something you can build on. Because there's no point in taking an antidepressant if you're not changing anything else in your life.'

INSIDER INSIGHT: DR SALLY LEWIS

Sally has been a medic for almost 20 years, firstly as a paediatric trainee and then, for the last 11 years, as an NHS GP. She's currently a partner at a West Berkshire surgery. She is passionate about the health benefits of exercise, both in a professional capacity and as the mother of two young children.

Do you prescribe exercise to patients?

Yes. There's an increasing emphasis on a holistic approach to medicine, rather than a patient coming to the GP, getting medicine and walking away again. A lot of diseases are influenced by general health – sedentary lifestyles, weight, smoking and drinking are issues – and there's no way any of the common medical conditions cannot be managed without exercise. There are exercise programmes to manage conditions like strokes, chronic pain and depression – the scope is broader than the ones we tend to think of such as diabetes and heart disease. Then there's exercise on referral, which might be set up in affiliation with local leisure centres. For some adults and young people, we support them joining subsidised exercise classes.

Shouldn't children be getting the exercise they need at school and with their families?

Well, it depends what kind of patient you've got. I see some people and my heart sinks. You just know that whatever you say, it's never going to happen. They're in the wrong socio-economic group, they're surrounded by the wrong influences, there are financial restrictions, there are so many children at home. The idea of them simply going for a run is just impossible.

Is the pandemic a wake-up call for people to be more active?

I'd like to say yes but I don't think it'll be a turning point unfortunately. For some, it has opened their eyes to what they can do when cinemas, bowling alleys and McDonald's are shut – they have to take their children for a walk. But there are different types of people. I see those who are active and think positively. I have one patient with five kids at home, including twins born during lockdown, and she was on the verge of post-natal depression. But she's started running and looked absolutely radiant when I saw her this week. Then there are those patients who often tend to have everything – depression, chronic fatigue syndrome, ME, chronic joint pains. If a person has one of those conditions, they'll often have the others. And you can never win with them. If you suggest they become active, they'll say they can't because of the pain, and on it goes.

Will we see GPs increasingly prescribe exercise as a preventative health measure?

Yes, you might see that if you're in the early stages of a disease – say if you're overweight and starting to present with joint pain or arthritis. That's an opportunity for the GP to say, 'Nothing's too bad here but unless you start being more active in your forties and fifties, your joints will get worse.' Also we do age 40+ health checks on people and that's a perfect time to say, 'Your blood pressure or cholesterol is a bit high, you're getting older, you need to up your game.' I've seen people then who've stopped drinking, taken up football and so on. The health checks give the GP a foot in the door to give that advice.

If everybody did 30 minutes exercise per day, how would that impact on your workload?

My God, if everyone did the recommended amount of exercise and ate their five fruit and veg a day, it'd be life-changing! If we can get people to lead more healthy lifestyles now, the positive impact on their health and the decrease in financial pressures on the NHS would be amazing.

Your Predictions – and hopes – for the future of sport and medicine?

As medics, we've got a lot in place to support exercise for preventative measures and for the management of chronic diseases. But we need to work together with other groups in order to get harder to reach people on board. We'd be foolish to lose the momentum towards being more active that the pandemic generated. We need school programmes, free facilities so everyone can join in, grassroots support for children whose parents can't pay for tennis lessons or football training, more things like the 'Cycle to Work' scheme and promoting safe cycleways. Doctors need help, otherwise we're banging our heads against a brick wall – we only have ten minutes with patients, after all.

The joining of the dots between physical health and mental health, recognising that exercise's benefits for the brain are as important as its benefits for the body, has become an increasingly mainstream idea in recent years. Yoga used to be the domain of Madonna, hippies and people who had spent their gap year in India, with its devotees mocked as cranks. Now Kerry's nine-year-old son practises it in his classroom.

Books about running used to be fixated on technique and performance; now there are just as many about the meditative, spiritual, anxiety-nixing qualities of pavement-pounding (if you're interested, try *Running Like a Girl* by Alexandra Heminsley or *Jog On* by Bella Mackie). If you've ever worked for a large, modern company, you'll know that the notion of employee perks now extends far beyond matched pension contributions and the odd free eye test. Employers provide lunchtime yoga classes, encourage staff running clubs and install showers. At one east London co-working space, they've fitted a showstopping, architect-designed yellow cycle ramp which allows you to ride straight into the building and down into the basement bike parking and changing-room area. Employers are, of course, not doing this out of the goodness of their corporate hearts. Healthy bodies mean healthy minds, which mean greater productivity, creativity and efficiency.

Even my notoriously hedonistic generational cohort, Generation X, seems to have got the memo. Back in our 1990s, although many of us were spending Saturdays on sports pitches, we spent our evenings at parties, gigs, clubs and raves, propping up bars and setting the world to rights. Turn the clock forward, and it's not just the stalwarts in the gym; we're now a generation of fitness fanatics, tackling the challenges of middle age – creaky bodies and a stress-spiking peak of responsibilities and workloads – with exercise. The ravers have become runners, getting their endorphin kicks from exercise rather than partying. Johnny Marr, the iconic guitarist with the Smiths, Electronic, The The, Modest Mouse, the Cribs and the Healers, now 56, is an excellent – if unexpected – example of this pivot. The idea of the louche, hard-living rock star is, he says, 'an out-of-date paradigm. When I first got into running that stereotype was one of the things I wanted to challenge in myself.' He started in his early forties, having 'grown tired of staying up late, taking drugs, drinking a lot of alcohol, all of that', building up to regular 30-mile runs around whichever city he was living in or passing through on tour at the time. 'Running is the friend of creativity. You feel clear, positive and you have energy and want to take on concepts and get projects done,' he says. 'It sounds a little corny but you find that distance runs can be a metaphor for things happening in your life. Where there is a parallel is sometimes when you're writing or recording a song and it's not quite there and you're about to give up. My experiences of running have taught me that you keep going, you persevere.' Many of his music industry peers agree – Kaiser Chiefs' Ricky Wilson is another keen runner, ditto Liam Gallagher, with the rasping voice behind 'Cigarettes & Alcohol' now extolling the virtues of a perky 6am 10k on Hampstead Heath. Singer Ellie Goulding, meanwhile, is a frequent *Women's Health* magazine cover star, something that would have definitely *not* been on the PR schedule of a popstar from a previous generation. When you add in the fact that millennials and Generation Z are, in the main, a far healthier bunch, it feels like there's a cultural sea-change in motion regarding how we view the benefits of exercise and sport.

INSIDER INSIGHT: **JOHNNY MARR**

A key figure in British indie music since the early 1980s, guitarist Johnny formed the Smiths with Morrissey before working with Electronic, The The, Modest Mouse, the Cribs and forming his own band, the Healers. Now 56 and a running obsessive, he's completed the New York Marathon and has been known to run up to 18 miles before playing a gig.

How did you get into running?

As a kid, I had an issue with a games teacher who used to pick on me. He'd make me go off and do long cross-country runs on my own. What he didn't realise was that I actually liked it but I pretended I didn't. So my love of running came from something that was supposed to be a punishment. I didn't do it for many years, apart from a brief phase in the early 1990s, and then got really into it in my forties.

What was your midlife running epiphany?

I was in Morocco with my wife, recuperating from an illness, and I had this amazing moment one night. I was sitting on the roof of the place we were staying, looking out over this stretch of desert with palm trees and the sun was going down – and I just felt like going for a run. Off I went, on the spur of the moment, running through the shadows of palm trees with the mountains turning pink in the sunset. I was surprised I got so far – I went five miles and it was one of those moments that all runners know about. The next day, I felt pretty good so I did it again.

That moment of euphoria, the runner's high?

Yeah. And I just really took to it. For a number of years, I'd been questioning my lifestyle. I didn't want to be the clichéd middle-aged musician hanging out in his mates' dressing room, raiding the rider. I just didn't really see that in my future. Because I'm a musician and I run and haven't drunk alcohol for 20 years, there's this assumption that I've had some kind drink and drugs hell and it's about abstinence. That I spent the 1980s dangling my children out of a hotel window, with Ozzy Osbourne. But actually the motivation isn't that. If I thought staying up late and taking drugs would help me make better music, I would do that. I'm not puritanical about it. The thing about running is that it wasn't about denying myself the life of a rocker, it was giving myself the gift of the life of a runner.

You're properly obsessive, aren't you?

Yes. I've always been like that about work and it's pretty handy to be obsessive when it's pouring with rain in Manchester on a Wednesday morning and you have to do a ten-mile run. My longest run was 30 miles but these days I'll do about 15 miles on a weekend. Sometimes when I was touring, I'd go for a long run, walk on stage and feel like I was vibrating, like I was two feet off the stage. And I've had moments when I've been running around cities that've been borderline transcendent. I'll be in a place and the breeze or the light will hit me in a certain way, a track will come on the headphones and it transports me back to the person I was when I was 11 or 12. That was the last time I felt that exerted, when I was climbing a tree, chasing someone,

running around being free, without adult concerns and responsibilities. These fleeting, almost mystical moments, you don't
expect and you can't go looking for.

Running has become fashionable in recent years – why do you think this is?

When I was a kid growing up in the 1970s on the council
estate, on the rare occasion that you saw someone running, it'd
usually be an old bloke in tiny running shorts and a vest, and
they'd be considered something of an oddball. But they were
ahead of their time. We live in a culture where it's so easy to be
over-indulgent that there has to be some recompense for that.
There's a lot of people who take up running because they've
gone too far the other way – they've drunk too much, eaten too
much, taken too many drugs.

Are your family runners?

My wife runs and we have a son and daughter in their twenties
and they both run too. That's something they've learnt from
me – the emotional benefits and discipline running can bring to
your life. Maybe they'll pass it on to their kids. I'm really proud
of that. In fact, I'm more proud of that than them seeing me at
Glastonbury.

Your predictions – and hopes – for the future of sport?

You'll see young kids, aged 11, 12, 13, out running more and
take that through their adult lives. Along with that will be
an understanding that running goes hand in hand with good
mental health. We are returning to who we were millennia ago,
when we ran as part of our nature, it was just a given. If you

let a toddler out of a car onto a piece of grass, they just take off. No one explains the benefits of running to young kids, they just do it instinctively. And I think the future is about returning to our instincts. A few years ago, running had a connection with vanity – people thought you did it because you wanted to look good. Now people know it's common sense. The attitude will eventually be, well, why *wouldn't* you run?

INSIDER INSIGHT: JOHNNY MARR

THE KIDS ARE ALRIGHT

We see this transition in the way sport is represented to children. Tom Palmer is an award-winning children's novelist who has also recently updated *Roy of the Rovers* – the much-loved children's stories about professional footballer Roy Race, which launched in 1954 – for a new generation. 'We made sure the team was very diverse, in terms of ethnicity and gender,' says Tom. 'We gave Roy a kid sister, who's a thorn in his side. I said, "We've got to make her a footballer too." And she became a highly significant character. By book six, she had her own book. She wasn't in the originals but it felt obvious we had to bring her in – women's football is so much more part of our world now. We also included players from different backgrounds. Kids respond really well to it. You go into schools and say, "This player is from Poland," and the Polish children like it.'

Tom believes that the capacity for children to engage with sport and activity, in particular for girls, has improved significantly. 'The main thing is boys don't take the piss out of girls like they used to a decade ago. When I do events, I do a quiz about football and reading, then we have a penalty shootout. Girls would be really reluctant to come up and do it. If they did, the boys would say, 'Well, she won't score.' And then if she did score past a boy goalkeeper, they would laugh at the boy. Now it doesn't happen now at all. Schools are kinder and more inclusive places.'

INSIDER INSIGHT: TOM PALMER

Tom has written 48 books for children, including a modern version of Roy of the Rovers. *His stories have been translated into nine languages and sold over 450,000 copies. In 2019 he won the Ruth Rendell Award for his outstanding contribution to raising literacy levels in the UK. The Leeds native is passionate about encouraging children to both read and play sport. When he's not writing, he goes fell running with his 16-year-old daughter.*

You've been going into schools to talk to children about sport for many years – what changes have you noticed about kids' attitudes?

This generation is kinder, more inclusive and have more empathy for everyone. Now you'll get girls talking proudly about being elite runners or rugby players in assemblies. They'd never mention it before – no one at school would know. There's a greater confidence there with girls. There's still much room for improvement but it's changed radically.

You often put girls front and centre in your books, don't you?

Yes, but it has proved hard in the past to get books about girls doing sport published. When I was trying to get a deal for *Armistice Runner*, which came out in 2018, publishers asked if I could change the girl lead character, who's a runner, into a boy because more people would read it. I stuck to my guns and eventually got a deal and it's been my fastest-selling book ever.

Your books are inclusive but how good is sport itself at being inclusive?

One of the problems is parental support. What happens if your parents won't take you to the sporting venue or to competitions or can't afford to or can't be arsed? Organised sport has become predominantly middle class for this reason. If you look at football academies, the children going into them have parents who are really supportive, who have cars and can drive 30 miles three evenings a week to take them to training. But if you haven't got a car or if you're working shifts, that's not going to happen. There's less access for poorer children, which leads to sport becoming elitist. A few years back, I read a piece in which Raheem Sterling talked about how he used to sit in a bank before school in the mornings while his mum, a single mother, cleaned it. He was so grateful to her. We used that storyline in *Roy of the Rovers* – Roy's mum has multiple cleaning jobs in care homes. Those stories, about parents making those sacrifices, need to be told.

Mental health in sport is a more open discussion now – do your books reflect that?

Yes. In a Roy story, one of the footballers is depressed. [*Armistice Runner* is about girl who is a fell runner – she has difficulties in her family and running gives her a lift.] In football stories in the past, you didn't read that kind of thing so much. There's much more focus on the person as an individual. There was this idea that footballers are just these flash individuals, who go around in their fancy cars, sleeping with whoever they want to sleep with but actually now we're seeing footballers as real people. However much you earn, misery is still misery, pressure is still pressure. We show Roy and Rocky under great pressure and how it makes them feel. The great thing about fiction is that it encourages empathy – you have a bird's-eye view of someone else's life, their point of view and their mental state. And so we can also see others around us in that way too. And that's got to be a good thing for society.

Your predictions – and hopes – for the future of sport?

The sports industry needs to work with schools and expand their programmes to reach children from poorer backgrounds – because you're not going to reach them through the parents. Schools can't afford the specialist sports staff and there are fewer sports clubs at school because teachers are under so much pressure. So you need sport clubs to provide the expertise – send coaches into schools – and pay for it. You've got to go to them, if they won't come to you. Leeds Rhinos rugby club go into schools in its part of Leeds and Leeds United also do it now. When you see it happening, it's wonderful.

INSIDER INSIGHT: TOM PALMER

Another hugely encouraging sign of our ability to rethink the way in which we help younger generations benefit from sport and activity is the increased provision of exercise-based mental health initiatives for children. And they are certainly needed – a 2017 Department for Education report noted that 8 per cent of British 5- to 10-year-old children had a diagnosed mental health condition, rising to 12 per cent among 11- to 15-year-olds.[46] Dr Martin Yelling, a former teacher and international runner (and husband of Liz Yelling, the double Olympian runner and Commonwealth Games bronze medallist marathon runner), is the founder of Stormbreak. This pioneering charity coaches teachers to use movement to aid children's mental health, in doing so equipping them with transferable life skills, such as resilience, motivation and focus. The use of the word 'movement' is important, says Martin. 'It's not about sport. We're not saying, "Go and play cricket to become more resilient." There's no scoring, no timings, no judgement. It's based on helping children understand that when they recognise an emotion or feeling, moving can help them respond positively to it. It's the same as a stressed adult saying, "God, I need to go for a walk" 'During the pandemic, with the support of Children in Need, Stormbreak created a suite of digital tools for children of primary school age to access their support, making the initiative as proactive as possible to support families without the means, time or knowledge to seek it out for themselves.

INSIDER INSIGHT: DR MARTIN YELLING

The former international steeplechaser is founder of Storm-break, a movement-based mental health charity for children, which launched in 2018. Based in Poole, Dorset, he's married to former GB Olympic runner Liz Yelling, with whom he has three children. Martin has a PhD in education physical activity and is founder and co-presenter of running podcast Marathon Talk.

What is the idea behind Stormbreak?

Adults will often say to children, 'Go outside and let off steam', and we're taking that notion and wrapping it in structure, theory and good practice. We say, 'Let's use this moment as an opportunity to talk about your mental health.' We might walk with the child, question them in a certain way about why they might be angry or upset, and listen to them. A stormbreak is taking a moment, it's a positive release that helps you regulate your emotions. It might be movement, singing, painting or playing music; there are various activities. We coach teachers on how to deliver this model.

How do you know if it's working?

We're building a digital tracker and we get evidence from children and teachers. We're seeing children managing breakdowns in relationships better or getting better at having open conversations. But it's a slow burn, it's not six weeks and done.

It seems like we've only recently made the connection between good mental health and exercise.

I guess so but, personally, I've been an exerciser for nearly all my 50 years and realise the non-physical benefits that moving brings. I have no desire now to compete at elite level but I still exercise because I recognise all the positive emotional benefits.

What's life like for an elite athlete?

The governing bodies and the media tend to focus on elite performance because of the spectacle of it and the engagement that brings. But it feels like there's been a shift away from this in the last decade. I see huge pressure on athletes as they progress through the system and then break down as they exit it. You've got to be pretty robust to take the battering – physical and mental – of life as an elite athlete and then transition out of that life. There's a lack of care, wellbeing and support. In essence, as an elite athlete, you do not create balance, you create a lack of harmony in everything you do because, if you don't, you're just going to simmer along. Your life is about being at the pointy end.

How can we increase mass participation in sport?

It's interesting how we've started to frame sport differently. Take parkrun, for example. People have been running around the park for many years. But what parkrun has done has changed the language around it. Previously we'd say, 'Running is good for you – go do a group run.' And someone might think, *Hmmm I'm not sure I can do this*, and they'd be at the back and not enjoying it. With parkrun it's very welcoming, inclusive and there's no focus on recorded times. It's a totally different attitude. It's about considering people's perceptions – the 55-year-old care worker who's been terrified of exercise her whole life, for example.

Your predictions – and hopes – for the future of sport?

With Stormbreak, it's about prevention. We're trying to create strategies for coping with mental health that will help children in 10 or 20 years' time. More broadly, during the pandemic, Garmin and Strava released wearable data stats that showed more people were going out being active for shorter times, which probably means they're people who are new to exercise. I certainly see tonnes of people out running who I've never seen before. I just hope it sticks and that surge in engagement for running and walking is sustainable. How are sports organisations planning to keep these new people engaged? There's an opportunity to be had but it needs to be considered.

One of the positives to emerge from the pandemic was the UK government's newfound willingness to help improve public health. Its motivation was clear – all the studies showed that being overweight or obese increased the chances of serious illness or death from COVID-19, something that Prime Minister Boris Johnson had first-hand experience of through his stint in an intensive care unit after contracting the disease. Plus, the government estimated that conditions caused by being over-weight or obese cost the NHS £6 billion per year. 'COVID-19 has given us all a wake-up call of the immediate and long-term risks of being overweight, and the prime minister is clear we must use this moment to get healthier, more active and eat better,' said a government spokesperson. 'We will be urging the public to use this moment to take stock of how they live their lives, and to take simple steps to lose weight, live health-ier lives, and reduce pressure on the NHS.' The initiative included GPs prescribing cycling, £50 fix-your-bike vouchers to get people back on two wheels, improved access to e-bikes for those who struggle on a traditional bike, and improved cycling infrastructure in towns and cities.

Could the horror of COVID-19 be a clarion call to the nation? When our lives have become literally survival of the fittest, will everyone get fit? As we have seen, Sport England's prediction is that a renewed enthusiasm might apply to a certain sector of society, the already-active and healthy got even more active during this period but people in the margins – those who are always hardest to reach – simply got left behind.[47]

ALL THE PEOPLE (SO MANY PEOPLE)

Partially, as Dr Sally Lewis explained, this inequality relates to underprivileged parts of society having the time or financial means to consider sport. It's also a question of lack of access to facilities to actually play sport. While private gym chains were able to remodel their facilities to exit lockdown and reopen for business as soon as the government gave them the green flag, things weren't quite so simple for public leisure centres up and down the country. Leisure trade associations told the *Guardian* that 1,300 of the 2,727 leisure centres funded by local authorities and 20 per cent of the UK's swimming pools were at risk of closing for good without increased governmental support.[48] Some applied for government loans to shore up their finances, only to find that local councils were not prepared to underwrite those loans. On the one hand Boris Johnson was encouraging the general public to engage more actively with sport, but on the other he was not able to provide the funds to keep facilities open.

It's easy to be critical of this apparent contradiction, although of course hospitals, schools and other areas of public investment were also in dire straits as 2020 turned to 2021. Sport facilities have actually always had a hard time proving their case for investment, and so, although many don't clock it, the public have been paying their own way when it comes to the creation of sports facilities up and down the country for a quarter of a century via the great white knight that is the National Lottery.

Funding from the Lottery has been a driving force behind this at grassroots level (and elite level too). It's rare to find a modern public sports venue that isn't emblazoned with its 'fingers crossed' logo. Running since 1994, over its first 25 years it provided £5.7 billion of funding to over 100,000 grassroots sport projects, creating opportunities for millions of people in the UK to get active, as well as funding the Olympic and Paralympic athletes to inspire them. This grassroots investment alone equates to £1,000 per UK resident.

It's not just the public themselves (via the National Lottery) investing in facilities, however. We are quick to gripe about footballers' inflated wages but few know of the Football Foundation, the Premier League and FA's charity, which builds and refurbishes grassroots football facilities with proceeds from the top-flight game. Mine and Kerry's local club, Thame United in Oxfordshire, is one such beneficiary. The team was formed in 1883, making it one of the county's oldest clubs, but by 2005 it was in serious financial trouble and evicted from its ground, just behind the town centre (land that was, inevitably, turned into housing afterwards). Following five years of homelessness and ground-sharing with local neighbours, in 2010, with substantial support from the Football Foundation, the club secured a new ground on the edge of town with eight pitches, a floodlit Astroturf training pitch and an 8,000 square-foot clubhouse, where Kerry often spends weekend mornings hiding with a cup of tea, when she should be on the touchline, watching her son play in the Thame Boys Under-10 side. We know from personal experience that United's new facilities, some of the best in the Hellenic League, are a thriving community hub. Not only do multiple teams of boys and girls playing at every conceivable age group make the club the focal point of local families' weekends, but the clubhouse is also used for a wide range of activities across our local community, from Jazzercise to coffee mornings, watching the big game in the sports bar to corporate meetings.

At a time of austerity and huge pressures on the public purse, we need to be more creative – just as we were with the creation of the National Lottery a quarter of a century ago. We need to find new ways to blend social need for sport with commercial opportunity, without expecting public money to save the day. One opportunity of this type has recently been missed. The

Football Foundation funded projects to the tune of £60 million in 2019, which is great work but, by point of comparison, if the FA sold Wembley Stadium, as it was keen to do, it could spend the proceeds on 30 all-weather pitches in every county across the land. This would create the biggest revolution that grass-roots football has seen since factory owners created facilities for their workers 150 years ago. However, in 2018, Shahid Khan, owner of Fulham FC, withdrew his offer to buy the stadium for £600 million after the prospective sale caused division within football's governing body. Opponents to the plan viewed it as selling off one of sport's crown jewels but, like many in the highest levels of the FA, I would question whether the real gem of British football was a piece of concrete, or the passion of a new generation of kids up and down the country inspired by Marcus Rashford and Steph Houghton. Kids who need decent Astroturf football pitches that don't turn into quagmires every time it rains. Councils need facilities like these too, as they don't need to be mown several times a week and can be almost continuously rented out to generate income, without fear of over-usage. There's no reason why a governing body should own a national stadium – it's not a venue manager, its job is to grow the game. In fact, the FA only bought Wembley in the first place in 2007 – ironically enough, with the help of National Lottery money.

As our cash-strapped nation moves forward, sport, like every other area of society, must be prepared to look at new ways of doing things and challenge tradition for tradition's sake. One sport that does a terrific job of being commercially successful and yet also reinvesting back into the grassroots of the game is tennis, where the All England Club, which runs the Wimbledon Championships tournament, generated the enormous sum of £52 million in 2019 to go towards grassroots initiatives. Each and every year it allocates the vast majority of its profits direct to the governing body of the sport in this country, the Lawn Tennis Association, which is responsible for growing the game, including building courts in parks, getting children playing and funding local clubs.

Separately the All England Club also has a charity arm, the Wimbledon Foundation, which showed how seriously it takes its duties to its surrounding community during the height of the pandemic. With the Championships cancelled in 2020, staff diverted their energies into opening up a kitchen on-site to feed local people in need, creating care packages for NHS staff and donating £1.2 million to local homeless charities and food banks. Tennis is often maligned as a preserve of the elite, but scratch below the surface and it leads the way in directing commercially generated funds back into the grassroots of the game. Those buying pricey hospitality packages at Wimbledon are essentially funding the park courts in nearby Bermondsey, which remain free for all to use.

It's not only tennis where these kind of models are thriving, often under the radar. Football has been relatively slow on this front but it is increasingly willing to give back to its communities. This is hugely powerful, because as a sport it has an ability to engage and enthral some of the most challenged (and often stubbornly resistant) areas of our community. Tranmere Rovers, the League Two football club, which is often overshadowed by its Merseyside Premiership neighbours Liverpool and Everton, is an exemplar. There has been some brilliantly creative thinking around how best to use facilities that are traditionally only open for a few hours per week, while simultaneously adopting unique approaches to solving some big societal problems. 'The council outsources some of its mental health work to us,' says Nicola Palios, the club's vice-chair alongside her husband Mark Palios, the ex-Tranmere player and former Football Association CEO. 'We get paid for that as would any other third-party provider and that's because we are so much better at engaging people, especially men, than your local NHS facility because we are a football club. If you're a 21-year-old man with suicidal thoughts or other mental health problems, you're not overly likely to turn up to an appointment at a clinic or surgery. Whereas if it's a group of guys, all in a similar situation, having a kickabout at the club, it's much more likely that they'll engage with it. They can support each other and there are mental health professionals on hand too. It becomes a bit of a virtuous circle because they're exercising at the same time so they're releasing serotonin in their brains, which improves mood anyway, plus the team aspect provides a support network.'

Tranmere's compelling programmes for the local community, which exceed what the public sector might alone be able to deliver, go beyond mental health provision. The club has also launched its own college. 'We were deliberately taking on kids who weren't necessarily going to be the most straightforward to deal with, the ones who had fallen out of the mainstream,' she says. 'We started it initially for the kids who got rejected from the football academies. That rejection really affects their lives because they get told they're going to be the next best thing since sliced bread until they get to 16, 17 or 18 and then they suddenly get hoofed out. A lot of them didn't really focus on their education because they were convinced they were going to be Wayne Rooney 2.0.'

The college is a huge success, with 98.6 per cent of students going on to further education or full-time employment. And, as Nicola points out, it's a set-up that helps the club too. 'It utilises our assets. And we've gone on to use some of those kids in our business. We started doing international work in China and some have gone out to work for us there for a year. By the time they come back they are radically different people because it makes them grow up so much faster. Then they have not only a qualification but some decent life experience as well.'

Activity like this works for everyone. Students with specific needs are provided with an education that understands and caters for them, which stops them causing issues in main-stream schools or dropping out entirely, and gives them new skills. Tranmere uses its stadium to generate an income outside of matchday and has a source of talent for the future of its business. Everyone wins.

INSIDER INSIGHT: **NICOLA PALIOS**

A former lawyer and highly successful businesswoman, Nicola Palios has been co-owner and vice chairman of League Two's Tranmere Rovers FC since 2014, along with her husband Mark Palios, ex-Tranmere player and the former CEO of the FA. They brought the club back from the brink of extinction with a hugely successful reboot that includes creative, pioneering community programmes.

Why did you decide on a community focus for the club?

The only way a club like Tranmere would thrive was being inextricably wrapped up in its community. And that meant doing a lot more than just the token 'we'll do a bit of kids football every now and then' for two reasons. Firstly, this was to ensure we had revenue streams that weren't dependent on success on the field. We wanted a resilient business that could weather a downturn. And we believed that you could use community work to generate revenue streams in that way, so it's not all purely charitable. The second reason is because we wanted to win the hearts and minds of the community, to get people to be proud of their club and give support when it was needed.

Why are you better placed to do this than your neighbours Liverpool and Everton?

When you live in the shadow of two Premiership giants, you've got to get hearts and minds because you're never going to have the glamour that they can offer. So you've got to approach it in a different way. We felt that we were much better positioned to offer genuine community connection than Premiership clubs. Their players are superstars and many aren't English so might not understand the local community or have that natural bond. It was noticeable when we got promoted that a lot of people said, 'If this were Liverpool or Everton, we'd be waving at the team from a balcony, but here we're partying with everyone.' We made a conscious effort to recruit players who were Merseysiders, which appeals to the players because they want to play at home, and also benefits us because they understand their own community and are more motivated to help. Our contracts oblige our players to give one day per week to community work. We've never had to persuade anyone to do this – they do it naturally because they enjoy being involved.

Do you find the newer generation of players more willing to be roles models, more community-minded?

We have always been a club where the players have been happy to do that. One of the most powerful things we've done is that after training the players would drop into the recreation centre and kick the ball around with whatever group was in there at the time. This got a really positive reaction, particularly in the groups with learning difficulties or disabilities.

Tranmere has an abnormally high retention rate of season-ticket holders. Why is this?

When we came in, we had a very ageing supporter base; a lot of season-ticket holders who are 80+ years old who have been coming to Brenton Park for the last 60 years. This is brilliant but it's obviously self-limiting and there weren't many young-sters coming. So we had a specific push to get young kids into the ground by lowering our prices to £2 for a kid's ticket and £30 for a kid's season ticket. Because the prices were so low, our supporters started buying £30 season tickets along with their own, to give back to the club for disadvantaged kids in the community. It's one of the things that captured fans' imaginations. Every year now we have 500–600 season tickets bought by our supporters to be distributed to kids in the local area who wouldn't otherwise be able to afford to come.

Your predictions – and hopes – for the future of sport? Could Tranmere's model be rolled out across football?

The chairmen of clubs need to understand that this isn't all about altruism because that's the block at the moment. They see their community arm as something that they've got to do for PR purposes but it's a drain on the club. So they keep it small but pretend it's bigger than it is, because they don't want the hassle and they don't want to have to put money into it. But it is a virtuous circle if you get it right. It will generate revenue for the clubs, in terms of them getting paid by the council, and also the community support, which in turn leads to more people coming through the gates. If chairmen understand that they would build it into their fundamental business model. We have a guideline, for example, that if we get in some unexpected money, we put a third of that into the playing budget, a third into paying down debt so that we're on a sound financial footing, and a third of it goes into infrastructure that supports the community and other commercial businesses. Most clubs would bung it all in the playing budget straight away, but actually if you can have other ancillary community things or commercial businesses that are generating revenues year on year that can support the playing budget, it's much better than just lumping it all on in one season and hoping it pays off. We've been talking to Alison McGovern, the shadow sports minister and a Wirral resident who knows the club well, to help her understand how you can replicate what we've done. Lots of football clubs are in deprived areas and so they can be really powerful tools for social good.

Sport's community initiatives are cropping up in unexpected quarters too. The private school sector is not generally feted for its efforts to connect with its local communities. But look a little closer and there are some signs that things are changing for the better. Just as Tranmere Rovers works with the public sector, private schools are increasingly collaborating with their local state counterparts.

Pete Bignell is director of sport and PE at Abingdon School, an independent school in Oxfordshire. He feels strongly that the private sector should be proactive in supporting its state counterparts in the local community. 'We have amazing multimillion-pound facilities and sometimes they're sitting empty – why can't they be used by local schools?' he says. 'At Abingdon we have a partnerships programme to work with our community. We've opened up our pool so three local primaries come in. We try to make it cost neutral – we don't charge them for use of the pool and they can walk to us and not pay for a bus. We just charge them for the use of instructors. We have a climbing wall so we did a climbing training inset day for staff from other local secondary schools. Now one of those schools has access to our climbing facilities.' Clear lines of communication are key here, says Pete. 'Sometimes private schools offer it and the uptake isn't great by the state sector. But I remember being on the other side of this, as a teacher in the state sector, and didn't feel I could ask either. It must be a two-way conversation. I'm a state-educated kid from London and, ultimately, we're all teachers trying to teach kids. As a sector, we can do more.'

While that is undoubtedly true, in the challenged school year of 2019/20 alone, 2,900 teaching hours were allocated by Abingdon School to their partnership with other schools in the town. It is possible to break down barriers between private and state schools so that everyone benefits.

INSIDER INSIGHT: **PETE BIGNELL**

Pete is director of sport and PE at Abingdon School in Oxford-shire, an independent school where he's worked since 2016. A keen amateur sportsman originally from London, he has also taught extensively in the state-school sector and is an examiner for A-level PE.

School sports in the independent vs state sector: what can they learn from each other? And does a school like yours have a duty to let local state schools share your facilities?

Yes, 100 per cent. But it's not always easy. There's a desire there but sometimes it's harder than it should be. Too many people think that the best teachers are in independent schools and that's a fallacy – there are rubbish and phenomenal teachers in both sectors. There's often more creative thinking in the state sector because it's a necessity and in the independent sector we can learn from that. And the state sector might be able to learn how we map our sports a bit more effectively.

What kind of initiatives do you have to collaborate with state schools in your community?

We employed an external rugby coach and we gave him a few extra hours, teamed him up with three of our students, and sent them in to local state schools to deliver rugby for a term. It doesn't hurt our students – they learn to lead and manage and that'll help their UCAS reference. It's a two-way street. The more of this kind of thing we do, the better.

Your school offers a huge range of sport – why is this important?

I've got 1,048 boys to consider and would rather they were all engaged in sports rather than 200 doing sport to a high level. We give free choice to boys from 13 and that's quite unusual. Each term they choose a different sport. Traditional sports have a certain priority – football, crickets, hockey, etc. But I don't refer to sports as major and minor – that phrasing is really common in independent schools.

Is it better to be generalist rather than a specialist in sport?

Children will probably move towards being a specialist as they get older. But lots of children don't know what they want to be academically – we study ten GCSEs and then narrow to three A-levels and then one degree. So why not do that with sport? If it's too narrow a range at the beginning, it's harder for children to find the thing they love. I don't mind if what you love is croquet or Pilates or tennis. What matters is that when you get older, you're still active.

So many people have horror stories about their school PE days.

Yep. We have to work hard to break barriers down for children. You're using the word sport a lot but I say 'physical education' and that's different. As a school we're putting the education back into PE, we're talking about physical literacy. How do you run, throw, dodge, catch, swim? I see swimming as a life skill with a competitive strand – I'm not trying to create the next Adam Peaty in my lessons but every boy needs to be able to swim. So when they're 18 and go to Magaluf on their boys' holiday, they can safely jump in the pool. This is where sport and PE are different – the latter is about fundamentals and skills.

You've taught PE to both boys and girls. How different are their attitudes?

The benefits of PE are the same for everyone but you need to coax them out in different ways. Maturation rates are massively different between girls and boys in their teenage years and we don't look at this enough. And we've been talking about offering traditionally male sports to females for years but no one has ever been brave enough to do it. But look at the rise of female football. We've been behind the times here.

Is body image a problem for female participation?

Body image is massive for girls. Changing rooms are a big thing – you're putting 30 girls – or boys – in a room to strip down to their underwear and change. That's tough, especially between the ages of 12 and 15 for a girl and 14 and 16 for a boy. And boys are far more conscious of body image now. You see it most with swimming lessons. We let them wear a pair of shorts rather than Speedos now. I've had boys asking if they can wear a T-shirt on top or come down to the pool with their towel wrapped around them. We have to respect that.

What's the answer?

Greater education about body image because Photoshop can ruin lives – kids are bombarded with these images on social media. Also, there's been a massive evolution in kit for schools in the last 20 years. Having more appropriate clothing, in terms of material and cut, makes a positive difference.

Your predictions – and hopes – for the future of sport?

I can see things like cross country coming back into vogue in schools after the pandemic. Before you'd ask a kid to go for a run for 30 minutes and they'd have said no. Now they're all going for runs. We've got a great chance to kickstart sports and physical literacy. I think sports participation will go up and all those local organisations that are volunteer-run will need support from governing bodies and grassroots funding for this.

INSIDER INSIGHT: PETE BIGNELL

There are obviously benefits for all of weaving together exercise and education at the heart of communities – as the London Olympic Park now demonstrates. Driven by the impetus of London 2012 Olympics, this once neglected, polluted area of east London now has an outstanding state school in Mossbourne Riverside Academy. Then there's Here East, an innovation campus that includes an arm of Loughborough University, Britain's most respected university for sport, plus BT Sport's HQ and many small businesses. And where sport has put down roots, art and culture have now followed: East Bank is a new project in the Olympic Park that will include sites for Sadler's Wells theatre, the BBC and the Victoria and Albert Museum. Work is slated to start in 2022, with the scheme receiving £385 million from the Mayor of London, £151 million from the government and £10 million from the shopping centre Westfield Stratford City towards providing skills, lifelong learning, jobs, and business and entrepreneur opportunities for local people.

This all dovetails with the prevailing direction of travel for urban planning – the notion of building mini villages within larger urban spaces, rather than discrete areas for offices, retail, restaurants, education, sport and leisure and so on. This approach certainly makes sense for post-pandemic lifestyles: many people do not want to return to long commutes, with all those wasted hours, preferring instead to continue with the flexible working practices that suddenly became the norm during lockdown. Many of us now want all aspects of our life – work, rest and play – to be catered for within the same local community. Professor Carlos Moreno, scientific director of entrepreneurship and innovation at the Sorbonne in Paris, talks of 'la ville du quart d'heure', the community in which all key facilities are within a 15-minute walk or bike ride. Moreno also calls for buildings to be more flexible and thus deployed for multiple purposes through the day, so, for example, the local school doesn't stand empty all weekend or all summer but is instead used by other members of the community. Nicola Palios and Tranmere Rovers are ahead of the game on that front.

It's clear that sport is no longer seen as a fun, optional add-on to people's lifestyles. It's an essential for all; a vital component in keep us fighting fit and healthy – physically and mentally – so we can face a deeply volatile and unpredictable world with strength and resilience. But we need to ensure there's both the will (as in we all take personal responsibility for our health) and the way (accessible schemes and facilities available to all) across all strata of our society for it to work. What we're starting to see is a slow, gentle, successful reworking of the role of sport at the centre of our lives and communities, which fits with our changing times. The result is that everyone – us as individuals, our families, our communities, our employers, the sports themselves, the NHS and the wider public purse – is a winner. A worthy goal, I'd say.

CHAPTER 7 / Taking Care of Business

JERRY MAGUIRE, 25 YEARS ON

The movie *Jerry Maguire*, starring Tom Cruise, Renée Zellweger and Cuba Gooding Jr, came out in 1996. Cruise plays the eponymous protagonist – a sports agent with agency SMI – who has an epiphany and decides that, rather than chasing the big bucks with star clients galore, he wants to focus on deeper relationships with fewer clients, so putting a bit of humanity into the sports business. SMI sees no place for this, and he embarks on a voyage of self-discovery (masquerading as a new business venture) with the odds stacked against him. I'm sure you can work out the rest – it was a Hollywood romantic comedy, after all.

There are three things worth noting about the movie. Firstly, the immortal line 'Show me the money!' thrown at Jerry by his sole initial client, representing the attitude of players and agents alike. Secondly, the way in which the sports industry is depicted – as Jerry puts it: 'It is an up-at-dawn, pride-swallowing siege.' Thirdly, as if to prove that point, the backstory of the movie was itself full of competing commercial agendas from the get-go. The film is credited with being the brainchild of Leigh Steinberg, himself a sports agent with his own business, and was the subject of exactly the kind of financial wrangles that are the bread and butter of the industry. According to the *Wall Street Journal*, sports brand Reebok and movie distributor TriStar Pictures fell out over an agreement for Reebok to provide merchandise and advertising support in return for being heavily featured in the movie.[49]

It's ironic that a movie about the sports industry ended up in a sports industry bust-up. In this case, life was imitating art. The success of the film also ensured that the general public were under few illusions about the dog-eat-dog nature of the industry – but also cemented the fascination that the general public have for that rough and tumble. Cruise won a Golden Globe, Gooding Jr an Oscar and the movie took $280 million at the global box office. The commercial sharp end of sport has done little to dispel the public perception that it's a bit of a mess ever since.

Twenty-five years on and the business of sport is still big news, with its own gossip pages and scurrilous rumours aplenty. I hear a lot of fair criticism of areas that still need to improve, but I also hear some opinions that are very outdated. The business of sport has now left its difficult teenage years behind. While it still might mess up a decision or two, and go off the rails at times, it is generally becoming more dependable – and sometimes even able to see beyond the next paycheque.

The problem is that it does a very bad job of telling that story. The industry tends to retreat to its bunker, sit out the air raids from the media and stick to what it knows. There's a certain insecurity in this insularity – many leaders in sport haven't been exposed to 'corporate big business' and would run a mile rather than have a conversation with the BBC's business editor about the impact of economics, or even just inflation rates, on sport. That fear is corrosive – and leaves the gossip to drive the agenda.

CHANGE OR DIE

So what is life really like inside the sports industry? How and why are things changing? Can't we all just learn to love sport exactly the same way that previous generations did?

Sadly, the answer is no. Time moves on. So where does this all leave the most traditional of sports? In fact, the smartest twentieth-century ones are busily reinventing themselves for twenty-first-century tastes, a necessary act of future proofing. They realise that in order to flourish, they need to relax their door policies, be inclusive and widen their communities. It's now or never.

Golf is one sport ripe for reinvention but, unlike the pace of change we saw from the England and Wales Cricket Board regarding the Hundred, golf's decision-makers were initially slower to react. Which is unfortunate because it's probably the sport that needs to change fastest in order to stay a permanent fixture of the British calendar. If you look at the big-picture trends, it doesn't look pretty. For starters, golf is very time consuming. As with cricket, the vast majority of people don't have time to play 18 holes of golf, an activity that takes around half a day at best. It's also very expensive – you need a set of clubs that might cost £200 and upwards, plus membership or one-off fees to play a round. Watching it on TV also costs money, as almost all of the sport sits behind a paywall on Sky Sports.

Beyond the time and financial barriers for someone to take up or even just watch the sport, the mere existence of golf courses is seen by some as controversial. An ever-expanding UK population and its accompanying housing shortage means it is hard to justify leaving thousands of acres of land accessible to only a few hundred members, no matter whether those members are funding their upkeep or not. Then there's the environmental impact of the cultivating those pristine fairways. Climate-change expert Dr Thomas Tanner pulls no punches: 'Golf is the most environmentally damaging sport per player, if you assume that otherwise the courses would be fields and trees. It's from watering all that grass and the fertiliser,' he says. 'This idea that a golf course is a green area and thus good for nature is nonsense.'

Golf has also been one of several sports to wake up to its lack of diversity. Even today, only 15 per cent of UK club members are female and it took until ridiculously recently – April 2020 – for women finally to be allowed to join what may have been the final men-only club standing, the Royal Burgess in Edinburgh. These factors, combined with an ageing member-ship base, mean that in recent years golf-club membership has been in decline, with numbers falling by 1.63 per cent between 2017–18. There's nothing inherently wrong with creating a private members club available only to those prepared to pay a significant fee, which in turn only makes sense if you're going to spend a significant amount of time there. The challenge is that it's very hard to create a viable business model for all but the very best.

The pandemic, however, gave golf an unexpected boost. England Golf reported that from May to July 2020, clubs gained an astonishing 20,000 new members; many of whom were younger people who were working from home and had more time on their hands in the evenings as they were no longer commuting, along with families looking for an activity to do together. It also helped that it was one of the first sports to receive the green light to reopen after the initial lockdown, thanks to its inherently socially distanced nature. (Tennis, another earlier reopener that doesn't involve close contact, also enjoyed a huge upswing in court bookings.)

So how can golf clubs maintain this out-of-the-blue momentum? How do you keep those fresh new participants engaged when lives return to something approaching normal? Clubs need to ponder how best to open up their facilities to the wider local community and increase footfall. If you can show people that you provide a third space where they can enjoy a lifestyle, in which golf is just one option, they are more likely to come. Children's activities, spa and gym facilities and community taster days are obvious ideas. They could also offer up usually empty buildings as co-working spaces (instead of a pint after work, workers could unwind by playing a round) or provide a route for a parkrun or similar. If National Trust venues can manage it, then it cannot be beyond the realms of possibility for golf courses to do the same.

There are also some interesting initiatives coming through – changes to the format such as playing 9 holes or 12 to make the game more time-efficient. Footgolf, meanwhile, uses a football (and obviously bigger holes!) on some golf courses so you don't even need to acquire a set of clubs to play. Topgolf, a US company with two sites in the UK, posits itself as 'sports entertainment', making its version of golf akin to ten-pin bowling, while Junkyard Golf, with five UK locations, is like playing crazy golf in a nightclub. Which will either sound amazing or awful, depending, most likely, on your age. Last time I visited the Oxford site, it was packed with teens and twentysomethings on a night out.

In sport (and beyond), there is a real art to balancing innovation with tradition. There is still absolutely a place for the latter. It can be an evolution rather than a revolution. The organiser of Royal Ascot, for example, understands that millennials and Generation Z are more experience-oriented than older attendees, so they have successfully rebooted their events, adding

DJs, street food and a day of diverse entertainment, to make it a coveted addition to a summer social calendar that will likely also include Glastonbury Festival. But their heartland attendees are still very much catered for and welcomed. At the other end of the age spectrum, the rise of walking football in recent years has reopened the game for older (and injured) players. It's the fastest-growing sport in the UK – in 2014, there were 200 registered clubs in the UK, two years later 1,000, and now 40,000 people play every week; many delighted with the resulting improvements to both their fitness levels and social life.

But you'll never keep everyone happy all the time. For every visitor to Twenty20 who loves the buzz, music and razzmatazz, there's a Test Match stalwart who prefers the slower pace of the five-day game. For every gang of lads on a stag night trying out Topgolf, there's a weekly ladies' fourball at their local club, a ritual that stretches back decades. Neither is more valid than the other.

For sports that trade on prestige, broadening their appeal can be challenging. Sometimes it's a case of relaxing and allowing curious newcomers to peek behind the velvet curtain. Corporate hospitality is one area that has changed markedly in recent years as sport starts to let its guard down. The traditional hospitality experience involved staid tables of eight who may or may not network with their neighbouring tables, as they sit down to a meal of multiple courses with the sport often relegated to sideshow. Manchester City's The Tunnel Club at the Etihad Stadium is a good example of how things have changed. Attendees mingle, munch on sharing plates stacked with grilled Padrón peppers and pumpkin gnocchi (no dodgy half-time pies here) and meet the players as they make their way to the changing room ahead of the match. They can then watch through a specially created window into the Tunnel as the players enter the field of play before the game. It's less formal, less traditional and more integrated than previous iterations of hospitality. Millennials aren't generally keen on anything 'corporate' but they do love a memorable day out.

YOU STILL WEAR NIKE?!

Whether or not you're a cricket or rugby fan, chances are that you lace up your trainers now and again for some purpose. And if that's the case, then change in the industry of sport is reaching you too. After all, from Michael Jordan to my ten-year-old daughter, we all have a say over what we wear when we play. The world has moved on from Nike's 'Just Do It'. Among groups of kids, the most likely reaction now to a statement like that is: 'Why?'

Since the days of *Jerry Maguire*'s Reebok spat, there have been a very small number of sports brands ruling the roost. Nike and adidas have traditionally led the way, with Reebok, Puma and latterly Under Armour heading up the next pack. They've managed to do a decent job of offering product that fits most areas of the sports market, hoovering up deals with the major sports teams and athletes, and dominating the major online and offline retailers in Britain. Not quite a closed shop, but one with fairly limited choice.

However, times are changing fast. Almost weekly, recession or not, new brands are entering the battle. There are a few drivers of this. Firstly, the market for sports clothing is growing – according to research published in pre-pandemic 2019, the UK sportswear market was set to grow by 20.9 per cent over the following five years to £6.7 billion by 2023, outperforming all other major sectors. That in turn is driven by the growth of athleisure as a category – sportswear to wear off the pitch, rather than on it.

Additionally, those traditional major sports brands that led the way in the early days of the sports industry belong to a different generation that are still playing sport, but aren't necessarily at the cutting edge any longer. As Generation Z develop increased spending power, they're unlikely to want to buy the same brands as their parents, let alone grandparents.

Finally, it is far easier for new brands to start selling when they don't need to use physical stores to do so. Digital democratises everything, and the clothing tastes of future generations are no longer dictated by the diminishing variety of high-street sports retailers. It is questionable whether a brand can be authentic or credible selling urban athleisure, yoga pants, golf shoes and simultaneously kitting out the England football team, whereas the online marketplace provides other choices for those who refuse the clothes shop. Sports clothing, as a result, is going through a renaissance of creativity, and also establishing a new consciousness when it come to the ethics of production. Generation Z grew up with the furore around sweatshop clothing production, after all.

One example of a brand that captures this new mood is Contra, the brainchild of parkrun founder Paul Sinton-Hewitt and its global CEO Nick Pearson. It produces its running tops and leggings ethically, using European factories, in response to revelations about mainstream sports brands using Asian factories with poor labour conditions. What's more, Contra takes a significantly different, inclusive, approach to sizing. 'We wanted Contra to represent fairness,' says Nick. 'Fairness in supply chain, manufacturing process and customer base – and to challenge those traditional stereotypes perpetuated by sports brands. They'll often use a divisive strategy – it's a popularity contest. "You can be one of the beautiful people if you buy one of our products." But if you haven't got a certain level of self-worth, you're driven further away from feeling that exercise is for you.' They drew on conversations they'd had over the years with both parkrun participants and – crucially – those who signed up to run but couldn't face it on the day. 'It might be a 45-year-old mother of three who's just getting back into fitness but felt intimidated going into sports stores to buy kit.' They recruited a diverse group of people to advise on Contra's design and fitting process. 'Some ambassadors said that going into a shop and asking for a size XXL was the most humiliating experience of their life, so we used that insight to define our sizing by letters,' says Nick.

INSIDER INSIGHT: **NICK PEARSON**

The CEO of parkrun Global, Nick has been with the pioneering international running community since 2015 and is responsible for developing strategies to create a sustainable business model. Drawing on his background in sports retail, he launched the brand's ethical, size-inclusive clothing label, Contra, in 2018.

Why did parkrun decide to launch a sportswear line?

We have 7 million parkrunners across the world now and felt one of the big opportunities for ensuring it could be sustainable was to find products of interest to the marketplace. It means parkrun can remain free and the community can choose to purchase Contra products, with profits directly supporting parkrun. We discovered the primary reason people sign up but don't run is because they feel they're not fit enough. Society has constructed an image of what active people look like – and it's not them. Sports brands have traditionally played a role in reinforcing this belief, or they try to address it in an insincere or patronising way. And if you're not of certain size or shape or age, it's hard to find gear.

What are the challenges of a brand with lots of sizes?

There has to be a limit to where you start and finish – you're never going to fit everybody. But we did our best. The cost of inventory is high as we need multiple patterns cuts. We wanted this to be a partnership that wasn't exploitative for all stake-holders, including the consumer. Most brands are profit maxim-ised – they'll say, 'What's the most profit I can generate from a customer?' But we said, 'What's the *least* amount of profit we need?' We don't need to work on traditional margins, we just need enough profit to donate to parkrun. A normal brand would push the customer into newer styles, with new products every season. But we don't drop styles, we keep them unless we need to improve something like the fabric. So we're not compelling the consumer to ditch old stuff and buy new for the sake of it.

What's the future for sports retail brands?

You'll get plenty more choice of niche brands because the route to market has been totally transformed and democratised for start-up brands. If you wanted to start something out of your back room, it's relatively easy to do that. The world has become smaller through tech and you're no longer reliant on a bricks-and-mortar retailer.

There's an interesting statistic about the average parkrun finishing time getting longer – what does this mean?

It was once a running event for runners but now we are a wellbe-ing organisation, committed to helping people become healthier and happier in their communities. It's about attracting *every-one* in that community. We're 16 years in and every year the average finish time has got slower, which shows a broadening of participation. That represents the role that parkrun has played in making physical activity more accessible to people who didn't feel it was accessible 16 years ago.

GPs have started 'prescribing' parkrun, haven't they?

It makes sense. The NHS should look to activities that encourage lifestyle change to help avoid people becoming sick, rather than dealing with the cost of medicating people who are sick. We teamed up with Royal College of General Practitioners in 2018 to encourage GP surgeries to sign up to a programme to support their patients to go to their local parkrun, where appropriate. It's been a huge success. We're still gathering insight but we believe it's an intervention that supports a healthier population in a positive, friendly, community-focused environment.

parkrun was forced to close down during lockdown. What impact do you think the pandemic will have had on fitness?

Our suspicion is the inequalities we've spent the last 16 years trying to address have probably been widened. The fit will be more fit, the inactive will be less active. We wouldn't be surprised if finishing times get faster for a while. parkrun will return with fitter people and we'll lose a group of people who were building up the courage to get outside. We will have to reinvest to get them involved.

All parkruns have an army of volunteers. What's the thinking behind this?

We aspire to redefine the culture of volunteering. There's almost a stigma associated with it: it's a chore, an act of martyrdom. We want to help people understand the positive benefits for you as an individual. It makes you happier, it makes you feel more valued, it gives you a sense of purpose. In post-COVID-19 Britain, volunteering will need to play a huge role. We'll have to rebuild society in economic turmoil like we've never seen before.

INSIDER INSIGHT: NICK PEARSON

There will be fewer jobs. Volunteering will support people's well-being and mental health, while offering opportunities to learn new skills.

Your predictions – and hopes – for the future of sport and fitness?

There is this view that sport is the answer to everything, that everybody is motivated by Lewis Hamilton, Paula Radcliffe or David Beckham. But we keep getting that wrong – some people are motivated by those iconic sporting heroes but equally there's a lot of people who aren't. Keeping on telling them that they should be doesn't help. Keeping on spending more money on more iconic sportspeople doesn't change that. There's a sector who'll never be inspired and motivated by aspirational sports stars and we have to acknowledge that. So make exercise fun, positive and empowering and that will help make it accessible to everybody.

In the coming years, more brands like Contra, which hope to provide a better experience for customers of all types and set themselves in direct contrast to the usual suspects, will emerge.

Castore, meanwhile, is a premium sports-clothing label set up in 2015 by two brothers from the Wirral, who have themselves played sport to a high level. Tom Beahon (who played youth football for our friends at Tranmere Rovers between the ages of 8 and 21) and his brother Phil had been frustrated by the lack of high-end sportswear for men, in a market saturated with mass-market brands.

Instead of signing a big-name athlete to just wear the gear, they've looked to an athlete as an investor in the shape of Andy Murray. Already a budding entrepreneur, Murray has pushed things a stage further (further even than IMG) by looking to own a part of the company whose apparel he wears. Having been kitted out by adidas and then Under Armour in recent years, he's evolved from being a trophy athlete to driving a challenger brand.

The Beahon brothers may sound like shrewd, experienced businesspeople. In fact, they launched Castore aged 22 and 25, having literally knocked on the doors of luxury fabric mills in Italy and factories in Portugal to ask for advice. Still under 30, they're a great example of Generation Z's total lack of fear in taking on Goliath. No wonder Nike and Co are doing their level best to avoid portraying themselves as the establishment.

One of the areas where the traditional sports brands are running seriously behind is women's activewear. I saw it for myself when I was in charge of buying some sportswear for the Two Circles team in 2013. Even with my wife installed as Head of Testing, it was difficult to find anything that both fitted well and looked good. Performance gear tended to look lousy and was very pink. So pink that my ten-year-old girl would have been delighted, but less so the women in our offices around the world who wanted sportswear they could wear to work so they could squeeze in a lunchtime run.

Fast forward to 2020, and the likes of Fabletics, Veja, Gymshark and a host of other fledgling independent brands, that often pick up huge traction on Instagram, are now making gear that has both function and form. Meanwhile, women's fashion retailers on the high street continue to launch fitness-wear lines. This has driven the growth of athleisure in sport and way beyond, to the point that trainers now appear more often than stilettos on the front row of fashion shows. Substance *and* style is a hard combination to beat. This is a movement that is likely to pick up further pace, based on the evidence of a report published in early 2021.[50] According to its authors, Robbert de Kock, President & CEO at the World Federation for Sporting Goods Industry and Alexander Thiel, a partner at McKinsey:

> Women's sportswear remains a huge growth opportunity. Overall, female participation in sport and physical activity is growing, largely as a result of women being more willing to see being active as an integral part of health and well-being. Pre COVID-19, women's sportswear as a category grew 40 per cent faster than the male category in the US and nearly three times as fast in the UK. While the overall market size of women's sportswear remains well below its male compatriot, we believe that sales of female sportswear (together with athleisure) will be a major driver of growth in the overall sporting goods industry market between 2020–23.

That's not just a trend, that's practically a revolution.

THIS GIRL ALWAYS COULD

While traditionally sports movies about women have been as poor as the kit that was available for them to wear, there was one outlier. Back in 2002, *Bend It Like Beckham* successfully told the story of an Asian woman, played by Parminder Nagra, starting to play women's football. It seems extraordinary watching the movie now how much women's sport has changed in such a short space of time. If the movie nudged the door ajar, generational shift has since blown it off its hinges.

When my younger twin sisters Em and Lou were growing up, football, rugby and cricket just weren't really options for them to play. For team sports, it was predominantly a choice of hockey or netball, and neither of those were on television. That meant they saw few role models of girls playing in teams. Parminder Nagra and her co-star, a young upcomer called Keira Knightley, offered a sense of what the future might hold. Nowadays my daughter follows the England women's cricket, football and Olympic champion Team GB hockey teams, and has their pictures on her wall. Quite rightly that translates into a sense of entitlement to be able to play new games, and to have the same opportunities as the boys.

Telling sport's stories truthfully is vital for hooking in more girls, says Rebecca Smith, the former New Zealand women's football international who's now head of women's football at COPA90, a London-based global fan-culture site. 'My sister and I started a production company because I thought the brand of women's football kind of sucked,' she says. 'It felt like it was ticking a corporate social responsibility box. The tone and way it portrayed the sport was very juvenile: "Look, women, you can have lots of fun!" You rarely saw players really kicking ass, having incredible skills, making tough tackles. The players are actually extremely strong role models. We wanted to show women as they really were and that needed better quality storytelling.'

INSIDER INSIGHT: REBECCA SMITH

A former FIFA Women's World Player of the Year nominee, Rebecca was part of the New Zealand international women's team that reached the quarter-finals at the 2012 Olympics. Now she heads up women's football at COPA90 in London, a digital site that celebrates football and its fans, with an emphasis on 'how football feels'.

You work in digital media – is that the way to bring more girls into football?

There's a massive opportunity in digital for sports in general but particularly women's sports that aren't generally in the broadcast market. The characters in women's football, the top players, are great. They're excellent at doing social media – they're savvy and they are really good at conversations because they have to be. They haven't just been able to focus on football from a very young age like male players have so they've become good at marketing themselves and the game.

It does feel like the new breed of male footballers are different though – more serious, better role models?

This is going to sound very cynical but most are just more aware of how to build a brand in a better way. Although I'm not talking about Raheem Sterling and racism here – he clearly believes in his message and is an incredible role model. On the women's side, I think they're purists – they don't make enough money to be millionaires who can retire off their football careers. They know they have to transition and work after their career ends. They legitimately want their sport to grow and they're willing to lean in to help it do so and be good role models who girls will look up to. There's more authenticity in the women's game.

How has women's football changed from the start of your career?

With the professionalisation of the sport, the number-one thing you need is the quality of the product, so players' fitness has increased dramatically. And because there's been more investment at grassroots levels in the UK, because there's been more role models, girls say, 'I can get to that level. There's a pathway for me. I can potentially make money.' What I find now though is a lot more girls have specialised at a younger age but they're not really happy. They get to 21 or 22 and they're like, 'We're here but still the sport hasn't caught up with us – we're still not on mainstream TV, we still don't have big deals, we're not working in conditions that are very professional.' So while that training has placed them at a very professional level, the rest of the ecosystem and the culture isn't quite there yet.

Thoughts on sport as a tool for social good?

There's not one person I've talked to about Netflix's Michael Jordan basketball documentary] *The Last Dance* who doesn't love it. The thing that cuts across everything – culture, religion, ethnicity, location, age, gender, sexuality – and appeals to everyone on a mass platform is sport. It has such a power to influence things in the right ways when there's so little else that can. That's only going to increase. Sport's roles models – and they are role models whether they like or not – they'll become a beacon for leadership. Not only because they're respected as athletes but because of the characteristics that sport teaches you. During the pandemic, I did workshops teaching businesses about the elite athlete mentality. So it's things like resilience. I let in a goal in the World Cup that had New Zealand knocked out of the tournament. How do you deal with that as captain of a national team? You live with it, you come back and score the first goal and drive your team forward because you have no choice. You can't curl up in a ball and die because you're back on a world stage again.

Your predictions – and hopes – for the future of sport?

I think the future's really bright for women's football in this country. It's getting there but it needs to be done in the right way, with proper investment. The Super League has grown but it's funded by the FA and sponsors so it isn't a self-contained economic entity. It's not run like a private business. There aren't many TV rights – they need to have more matches on TV and to make the production higher quality – things like more cameras, for a start! And the decision-making bodies need to be more diverse. I've worked with the FA and FIFA – it's all the same type of people, middle-aged White men. You need more diversity otherwise you're not making the best decisions for everyone, you're just making them from your own perspective.

As UK Sport's Sally Munday says of the Olympic champion hockey team: 'They've changed the perception of the sport. For too long it was considered to be a butch thing. They've showed that being strong and athletic is beautiful and positive. And they started off a change in attitude towards women's sport, which was then capitalised on by England's women winning the cricket World Cup in 2017 and the netball at the Commonwealth Games.' She continues: 'For years we've had broadcasters saying, "People don't want to watch women's sport," but 10 million people tuned in to watch the women's hockey team win gold in the final at Rio 2016, in a game full of drama and excitement.'

Happily, my own daughter Niamh has never really known sport any other way. While she expects – and mostly receives – the same opportunities as boys of her age, they need to be presented in very different ways. The penny is finally dropping that women of all ages tend to value different things in sport and exercise to men. From a very early age, their drivers are simply totally different.

Perhaps the best example of this in the last ten years has been the development of the LEGO Friends toy range, created by the manufacturers of LEGO ten years ago to appeal specifically to girls. This was no overnight success – they had made several failed attempts to launch a product designed to reflect the realities of how girls play. Beneath the superficial (and slightly stereotypical) changes of colours to more pastel colours, there were two far more important changes in their approach with LEGO Friends.

Firstly, having watched groups of girls, they saw that girls loved to build models just as much as boys, just differently. Boys, they observed, tended to build in a linear way – building rapidly to complete the task of creating a kit to look just like it was on the box. Instead, girls preferred to stop along the way, to tell stories long before the model was complete. In response to this, LEGO bagged the pieces in its Friends ranges into smaller sections, so that girls can begin playing various scenarios without finishing the whole model. I notice this with my daughter who has had enormous amounts of fun with several kits where some of the small bags have yet to be opened at all. This has the added advantage as a parent that there is far less risk of the excruciating pain of standing on odd bricks, so I am all for it.

The second key change was to create a specific set of female figures, each with their own backstories. These replaced the generic square figurines much loved by the boys while the girls, they found, just could not identify with. This identification is fundamental, LEGO found, because girls were much more likely to project themselves onto the life of a figure, whereas the boys played with their little yellow friends in the third person and rarely tried to 'become' them. LEGO design director Rosario Costa told *Bloomberg Business Week*, 'The girls needed a figure they could identify with, that looks like them.'[51] They knew they were onto something when girls started saying, 'I want to shrink down and be there.'

The launch of the Friends range in 2012 was controversial, with consumer groups complaining that LEGO was reinforcing gender stereotypes. However, when you strip back the projections of adult arguments on to kids' play, the truth is girls love it, and that a new generation of girls is indulging in active play when (like my daughter) they had previously had little interest in playing with their brothers' sets. Kids will not stay with something they don't value and LEGO doubled its sales targets in the first six months. Several years on, Friends remains one of their top-selling ranges.

Scary as it may seem, young girls who may have been ten years old when they received one of the first LEGO Friends sets for Christmas when it launched in 2012 will now be starting to enter the workforce. They are the first generation who will have grown up with toys and broader forms of entertainment that started to be driven out of an understanding of their need for sociability over speed of outcome, and the importance of being able to project themselves inside a community rather than feeling like an outsider. No surprise then, that options for 'play' for twentysomethings are starting to cater to these same elements. UK fitness chain Frame was set up by Pip Black and Joan Murphy, specifically targeting women in central London who might have traditionally felt that sport in general, and the gym in particular, was not for them. Pip and Joan made a number of diversions from the traditional gym model to make this work. Having cracked the recipe, they are expanding Frame quickly and have developed a community of committed gym-goers (or 'Framers') in their seven locations across the city.

The Frame approach is very different from the traditional gym model. For example, guests attending classes can select them based on mood. This isn't all high octane and energy – there are classes to cater for visitors feeling 'drained', 'stressed' and 'fragile'. Instructors for classes are selected based on their ability to engage and fit in with the member community (much like the logic for the LEGO figurines), rather than because they are big-name influencers.

Traditional gyms tend to rely on joining fees and ongoing direct debits after they hook new customers. Having welcomed a new joiner, typically gyms will only work for a certain amount of time at persuading their members to make best use of their membership. After that, they try to avoid 'waking the dead' – a phrase they use to describe reminding lapsed members they have an expensive direct debit going out every month. Instead, Frame and other new gym chains offer 'pay as you go' smart cards, which work in the same way as an Oyster card on the Underground. Their clientele can then pace themselves, just like the young girls making their Friends kits.

Most importantly, for a generation of women who might not necessarily have been gym members before, the first statement on Frame's promotional video is: 'We don't take ourselves too seriously.' The aim is to be welcoming, inclusive and cut through the nonsense talked about physical exercise. 'No guilt trips, no body shaming, no airbrushing, no body shaming,' they promise, speaking exactly the same language as the 'This Girl Can' campaign. 'Some days we smash two classes in a day, others we lie on the mat and pretend to meditate.' This is a world away from a cohort who, as kids, would have built a LEGO model as quickly as possible to make it look like the picture on the box. This girl always could – she just needed to be able to engage with sport on her own terms.

TAXI TALK

These days I rarely admit to a taxi driver that I work in sports. I know if I do, it's likely I will need to defend what I do for a living because, believe me, everyone has a view on sport. Here is my list of the Top 5 cabbie complaints about my industry. If you don't work in sport, I'll hazard a guess you'll nod in agreeance with some of these too.

1. Sport is too elite nowadays – we can't identify with the athletes

Well, it's true that sport at the highest level is hugely compet-itive. I once tried to run a marathon on a treadmill at the pace that the winner of the London Marathon would run and lasted about 200m. But is that too elite? I think it's a good thing – I want my ten-year-old daughter to be able to watch amazing cricket on TV and wish to emulate it, for professional athletes to help her to dream. The key is to tell the stories about how the athletes became exceptional. Their standard is not out of reach, people can do amazing things, it just takes commitment.

I do think it's true that it has not been easy to identify with sportspeople in the past but that's changing. The new breed are a lot more in touch. Ridiculously talented – undoubtedly. But also focused, committed, socially aware and brave. If we can't identify with those qualities, maybe that says more about us than it does about them.

2. It's also too upper class – that English cricket team all went to Eton, you know

Actually, most sports don't skew posh at all. Sports like cricket and rowing do have issues in that regard – principally because the facilities, equipment and specialist coaching required are difficult for state schools to provide, and it's expensive for parents to provide support outside school.

There are some brilliant schemes, like the MCC Founda-tion in cricket, that are trying to offer more opportunities for kids from inside the state-school sector, and, to the credit of the private schools, they continue to seek talented kids to join on bursary schemes. However, this is likely to be a continual challenge when state-sector school budgets are too tight to mention. This makes identifying talent and strengthening the links between state and private schools, as we have heard about in relation Abingdon School, even more important.

3. British sport isn't British any more – there are too many foreigners coming over here and taking the places of our kids

This one annoys me the most. It's a view that tends to come from football fans. I'd usually ask the driver who she or he supports, and which players they would not have brought to the club. Typically you'll find they're less concerned about the star names, but the 'journeyman' (cab drivers seem to like that word!) pros. They argue – with some justification – that British kids find it tough to progress when their way is blocked by international players.

There are a few counter-arguments to this. Firstly, we have had an open labour market. It is just as easy for British kids to play in Italy as Italians in Britain, if they have the drive to succeed. Secondly, football in England has benefitted from a revolution in facilities and profile in the last ten years, without ramping up ticket prices nearly as quickly as people would have you believe. That's principally due to increased revenue coming from international broadcasters who recognise the global appeal of the Premier League and its labour market. Much as we would like to, we can't have our cake and eat it.

However, the chat is a little easier post-pandemic – as I explain that financial Armageddon in football means that no football club in their right mind will plump for signing international 'journeymen' if they have talented local kids who can do the job.

4. It's all about money nowadays – it's all anyone cares about

I refer you partly to my last answer, m'lud! It's definitely true that sport is a business. And the truth is that it always has been. But having worked in the industry for 25 years, I can promise a few things:

i   I have never met anyone who is just interested in the money. If they were, they wouldn't work in an industry where salaries tend to be 30–40 per cent lower than other sectors and where weekends tend to be the busiest days of the week.

ii   Money has to be a consideration, because there is nobody else to pick up the pieces. The government can't afford to bail out a team going under (as we have seen through the pandemic).

iii But money is not the only consideration. Chelsea could sell tickets for three times their face value. Nobody told Harry Kane he had to sponsor his local team and give the exposure to charities. Increasingly clubs are aware of their broader social responsibilities and the communities they live in.

iv   Not even the most commercially orientated of teams can exist without a local fan base and a vibrant league. If money was no object, Premier League football teams would play half their games abroad.

5. They're all on drugs anyway

No, they're not. A minority are. It's true that drugs remain a threat to the credibility of sport, in particular those sports with a large strength or endurance component to them. This doesn't make me want to give up, though, any more than seeing someone else flouting lockdown rules made make me want to do the same.

What has improved, however, is our ability to find people guilty after the event – for example, taking samples to be tested at a later date once medicine has developed. For that reason, the risk inherent in drug taking will increase rather than decrease. I see the work going into ensuring the playing field is as free of chemical intervention as possible. The best thing we can do to ensure that remains the case is to fund these organisations properly, as the credibility of professional sport depends on it.

Often at the heart of my taxi drivers' various complaints is a sense that sport is getting too far away from the fan, and a feeling that money and technology are playing a role in this. I have always found this ironic because there are so many ways in which technology is helping more people watch *and* play sport, the pandemic experience being an obvious case.

Technology's involvement in sport tends to start at the elite end. Sport is a high-stakes battleground for new technologies, and often the proving ground for them. The field of play has changed beyond all measure in the last 15 years. 'The single biggest change in the sporting landscape in recent years is how technology has opened up to the sports world and empowered the potential of community,' says Michael Payne, a former long-serving IOC marketing director and author of *Olympic Turnaround*, which details the evolution of the Olympic Games during his tenure from near extinction and bankruptcy in the early 1980s to a hugely successful global franchise. 'Sport has always been about community, whether it's about a fan base or the members of your local cricket club. Tech and the multitude of new platforms have empowered the fan and participant to have a whole new level of engagement on an active basis rather than passive basis.' Players are fitted with heart-rate and distance tracking technology to understand how they are performing. Equipment is painstakingly analysed to understand where any competitive advantage might lie. Owen Slot describes this process as related to Team GB, Britain's Olympic team, in his book *The Talent Lab*. He says that British investment in this space started in earnest for Beijing 2008, focusing on technology to help athletes go faster. Over time, with low hanging fruit like aerodynamics covered, this has transitioned to broader programmes that support the whole process of preparing for competition. For example, a specific project might consider how best to minimise the number of training days an athlete loses to injury or illness, how to reduce the risk of saddle sores for cyclists, or prepare athletes for the unique levels of heat and humidity weather conditions in Tokyo.

Team GB has led the way for Olympic nations in its advancements, supported by significant investment from the Department of Culture, Media and Sport, the National Lottery and the English Institute of Sport. There are hosts of projects of this nature just beginning to bear fruit. I hear a little about these because of my role at the English Institute of Sport, which leads the British technology agenda for the Olympic Games. Almost as impressive as the innovative projects themselves, however, is the secrecy within which any level of detail is shrouded.

The growing importance of technology in delivering success is also true off the pitch. The biggest sports leagues have global followings who they are in contact with at the touch of a button through digital media (often with the help of Two Circles, the business I co-founded). Live footage is transported in real time, as players' heart and sweat rates, distance covered on the pitch and so on are reviewed and measured in a similar way. Managing all of this technology does not always come easily for sports. Fortunately there is no shortage of technology companies wanting to use it as a shop window. The likes of Microsoft find it much easier to sell their wares by explaining their work for Real Madrid than for a standard (but slightly less exciting!) insurance or banking client.

Sometimes, however, these swanky new bits of kit are not quite all they seem. The first ever photo-finish camera was paraded at the London 1948 Games as an innovation by watchmaker Omega; however, organisers had installed officials at the finish line with stopwatches and they were the mechanism that decided finish times and medal placings as the kit was not yet accurate enough.

Overegging the role of new technology continues to this day, not least as sport is not as easy as it seems for the biggest tech companies to grasp. At the Winter Olympics in Nagano in 1998, the Games generated 1 terabit of data, which itself was five times more than the preceding Lillehammer Games. As Michael Payne writes in *Olympic Turnaround*, the requirement for 1 terabit of data storage made IBM seriously consider the costs of continuing as a partner to the Olympic Games. To put the pace of change into perspective, the size of storage that made a global technology company baulk as recently as 25 years ago can now be bought for £14 on Amazon.

INSIDER INSIGHT: MICHAEL PAYNE

A professional freestyle skiing champion in the 1970s, Michael was the International Olympic Committee's first marketing and broadcast rights director. He wrote Olympic Turnaround *in 2005, which unpicks how the Games shook off scandal and bankruptcy to emerge as a one of the world's biggest and best-loved brands. Michael has been recognised as one of the 50 most influential marketeers in the world and is a senior adviser to some of the biggest sports businesses in the world, having brokered more than $25 billion worth of deals in sport during his career.*

What have been the biggest changes in the sports landscape since you wrote *Olympic Turnaround*? Has anything surprised you?

The digital space is allowing the empowerment of community and a more focused dialogue with the sports fan. I competed on the freestyle skiing world cup circuit many years ago and recently someone launched a new Facebook group, which meant I started connecting with people I used to compete with 40 years ago. Each morning I watch videos on half a dozen specific extreme skiing sites. I would never have had that opportunity before. There have always been sports that frankly weren't important enough to warrant their hour in the spotlight on the TV network but still had passionate followers. Now you've got the mechanism to bring together a substantial worldwide fanbase.

What would be on your action list for the Olympics for the coming years?

There's the short-term issue of still being able to deliver Tokyo in the shadow of the pandemic. But a really big crisis can be a great way to achieve a lot of things you wouldn't otherwise be able to achieve. At the start of the pandemic [President of the IOC] Thomas Bach – whose motto is 'change or be changed' – wrote a letter to the Olympic movement talking about the opportunities that will arise from the situation. I lived through – and still bear a few scars from – the 1999 bidding scandal that surrounded the 2002 Salt Lake City Winter Olympic games. That crisis very nearly collapsed the IOC. I would go into the office each day and not know if the organisation would survive the day. We ended up embracing and putting in place a reform programme. We pushed through a series of reforms in six months that would otherwise have taken 30 years.

Where are we at with doping in the Olympics?

I'll make a few observations. Define doping. I sat on the IOC board for 20 years and saw the President of the company turn around to the scientists and say, 'Give me a definition.' And I've never heard a definition that didn't require a PhD in biological chemistry. Say you're running, you fall over and twist your ankle but you have to compete tomorrow so you take a painkiller injection. That's legal. But taking certain other substances is not. Where is the line? And why do the media go absolutely batshit if someone in the Olympics is caught doping, having taken the wrong cold medicine? But if you look at professional sports, the media and the public couldn't care less because they're being entertained. Why does it matter so much one day if it's the Olympics and no one cares the next day if it's Major

League Baseball? I'm not passing judgement, I'm just putting it out there.

What are global sports events' environmental responsibilities?

Sport has an important role to get the message out there, to show the way, but don't necessarily expect sport to provide all the solutions. You have to find a balance. The staging of the Olympic Games in Beijing was a massive catalyst to cleaning up the environment and for the Chinese having an open debate for the first time about the importance of environment. The IOC has just built its new HQ in Switzerland, which reuses water from Lake Geneva and is one of the most environmentally friendly buildings in the world. Because of the profile of the organisation it was an important statement in terms of leadership and showing the way.

Post-pandemic, there's a governmental drive to get Brits fit. Thoughts?

I've always believed the IOC should drive the role of sport in an educational agenda. The values learnt from sport – team collaboration and fair play – should also be part of the global education curriculum. It's been very ad hoc in terms of which governments encourage physical activity as one of the basics of education. I've argued for a long time that the IOC really should push this. President Bach gets it and is now driving that forward.

What are your predictions – and hopes – for the future of sport?

I feel very positive. Sport is arguably the most important entertainment sector out there. There is very little content as powerful as sport; little else that cuts through the clutter and connects with people. And now the fan has lots of choice. In the past, sports would sit back and say, 'I am who I am, so you'll watch me.' But now they have to earn the right to keep the fans engaged, they must treat them like proper customers otherwise they'll move on. In terms of participation, many people are increasingly aware of their health, have more spare time and more disposable income to invest in their passion and have the platforms to connect with like-minded people, so many sports will grow. As for engaging the people on the margins, the first question is – are they watching any sport? Are they still watching their football club? If I was the football club what social programmes should I be offering to local communities? This comes back to sport as a pillar of society – what is the responsibility of sport to give back?

While there will always be hiccups at the frontier of innovation, modern sport relies on technology to share its stories and keep us entertained around the world, as lockdown showed very clearly. This is also true of our own sporting pursuits. While some prefer to keep their leisure activities to themselves, many others prefer their sport social. Smartwatches and recording tools like Strava are a source of mutual support and challenge for many. I enjoy them as a means of connection to others, as most of my sport is done around dawn before anyone with a modicum of common sense would want to run with me. It seems I am not alone – in two studies published in 2015 and 2017, a researcher from Ghent University collected activity data on more than 4,500 public Strava profiles and found that social interactions (likes, replies) spurred users to post more activities – essentially to become more active.

It's not only for those of us looking for a social media encouragement where technology can help us play more. It is also happening with equipment, in particular Paralympic equipment.

The first Paralympic Games, held on the lawns of Stoke Mandeville Hospital, Buckinghamshire, in 1948, saw two ex-servicewomen and 14 ex-servicemen competing in an archery competition. The equipment they shared was made up of heavy, unwieldy wooden bows and arrows. They were seated in cumbersome hospital-issue wheelchairs.

The early days of the Paralympic movement relied on sports that could be played using whatever standard-issue equipment was available. Founder Ludwig Guttmann created the sport of wheelchair polo, which used basic wheelchairs, a puck and shortened walking sticks. Unfortunately by this time he had unleashed a significant competitive spirit among Stoke Mandeville's patients, and the sport became too violent for it to continue. He replaced it with wheelchair basketball, still one of the most iconic Paralympic Games sports.

Although over 70 years have passed since the inaugural Paralympic Games, disability sport has only started to truly embrace technology in the last 20 years or so. Peter Norfolk OBE is Britain's most successful Paralympic tennis player, having won gold and silver in Athens 2004, gold and bronze in Beijing 2008 and six Grand Slam titles. 'When I started my tennis career in the 1980s, we had to learn how to build the right equipment the hard way,' he says. 'We took a hybrid everyday chair and tuned it on court. Now we use lightweight titanium chairs, with bespoke alterations of footgait, backrest, bearings, casters and wheels – we like to think of them as the Formula One racing car of wheelchairs!'[52]

Not all countries, of course, can provide the same amount of support to their athletes. Clare Griffiths, who has played for the British wheelchair basketball team at five Paralympics, told me, 'Access to a sports chair can ensure a beginner is able to enjoy the sport the first time they have a chance to play. Chair set-up, seating and strapping all have a big impact on balance, agility and mobility.'

Not only is faulty equipment dangerous, it can also put the result in doubt. Wheelchair basketball rules state that an athlete must fix any equipment malfunction within 50 seconds or else that player must be substituted. Leading-edge technology is important, but so is having equipment that is robust enough to last the course. 'Chair maintenance is critical,' says Clare. 'It doesn't happen very often, but if a chair frame breaks it is likely that you are out of the game.'

The creation of this leading-edge equipment is now big business. The market leader, German business Ottobock, focuses exclusively on the development and production of prosthetics, orthotics and wheelchairs, with its sales topping 1 billion euros in 2019. Most excitingly, technology developments are likely to revolutionise its ability to help even amateur athletes stay active, so not just the very elite will have its equipment. For example, 3D printing should mean that all athletes should be able to have bespoke orthotics made. Robotics may even enable artificially intelligent prosthetics, where athletes can replicate the fine motor skills of able-bodied athletes.

The next frontier of medicine and technology will hopefully also help us to enable individuals with mentally health issues as well as physically disabled athletes to enjoy their sport. For example, the more we understand about how the brain processes information, the better we will be able to design technology to solve the challenges that athletes with mental health issues face. This could mean installing visual or verbal cues into equipment to remind those who struggle with memory how to perform a certain task in competition.

As in all walks of life, technology in sport has the capability to do both good and harm. Well harnessed, it can bring us closer to our heroes, and make our own amateur pursuits more enjoyable. We can't put the genie back in the bottle, and so need to proceed with our eyes wide open.

Unfortunately, however, there is one other area where we cannot turn back time, but the potential risks of inaction are even worse.

THE GREEN MACHINE

One of sport's biggest challenges today is facing up to its responsibility to the environment. Of course, a gentle jog in the park doesn't do any harm, in particular if you are kitted out with gear from new-kid-on-the-block British brand Presca. It has produced sports gear that is fully recycled (from plastic bottles, no less) and completely recyclable (via a scheme it runs to take back old clothing and put it back into its production line). We will see far more of this type of clothing with a conscience enter the market, throwing down the gauntlet to Nike and its fellow big hitters.

Some sports are under particular pressure in terms of their impact on the environment. For example, there are real tests ahead for international motorsport – not only the carbon footprint its events create, but also the creation of a shop window for a means of transport that we need to wean ourselves off to enable a healthy planet. Some newer codes – for example Formula E – are emerging that aim to reduce the carbon impact of the races themselves; however, they are still flying containers around the world for public spectacle.

Formula One has promised that all its races will be sustainable by 2025 and pledged to achieve a net zero carbon impact by 2030. 'Formula One was the first sport to take carbon offsetting seriously,' says climate-change expert Dr Thomas Tanner, director of the Centre for Development, Environment and Policy at SOAS, University of London. 'They signed up to the emissions offsetting scheme for the whole caboodle – not just the cars zooming around on the track burning off fuel, it was about getting all the kit there and the spectators too.' The pledges are laudable, but the sport is likely to need to move quicker than that to avoid tighter regulation that would take things out of its hands. The pandemic in fact forced Formula One to fast-track a host of innovations to adapt its formats to changing times – for example, two races at a single destination. This kind of activity is likely to become the norm for many sports at an international level. COVID-19 created the permission for sports to try things in the name of the short-term health risk to populations around the world – all that will change is that formats of the future will be driven by the longer term health threat of climate change. This is going to be a significant change required of the sports industry in the next ten years. By the time Generation Z are heading up the sport this will be the only way of doing business. While the pandemic has shielded the issue from view in the very short term, mitigating climate change will be another fundamental aspect of the sports industry's maturation.

INSIDER INSIGHT:
DR THOMAS TANNER

With over 20 years in his field, climate-change expert Dr Thomas Tanner is director of the Centre for Development, Environment and Policy at SOAS, University of London. He's worked all over the world, including extensively across Asia, Latin America and Africa, and his previous roles include country negotiator in UN conventions on climate change. Having grown up in the north-east of England, he's a die-hard Newcastle United FC fan.

How big an issue is the global sports industry when it comes to climate change?

It's not seen as being a relatively problematic industry. It's not making stuff and transporting it around the world. The accumulative impact of goods is so much more than that of services. And if you think of the people who travel to global sporting events, there are very few of the world's population who actively attend. That said, every tonne of carbon counts. Forward-thinking football clubs are building in sustainability when it comes to redeveloping stadiums and training facilities and there are now green rankings of Premier League facilities. But I don't see any evidence of them intervening in things like the carbon footprints of fans travelling to see them. The clubs could facilitate or subsidise coaches that'd be lower carbon than everyone driving or flying on their own.

What should our personal responsibilities be?

Let's look at the impact of participation events, things like parkrun becoming so popular. If you think the consumer should take action, it's on me to lobby the organisers of my parkrun to encourage or incentivise people to use public transport to get there. Can you get a green star on your parkrun profile for not using your car? Those kind of nudges are good. That's about empowering people. My experience has shown that agency is really important. Putting solar panels on your house isn't just about saving money, it isn't just about helping Britain to save the planet, it's about you feeling like you're actually *doing* something. You're saying, 'This is part of my climate pledge.' The rise of open-water swimming is another one to consider – everyone is driving to those places; they're not getting the train to some river in the middle of nowhere.

Can you foresee a future when skiing will become a pariah activity?

I don't think so. It's always been a high-carbon activity but people just don't care because it's such fun. The much stronger driver is the increasing lack of snow. When I first started in climate change, we were doing studies around the world – observing rising sea levels in Bangladesh, permafrost melting in Tibetan China and so on; these really direct signals of climate change. But Europe was quite insulated. With skiing, the tourism signal was the only thing we really had – even 20 years ago the sector was being impacted by the increases in temperature. The lower lying resorts were really starting to struggle and were starting to adapt to become summer resorts too for financial sustainability. Although maybe they'll just buy more snow machines or people will just go to higher altitude resorts.

What are your predictions – and hopes – for the future of sport?

Emissions from flying are really important. It's become normal to, say, fly to the Florida Open for a long weekend, at the drop of a hat. It's not that big global events won't happen in the future but we'll hopefully be more mindful about how we get there. There's that Swedish term *flygskam*, which means flight guilt, the idea that everyone should be ashamed of, and stop talking about, where they've been. Currently this is only a concern among a really small proportion of the population. But things are changing. We might see carbon taxation or something like permits that allow you to fly once every year, with everyone having the right to burn a certain amount of jet fuel. If you want more, you have to buy someone else's allowance. Radical ideas do have a place at the moment. And temperature changes may affect the sporting calendar. The ski season will start later and, in places where it's getting hotter earlier in the season, you'll see a change in football. Remember the drinks breaks we saw when, after the first wave of COVID-19, they restarted the Premier League in the heat of the summer in 2020?

INSIDER INSIGHT: DR THOMAS TANNER

Beyond the impact of travel, sports venues themselves are starting to show signs of revolution. In 2018 the United Nations published data that suggested that 55 per cent of the world's population is now urban. By 2050, that figure will have risen to 68 per cent – 6.7 billion people out of an anticipated global population of 9.8 billion.[53]

When you fly into one of these city centres (although at the time of writing no one is flying anywhere), one type of building tends to stand out beyond all others. The trick of perspective can make skyscrapers seem fairly unremarkable, and yet it is impossible to miss the sports stadiums. They stand out as green rectangles with intricately built surrounds; the grass often seeming incongruously luxurious amid the rail lines, roads and houses packed around them.

In truth, the relationship between sports stadiums and their local environment has often been uncomfortable. Even within the triumph of the Queen Elizabeth Olympic Park in Stratford, the Olympic Stadium (now renamed the London Stadium) has engendered controversy, due to its current role as the home of West Ham Football Club. Some people think a private enterprise shouldn't be allowed to benefit from something built with taxpayers' money.

That said, the pandemic also reflected the significant progress made reversing things in the other direction, from private ownership to public usage. One former Olympic venue – ExCel London – was transformed into an NHS Nightingale Hospital for the potential use of thousands of patients. Lord's Cricket Ground, Chelsea's Stamford Bridge and many other facilities were made available to healthcare services. Across the country, sports stadiums started to re-embed themselves in the local communities they were built to serve.

As we learnt from Tranmere Rovers FC's co-owner Nicola Palios's creative use of the club's facilities, this is a trend that has been developing for a while. Sports organisations started to realise that it is a disservice both to their local community and their balance sheet to have their facilities stand empty for 340 days of a year. The leaders in this space have traditionally been those sports that have found it tougher to make ends meet on those matchdays, with long off seasons to contemplate. Edgbaston Cricket Ground in Birmingham has won awards at the Asian Wedding Awards, integrating itself into its local Asian community, who also happen to be mad on cricket. Saracens Rugby Club in London has even built its own free school. Harlequins, meanwhile, has thought carefully about getting best use of the facilities it already has, creating a serviced office business to use hospitality areas outside of matchday. Harlequins has also laid an AstroTurf pitch in the off-season to welcome England Hockey to play international matches on the ground.

The next step will be the transition to permanent all-weather AstroTurf-type pitches, in short supply up and down the country while local playing fields are at a premium. Opening up pitch facilities for greater usage by the local community will also create more impetus for ancillary facilities like catering.

The ultimate opportunity is to start a new building from scratch. Tottenham Hotspur took things to the extreme with a grass football pitch that can be wheeled away and replaced by an AstroTurf one for American football fixtures. Football club Bristol City's renovation of its stadium included the placement of solar panels on the roof –, which more than offsets the club's own power usage.

In a leafy part of south London, another game-changing project is soon to be underway. The All England Lawn Tennis and Croquet Club is soon to undergo a revolution in its footprint, having reclaimed the lease on the golf course it owns across the road from its current site, in what is reported as having been a £65 million deal. The 73-acre site will enable the expansion of its historic Wimbledon Championships' footprint and also continue the significant work it already does to contribute to the community through its foundation. As Matthew Campelli says on the *Sustainability Report*'s website, 'When a stadium opens itself up to being the nucleus of the city it inhabits, it can become a crucial part of a neighbourhood's regeneration – even encouraging citizens to stay, work and raise a family there.'[54]

Tokyo is an example of a metropolitan area where this kind of thinking is being applied with significant impact. The Japanese use a process of *machizukuri*, by which citizens work with city planners to help the place in which they live best meet local needs. The Japanese capital has an increasingly ageing population. The 'villages within the city' that are being designed bring together shops, physical activity areas, public amenities such as doctors' surgeries, cafés and so on into one hub ... and in doing so move away from the traditions of city planning that have tended to produce business, retail, entertainment and residential districts. The French idea of the '*la ville du quart d'heure*' we mentioned in Chapter 6 has legs, it seems.

Even if this is stretching the realms of the possible in certain areas, planners are starting to take a far more enlightened approach to town planning in the UK, too. The founders of Frame, for example, say they have noticed a significantly different attitude from landlords for their London gyms since they noticed that local fitness facilities have a significant impact on the desirability of their properties overall. For similar reasons, sports-based entertainment destinations that offer the chance to play as well as drink and eat – the likes of Flight Club, an interactive darts experience – are also highly prized in new urban locations. Younger generations are less likely to see alcohol as the foundation of a night out. A 2018 report from Berenberg Research found that respondents in their teens and early twenties were drinking over 20 per cent less than millennials (who themselves drank less than baby boomers and Generation Xers) did at the same age.[55] Given this trend, it is becoming increasingly important to give opportunities to 'play' on a night out, too.

Some sports brands have picked up on the hardwiring of sport into new urban environments. In adidas's case, it has focused a significant amount of its whole marketing budget on a hyper-local level in specific cities, and developed initiatives like running clubs or street-soccer competitions that genuinely add to their local community. adidas knows full well that the moment it loses its place in the chat on the street among the key urban audiences that influence wider opinion, the brand will lose its relevance. This is a fight it cannot afford to lose with Contra, Castore and Co nipping at their heels.

The city, of course, thinks differently to the countryside. For adidas, it's far more important to gain credibility with 20 influential skateboarders in Brixton than 2,000 teenagers in the Home Counties. For town planners, the opposite is true. Outside of London, sport has a key role to play in regenerating town centres. In future, retail spaces are likely to see the development of sporting experiences to add value to shopping centres, and maybe even distract the kids while their parents shop.

New housing developers are certainly starting to realise that parks and open space are just as important in the choice of a new home as an extra few feet on the back garden. Some even advertise proximity to a parkrun as a key advantage for their new developments.

SURVIVAL OF THE FITTEST

The pandemic was not pretty for so many areas of British business, and while sales on Fitbits and Garmins increased as the fit got fitter, all was not well for the sports industry as a whole. The strength of many organisations who had led the way through the 60 years of the sports business was put severely to the test.

Sport was hit first and hit early. All of the trends that had been bubbling under at the turn of the decade hit fast forward. Take your average professional sports team, for example. Ticket revenues disappeared as events were cancelled. Broadcasters started to look for money back from leagues, who in turn had to claw that rebate back from their member teams. Sponsors renegotiated their contracts as their logos were not on display and there was no hospitality for their guests. All at the same time as their biggest and most expensive assets – their playing staff – were sat at home.

Teams started reacting to the need to balance the books for the long term. Clubs began to get sharper on their player costs, which had become far too high to be sustainable. 'Clubs will probably run with slightly smaller squads,' Dan Ashworth, Brighton & Hove Albion FC's technical director, told the *Guardian*. 'There will be less money in the game. Less money for transfer fees, for agents' fees, for salaries and wages. That's for sure. There has to be because we've all taken a hit. But we're doing our best to crack on and try to prepare for every eventuality.'[56] New technology started to fuel that shift to efficiency, such as the online player-trading platform TransferRoom, which allows clubs to make transfer and loan deals online and reduced the dependency to some extent on player agents.

In truth, if professional sports teams cannot remodel themselves to survive post-COVID-19, then they were probably living a little beyond their means beforehand. The BBC, based on research conducted with Deloitte and Vysyble, reported that professional football clubs in the Championship division ran up £307 million pre-tax losses between them in 2017–18, and spending on player and staff wages alone exceeded total revenue by 2011.[57] You clearly can't run a business long term when you are spending more than you are making, and the challenge for all clubs is to re-engage with their local communities so that football is only part of the story they tell. Painful as it may be, the end product of the pandemic should be a leaner and more sustainable state of play.

This disruption, of course, hits the whole ecosystem. Mark McCormack's IMG, the original sports agency (recently renamed Endeavor) was reported by *Variety* to have borrowed $260 million to see them through the crisis.[58] While that will keep the lights on in the short term, the challenge is that none of the TV productions, events and player representation will ever be the same again, and they are all lucrative areas for the business that McCormack built.

One area of growth, however, that has been broadly protected is women's sport. The Football Association, for example, committed to retain spending on the women's professional game at pre-pandemic levels, while having to cut costs elsewhere. Parts of the media questioned whether women's sport would lose the head of steam it had built up. The reality is that sports will continue to invest in their growth areas and choose to save money in areas of their sport that were not growing at quite such a pace. When times get tough, not many businesses will choose to cut costs in the parts that are growing furiously. Consultancy firm Deloitte predicted that, '2021/22 may prove to be the breakaway season for women's sport revenue'.[59]

Within this wholesale consideration of the 'way things have always been done', at least as many opportunities as challenges are cropping up. While Roger Federer called out the men's and the women's tennis tours as organisations that might be more sensible merged into one, Andy Murray too continued to focus his efforts on pushing gender equality, having been a constant advocate in this regard since hiring a female coach in 2014.

Opportunities don't always have to come in new sports or formats, they can also involve revisiting previous ones, once changing attitudes and demographics bring them back to the fore. One of tennis's greatest strengths is the ability for both genders to mix and play together – and yet they don't maximise it. Mixed doubles has somehow fallen into being 'filler content' for the Grand Slams. Andy Murray picked up on this in an essay on equality he was invited to write for the International Olympic Committee, noting:

> When I played mixed doubles with Serena Williams at Wimbledon last year, it was a good example of how the format draws a different crowd to the sport. Normally when I win or lose at Wimbledon, people will come up to me and say 'Well done' or 'Bad luck'. But, with Serena, so many people said, 'We loved seeing you and Serena play together. It was brilliant.' People enjoy seeing that, and we should promote it. How can you not see that it's a good thing?[60]

The legacy of the pandemic is a rupture in the professional sporting landscape, but its effects had been on the cards, anyway. Big sports and events will thrive if they can navigate their offer to a customer base full of millennials and Generation Z, but without disenfranchising the older generations who have larger spending power for the foreseeable future. The Olympics needs the new sports to land well, while still playing to the universality and tradition that is its strength. Cricket in England needs to thrill through Test Matches and the Hundred in equal measure, but for different audiences, each of whom need to reconcile themselves to the fact that neither of them owns the sport. The Premier League needs kids to care and see themselves on the pitch one day – whether they are growing up in Sheffield or Shanghai – and their parents have to be able to afford the right to watch the games live alongside them.

New ideas and economies will step into this environment and will be desperately needed to bridge the divides our public debt has created. Whether This Mum Runs is a business, a social enterprise or closer to a charity is irrelevant – it works. If Liverpool FC makes the numbers work and thrive in its community by being the best side in Europe, good luck to that club. Many sports teams will necessarily go back to being tools for advancing the agenda of the local area, like they were in the times of the Industrial Revolution when they first began. And they will be all the better for it.

So what would happen in a remake of *Jerry Maguire* now? Well, it's very likely that Jerry would find it much easier to build a business representing athletes who want the personal touch. His first athletes would still demand fair pay for a job well done but have far broader aspirations as to how they utilise the privilege of fame. Jerry might well focus on fast-growth sports. As a result, three-quarters of the athletes he would choose to represent would be women.

Jerry hired Renée Zellweger's character as his PA in 1996. Nowadays he'd sort out his own logistics, and she'd become a specialist in setting up players' foundations. They'd run a virtual office, of course, preferring Zoom to airport terminals.

Both would still be working 14-hour days – but never miss their children's bedtime story.

Jerry would have comfortably found a new breed of athletes looking to take a different tack on their careers. He'd spend as much time helping them articulate their point of view on social issues as sorting out their new contracts. He'd be less attuned to spotting the signs of alcohol influencing their behaviour than the impact of media pressure and social media on their mental health.

Jerry's business would try to build athletes for their lives beyond sport. Its services for players would recognise that its athletes want to build a life through sport. It might offer such services as nutrition, strength and conditioning, and psychology support; social media management advice; personal brand building and charitable partnerships. There would be less focus on 'Show me the money!' today. It'd be more 'Build me a support network!.'

This far broader, more holistic scope is how the most forward-thinking agencies of today think and operate, among them 77 Sports Management.[61] You might not have heard of the company but I bet you know one of its co-founders. Andy Murray again. His agency focuses on up-and-coming athletes, and unsurprisingly counts just as many women as men on its books.

HARDER THAN YOU THINK

An exciting future beckons. What is clear is that whether talking about disability or dividends, Olympics or Orient, sponsorship or streaming, commercial growth or climate change, sport needs to be very clear what it stands for. The bravest will not only survive, but thrive. Those athletes, teams and sports that crack the Sporting Recipe – creating something that society craves, working in tandem with the community (whether that be local or global in nature), and doing so in a way that makes money – will lead the next decade and beyond.

History tells us, however, that changing times are hard ones to lead through. They don't always make you popular. If you've seen the smash-hit musical *Hamilton*, you'll know that Alexander Hamilton was the First Secretary of the Treasury of the United States. He was a leading voice for governmental reform in challenging times, changing the model for the United States in several ways, not least introducing the nation's first tax on a domestic product (the infamous, and deeply unpopular, Whiskey Tax) so that the United States could finance its military without going further into debt.

Hamilton's legacy lives on in a quote that is very apt for the times sport finds itself in now: 'If you don't stand for something, you'll fall for anything', a quote that features in Public Enemy's mesmerising 'Harder Than You Think', the soundtrack to Channel Four's coverage of the London 2012 Paralympic Games. Working in sport is indeed harder than you might think. But it's also a privilege. Those sports that are clear in their purpose and direction won't fall for anything that the next decade throws at them. They'll comprise a diverse team, make tough decisions, change before they have to, and be more attractive to future generations as a result. Bring on the revolution.

CHAPTER 8 / Fast Forward: Ten Predictions for the Future of Sport

I'm not a big gambler. I find watching sport exciting enough without the need to spice things up any further. Sometimes too exciting, if it's my kids competing.

I partially retired from gambling after one miraculous, long-odds bet on the exact result and first scorer as Chelsea won the 1997 FA Cup final. The £500 proceeds saw me through the first half of my final term at university, which was fortunate as the coffers were totally dry by that point. It also happened to be the point Claire and I got together. Thanks to Roberto Di Matteo's first-minute wonder strike against Middlesbrough at Wembley, I had enough cash to see me through some decent early dates with my now-wife. It's a funny old game.

I retired from the occasional flutter completely when we co-founded our sports agency Two Circles in 2011. Putting our mortgage on the line, based on our hopes about where sport might head next, felt like quite enough gambling for any family. Even so, I do still like predicting what the future holds. My dad and I did manage to get a fair amount right between us in our book, *Britain and the Olympic Games*. We suggested that the country would eventually lose its heart to the 2012 Games despite the naysayers; that London's Paralympic Games would create a step-change for how physical disability was perceived in this country; that the Games would regenerate Stratford and the surrounding east London area for the long term. It wasn't only positive stuff, though – we noted that doctors' then-niche warnings about sugar addiction and diabetes would start to become mainstream topics of concern and heap further pressure on an (already) cash-strapped NHS.

We didn't by any means get everything right. We predicted Rio would take London's lead in 2016, using the Games for social and economic regeneration. That was the plan, but the reality was sadly different. The Games themselves were a real success, but the impact afterwards desperately sad, as Brazil struggled from crisis to crisis, and their stunning regeneration of a whole area of suburban Rio fell forgotten by the wayside. The Rio Olympics (and Brazil's 2014 FIFA World Cup too, for that matter) are a warning for all of us – everything can be pointing in the right direction, and still, you never quite know.

One of our best predictions was that parkrun's rise would continue apace. We wrote about the experience of turning up for the first time:

> There is a buzz of conversation between the regulars as you arrive and those who are able wander over after the event for a coffee at the park café. The event feels surprisingly communal. It might be a different structure to the traditional running club but it is no less valid as a facilitator of mass participation sport.

Reading it back, it feels as if we were almost looking to justify the existence of parkrun as an alternative to the more traditional running club in growing running participation. When I first ran a parkrun in March 2010, it was a relatively new kid on the block. While it was growing quickly at the time, it was a slightly niche idea. Success was by no means guaranteed.[62]

So how did we know change was afoot? Well, from the minute I entered Black Park near Slough that sunny spring morning in early 2010, clutching my printed barcode, I could see clues all over the place. The parkrunners were more racially diverse than competitors in your average 5k road race, more mixed in ability and age range. There were families running together. There were queues to put a £1 coin in the council-run parking meter. The lady running the café had opened up at 8.30am and said that from 9–10am on Saturday was now the busiest hour of her week.

The rest, as they say, is history. Just before the pandemic struck, on 20 January 2020, parkrun involved 685 events, 195,818 athletes and 15,914 volunteers on a single day around the world. Not only are there more parkruns, but the number of people taking part in each parkrun has more than doubled. Fortunately, both the growth and the chatter that continue at the café suggest that there are no signs of its success ending. Black Park has been able to refurbish its car park, and there are now three people serving coffee on Saturday mornings.

That's the thing with trend spotting – it's partly a case of looking at the data, but it's also about people-watching and listening hard. In the case of parkrun, the biggest clue, however, came in the form of the people who were obviously regulars. They weren't the string-bean-shaped, elegant runners who were already warming up half an hour before the start of the run, the kind of people you might more often see at the traditional running club. Instead, the parkrun regulars seemed to be 'normal' folk of all shapes and sizes, who had clearly found something compelling in this form of exercise to keep them coming back week after week.

In 2010, we didn't have any kind of theory to test parkrun against, just a sense that the model was built for twenty-first-century sport. Now we do have a theory, the Sporting Recipe, and with the benefit of hindsight we know that parkrun is the perfect fit: popular with runners from all walks of life, accessible for all in local parks and paid for by others (sponsors and buyers of Contra). It felt ripe for success back then – and it was.

With the benefit of that experience – the ones we got right, and wrong – and now armed with the Sporting Recipe, I've spun the wheel again, over a decade on. I've talked to hundreds of people, watched and listened to thousands more. Sport being sport, I've heard hundreds of theories in pubs, at the side of kids' football pitches and on radio phone-ins, many of which conflict with each other. Ultimately this book has been about trying to make sense of those.

What follows are ten predictions for the ways in which I think sport will change. Some may happen within 10 years, others may take 20. Some are backed by strong data or the consistent viewpoints of those experts we have interviewed for this book. Others were simply inspired by observing things, such as the ways in which my kids interact with their mates.

Whatever the inspiration, all fill a need in our environmentally, socially and economically challenged world.

1. SOME WILL DO SPORT, BUT ALL WILL PLAY

In the mid-1990s, I spent hours in my college bar arguing with friends about whether darts was a sport or a pastime. Some thought all sports had to be both physically demanding and require skill, others were comfortable that skill alone was enough. Twenty years on, that conversation just wouldn't happen. That debate was a twentieth-century one and deserves to stay there.

Things have changed more fundamentally. This is a bigger shift than simply moving the definition of sport to encompass the likes of parkour, street dance and Jazzercise. At some point in the 1980s, people stopped caring whether a sportsperson was an amateur or professional, and the same fate will befall the question: 'Is that actually a sport?'

In the future, the only question that matters will be: 'Is it fun to play and watch?' People just won't care whether something is, or isn't, defined as sport. Breaking, an activity traditionally defined as dance, is in the 2024 Olympics in Paris. Come 2024, some will roll their eyes at this. I'd be inclined to repeat the IOC President Thomas Bach's remark: 'Change or be changed,' and remind them that the Olympics has always iterated that its list of sports will change with the times. Tug of war, rope climbing and pistol duelling, for example, all featured in the twentieth century. So did the Cultural Olympiad. From 1912 to 1948 Olympic medals were awarded for works of art inspired by sport. So, really, we need to relax. If the Olympics is to remain the pinnacle of games, innovation must be a constant.

It's very easy to throw out lazy opinions about what kids today enjoy and change our sports to reflect that. That's a dangerous route to take, as many of the traditional statements older generations tend to trot out can be nothing but excuses. 'Kids today like shorter content so we need to make games shorter' is a classic. But kids don't have a problem playing *Fortnite* for four hours straight. 'Kids don't want to watch, they want to play themselves' is another. Yet they're also happy to watch YouTube clips of other people playing *Fortnite*. I also hear a lot of predictions that traditional sports with strict rules will die out in favour of freestyle activities. I don't buy that, either – in some formats of *Fortnite* there are firm rules and scoring systems, and it's the competitive tension around a commonly held set of rules that drives the game. In other parts of the game, I notice my son enjoying a free-style wander through a virtual world. It's up to each individual to choose how they want to play on any given day.

What does that all tell us, then? Well, future generations will still want to compete – and watch others do so – with the objective of winning and losing. For many, the winning and losing will remain a fundamental part of sport's value, with strict rules enabling those highs and lows. In some areas of sport, the rules will need to get tighter rather than looser – how bouncy can an athlete's trainers be, for example, before they have an unfair advantage?

'Sport' as a word will likely become far narrower in the way in which it is used – focusing on competition. It may even become an anachronism entirely. For many more, however, it will all come back to 'play'. Many don't want or need rules, medals or personal bests. People will love to play and come alive when they can get actively involved in a compelling experience that takes them outside their day-to-day. Some will want to compete, others won't. Neither will carry a badge of honour. We will finally and belatedly stop looking at sport through an outdated lens and start playing on our own terms.

2. LOCAL TEAMS FOR LOCAL PEOPLE

When it comes to climate change, Greta Thunberg represents the views of generations to come. I've never met a child or young adult who disagrees with either Greta or Sir David Attenborough. Generationally driven change is an inevitability.

Playing at its purest is, in theory, about as wholesome and environmentally sound a pursuit as you could expect – principally outdoors, working body and mind, encouraging interaction with others. It's when organised competition gets involved that we start to become a source of environmental problems, whether that's travelling to watch the men's World Cup finals in Qatar, or a 200-mile round trip to take your kids to play regional cricket.

Change will necessarily start concurrently at local and global levels. If professional sport is going to be supported by new generations, it needs to be less reliant on frequently flying competitors and audiences around the world. This will mean competitions will need to be more nationally and regionally led, feeding fewer (but even higher profile) global competitions. Tennis Grand Slams and the golf Majors, for example, will continue to attract global fields but tennis will be pressured to regionalise its professional tours below that, just as golf is structured today. This pressure will not only be from new generations of fans, but also politicians as tomorrow's voters come of age.

While this seems unlikely in 2021, with the forces of sporting globalisation firmly at play, it will happen. I think it will happen much like the push towards equal prize money between men and women over the last 20 years – a trickle, and then a torrent to the point that change is inescapable. Whether it's athletes or organisers, the air miles accounts of global sport will take a significant hit. That doesn't mean sport can't be globally connected – but there will be a new emphasis on domestic and regional delivery. A qualifying group for a European Football Championship doesn't need to be played across a whole season, for example – it can be played in one location over two weeks.

While there will be downsides, there will also be upsides. The world's highest profile international competitions – the Olympics and the FIFA World Cups – each take place every four years, and most international sports will be pressured to follow suit. Many sports industry experts are already starting to wonder whether 'less is more' – the biggest global sports events will continue to grow, but principally because global competition will once again revert to being a cherry on the cake.

Most importantly, even if they have global aspirations, athletes and teams will need to be far more connected to their local communities. Local teams will need to support sport in schools as active mechanics to find talent and new ways of growing local fan bases. Forward-thinking ones will find new and different ways of integrating their stadiums and facilities into the local communities, many building on their experiences during national lockdowns. At times, even national level competition will be under question. With money too tight to mention, it is very likely the lower tiers of English football will be regionalised, just as they are in Germany. Some clubs may have be declared bankrupt before they start back on this journey, reinstated by the force of will of their local communities.

The most successful local teams will become as fundamental to the development of sustainable local communities as company playing fields were 150 years ago when workers first started to get meaningful free time. They will provide a social need through closer connectivity with their local community and find a newly sustainable way of operating as a result. Towns will be proud of their teams once again, and they will likely be playing close by a little more regularly, too.

3. THOSE WE TRUST WILL CHANGE OUR NATION

We live in a digitally driven era of suspicion and conspiracy theory. Distrust of media, politicians, business – authority, essentially – has rocketed at the same time as we are entering a new level of financial hardship.

This does interesting things to our perception of athletes' performances regarding drugs. At the beginning of the twenty-first century, as cyclist Lance Armstrong's past misdemeanours came to light, we entered a period of base mistrust, which did material damage to many sports' reputations and viability. Sporting authorities and anti-doping technology seemed permanently to be two years behind the ingenuity of athletes cheating the system.

Times are changing, though. Savvy athletes will increasingly realise that their long-term credibility, financial viability and even their own mental health depends on them proving they are clean athletes. The emphasis will increasingly be for the athletes to prove they are innocent rather than authorities to catch them out, given the public perception for endurance sports such as athletics and cycling is likely to remain a world of 'guilty until proven innocent' for some while yet. The driver of this won't just be the rules, but market forces. Some athletes are already making all their blood tests and doping records public. This comes at a cost to privacy and shouldn't be necessary, but in general athletes will view this as a price worth paying.

This will be just one part of a more general toughening up of the public's view towards heroes in general, and sports stars in particular. Through Sterling and Rashford, we have already seen a benchmark for the level of social contribution that athletes can provide in Britain. We have seen them stare down the tabloids and even the Prime Minister. This sets the bar higher for our expectations of athletes as role models, but has also shown the potential positive impact on those who can jump over it.

It's not just footballers, though. Jessica Ennis-Hill is such an enduring influence on the British not because of her London

2012 Olympic gold medal, but because of her efforts to come back and compete as a working mother. A good friend once met Jess for a working commitment, and the athlete's opening gambit was, 'Hi, I'm Jess. I'm a bit in shock right now, one of my best mates has just split up with their boyfriend.' Completely natural, and no airs and graces. Authenticity wins every time nowadays, and it's no surprise that she is often used by organisations hoping to help people break down barriers and their fear of giving sport a go. Generation Z fundamentally prize authenticity beyond all else. This can come from athletes like Jess, but also from a YouTube account of a kid looking to become a pro footballer or her dad to planning to jog 5k.

Inspiration ultimately starts with the thought, *If they can do it, so can I*. The sooner we understand that athletes of all types can inspire, the sooner those who follow This Mum Runs, but have not yet attended a session or engaged with the community, will finally put on their trainers, pluck up courage and give it a try.

4. WE'LL ALL BE IN THE GAME

When it launched in 2000, *MTV Cribs* was a formative moment in pop culture. It enabled the sons and daughters of the original MTV generation to see inside the picture-perfect houses of some of the world's biggest music stars. Such was the celebrity-obsessed culture of the day. Two years later, I was working at MTV and helped build *MTV Football Shorts* – much like *MTV Cribs*, it was a show that offered viewers the chance to see inside a world of luxury and privilege with the biggest football stars in the world. Two decades on, and the show hasn't aged well. Its staged inauthenticity is the complete antithesis of today's zeitgeist. No surprise, then, that MTV's announcement during lockdown of the launch of *MTV Footballers' Cribs* was met with general indifference.

While social media allows us permanent inside access into the worlds of our heroes, in the most part that enables proximity and interaction rather than reinforcing the extent to which sports stars are from a different galaxy. Sports-specific technology has helped that – I can see how quickly I am running on the same course as professional athletes who use Strava, and even go on to the digital cycling world of Zwift and watch Tour de France champion Geraint Thomas fly past on his bike while he livestreams the action on YouTube. While the physical performances are superhuman, the humanity of the athletes becomes far more obvious when I can be up close and digital.

There are more clues here if you actually watch *Fortnite* (or *Roblox*, my daughter's favourite). Whether kids are playing alone or alongside mates with their headsets on, they insist on hearing the story behind the action. My son is a cricketer and he'll switch on to watching cricket live the moment he can listen in to two players giving each other stick on the pitch via a microphone set on the pitch. It's not going behind the scenes with a manicured view of reality like MTV is promising – it's being right there, 'in the game'. And that's what is compelling. Of course, providing this level of access is not easily done. It is possible, but with a bit of give and take. I learnt a lot about real life while standing at the side of the pitch, at the age of ten, watching my dad play football. It was a real privilege to spend most Saturday afternoons with a group of 20- to 35-year-old men, supporting, laughing and, yes, maybe occasionally learning the odd new word. I think we over-sanitise the experience for future generations at our cost.

Broadcasting sport will need to keep shifting away from a focus on thinking about making shows for a TV screen being watched by 2.4 million people in their lounge, and more towards building experiences for networks of connected people, whether they are watching virtually but chatting with headsets on, or together in front of a big screen at the club or pub. Screens in this new world will be predominantly very big and very small, rather than TV shaped. As viewers, we will need to then recognise that it is people's livelihoods playing out in front of us. It's stressful stuff, and sometimes uncomfortable viewing. It's fine if we do want to get inside the game, but we need to realise it's not always an easy place to be.

Not only will integrating regular people and the professionals become the norm digitally, but it will also increasingly be an important part of live events – offering the chance for mere mortals to take part alongside top-end athletes wherever possible. The Paris 2024 Olympics organisers are planning a marathon on the same route as the elite race, just a day afterwards. There are also plans afoot for an urban sports park offering the public the chance to showcase their own skills, while the best of the best at BMX and skateboarding are trying to win Olympic gold. This is a natural, if logistically challenging, evolution. It will bring our heroes back down to earth after a period of seeming untouchable. Just like Jessica Ennis-Hill, the closer they get to us, the more we will realise just how extraordinary their talents really are.

This kind of collaboration also represents the future for global sporting events – not only during them, but afterwards, too. In 2020, parkrun agreed a deal with the global governing body World Athletics to leave community health legacies by creating a series of permanent parkruns in the host cities and countries of world championship events, including the World Championships Oregon 2022 and Budapest 2023. parkrun will help World Athletics by leaving something permanent behind when the show leaves town, and World Athletics will help parkrun with the politics, permits and power to make things happen quickly across a whole city.

5. SPORT TECH WILL NOT JUST BE FOR CHRISTMAS

Much as some of the old guard might not like it, sport does not have to mean getting muddy or even going outside. In the 1970s and 1980s, aerobics broke the mould for what Britain considered exercise, and even created TV stars of the instructors on breakfast TV. Their star waned a little as DVDs took over the home-fitness regime, enabling exercise behind closed doors. But the DVDs didn't enable sociability – a problem solved by gyms filling a void Britain never knew it had. There are now close to 10 million members of gyms up and down the country.

When the gyms shut as a result of COVID-19, Joe Wicks showed a generation that there were, in fact, no excuses – it was perfectly possible to exercise with a very small space and a wi-fi connection. Not only that – being in a space with tens or even millions of others doing the same thing was actually pretty fun – in particular for younger kids, who the government had been terrified were getting increasingly difficult to entice off the sofa. Even those who grew up loving the school cross-country run realised that in a world where there were limited alternatives, technology could help them get their daily fix in a non-invasive yet social way. The pandemic helped us understand that technology could improve our experience of exercise in our nation, not destroy it.

This evolution was important, because previously technology had been very focused on the performance end of sport – widgets to track how fast a tennis player could serve, smartwatches to track pace for keen athletes, apps like Strava to track and showcase their progress, social media influencers with sixpacks to set a challenging benchmark. Sporting technology had mostly been just as scary and daunting as the sport itself. Coupled with this, there had been an understandable media narrative that, more generally, laptops, electronic games and so on were making Britain less healthy. All in all, technology and sport didn't mix in the mainstream. Even when they tried – initially via the steps counter – many felt weighed down by the responsibility to move. Beyond the hardcore, many smart-watches and step counters were bought for Christmas but didn't last long into the new year.

It was only during the pandemic that we came to see that technology could be a help as well as a hindrance. While it still wasn't for everyone, it gave people the autonomy to exercise on their own terms, the belonging to feel part of a community (even if exercising locked down in a tower block), and the confidence to do so in a low exposure way, often with only the cat or dog watching on. These three factors comprise what psychologists call the theory of self-determination – basically, factors that motivate us intrinsically to do something, as opposed to external forces.

Therein lies the future for technology in sport – as much for the mainstream as the medallists. While steps, pace and miles per week were motivating for the hardcore in the early days of digital technology in this space, the biggest shift we will see in the next ten years will be the opportunity for the less elite, and yet more in need.

6. THE NHS WILL DISCOVER AN ACE UP ITS SLEEVE

The quicker our adoption of technology in daily life increases, the sooner we will be able to reap additional benefits in terms of the insight it provides into our health and wellness. This starts on quite a basic level – my smartwatch takes a measure of my resting heartrate overnight. I know if it's higher than usual that (unless I have had a few beers!) my body is very likely fighting a bug, so I won't go out for a run that day and will make sure I hit the zinc and vitamin C.

Although that's a pretty simple example, it does have big implications. During the pandemic, data was used in important ways to manage the spread of disease. For one of the first times ever, mainstream Britain started to debate infection graphs and recovery rates in great detail. We all learnt that using data to predict health patterns is complex, but that when it comes to health, understanding only comes from keeping score. Not least for a cash-strapped NHS. Data can and will do so much to inform all of our health into the future.

This will inevitably start with the sporty hardcore – the Oura ring I have described being a good example. Smartwatches will not only track our sleep and exercise as they do today, but be hooked into our fridges to tell us what to eat and drink afterwards in order to help us recover from exercise while protecting our immunity levels. We will be able to use data from our fridge to automatically order food stocks that need replenishing, or even have our phones suggest healthy recipes based on the fridge contents, taking into account the use-by dates.

While most of this is possible today, the next ten years will see this kind of activity become mainstream. Over that time period, UK online shopping is projected to grow from around 20 per cent of our purchases to more than 50 per cent. Any smartphone can be used to track a resting heartrate. We can use watches to track the quality of our sleep, and apps to track how stressed we may feel. The healthcare revolution in the next ten years will not necessarily be about finding new data, but combining and interpreting things we already know. If we start to learn more about nutrition, health metrics, sleep patterns and exercise all in one place, we can go a long way to preventing many of Britain's most common illnesses. In ten years' time I won't only hit the vitamin C and zinc if my heartrate is high, I will also have learnt the various other ways in which my personal body response fights infection at that moment.

The truth is we are only just scratching the surface of what is possible in this area. In late 2019, Germany passed its Digital Healthcare Act, which enables the prescription of software and apps to patients as part of their treatment.[63] The first apps that have approved provide support for conditions such as obesity, insomnia and osteoarthritis. In early 2021, a business called Quantum Operation from Japan started showcasing a tool that can establish the amount of blood sugar in your body without requiring a needle, so enabling people to learn far more easily how to manage or even avert diabetes. The answers may not even be solely within our own bodies. For example, one of the most promising areas of research in British medicine at the moment is driven by the charity Medical Detection Dogs, which trains dogs to detect the odours of specific human diseases. It is at the forefront of the research into the fight against cancer and helping people with life-threatening diseases. We are naive if we think there isn't lots still to learn.

As healthcare and sporting activity become necessarily more joined up, we will also start to become more able to prove the impact of sport in medical rehabilitation, both physical and mental. Studies that can empirically prove the impact of Stormbreak in a classroom, or local sports clubs on child obesity and diabetes, will emerge in the next few years. The results of research of this sort will change the way government thinks about the total impact of £1 spent on sport as a means of illness prevention. Once the case is secure, we will see more focus on extended projects that enable deeper collaboration between the public and commercial sectors making their mark across the country. The Cycle to Work scheme offered by the UK government to all employers is a great example of the kind of model that will be used more. The government provides a tax break to those wanting to buy a bike to get to work, which sells more bikes for happy retailers. This also means employees get healthier riding to work rather than sitting in traffic jams, which keeps them in the office and out of needing NHS treatment. The bike trips also contribute to the environment. Everyone is a winner. What will happen next is that we will be able to definitively prove that the government's loss of tax receipts by making the bike purchase tax free is recouped by the corporate tax from people's increased productivity, plus the saving made on the NHS patient bill. That level of connected thinking should change the way our leaders think about sport for good.

7. PARENTS WILL BE SEEN BUT NOT HEARD

The more we learn about the impact of exercise on physical and mental health, the more the impact of inactivity becomes clear. Happy kids are kids who move, ideally alongside their peers. Things have been slowly changing for a few years. Forest nurseries and schools have been launched with some great results – echoing Stormbreak's conviction that kids need to move to be happy, healthy and learn most effectively. The results speak for themselves, and as this happens the need for parents to ensure their kids are active is going to significantly increase in importance. A YouGov parents' survey published in late 2020 found that almost two-thirds of parents believe that the wellbeing of pupils is more important than their academic attainment, and more than half also agreed that pupils' wellbeing is likely to be better in schools that prioritise sport and physical activity.[64]

A child who eats vegetables, helps around the house and likes nothing better than to curl up with a good book may be parental bliss, but we now understand that this alone is just not enough. Kids don't need to play organised sport, but they do need to be outside in the sun, playing with other children and raising their heartrates. The challenge, however, is that parents have always been a competitive bunch, and many have not really read the memo correctly. Instead of focusing on getting their kids outdoors and muddy, smiling and active, many prioritise sharing pictures of their kids winning stuff. Children aren't daft, and in turn they focus on trying to become what their parents notice and value.

As a parent myself, I know this isn't easy. I want my kids to be able to reap the rewards of the work they put into their sport, and if they've put the time in, then I will want them to feel it's been worth it. But that's where it needs to stop. It's natural for parents to be proud, but we need to post pictures of kids in the layers of dirt, the mud-bath that used to be a lawn and a washing pile the size of Big Ben rather than posing with a trophy. The trophy photo *is* important – for the kid to remember a day when the hard work paid off, not for their parents to use as a bragging tool. The challenge for parents is to expose their kids to more opportunities to be active and play but letting them grow into competition – or not – and specialise – or not – at their own pace.

One initiative that started in football has been to try to keep parents away from the field of play via mandatory temporary fencing. In theory it gives the coaches and referee space to support the kids, without the overly pushy parents bellowing away from the sidelines. This kind of initiative is set to continue.

I spoke to one sports coach who told me that the sessions she had run during partial lockdown (when parents had to stay in the car and were not allowed to be pitchside) were among the most effective and fun she's held. She noticed the kids relaxing and smiling more. Sad as it is, I think this is the future. After all, there is a reason why parents aren't allowed in the classroom!

Of course, this level of parental intensity is a world away for those who have to work long hours to keep the family afloat, or who don't have transport to get their kids to their fourth sports session of the week, let alone the time to watch them. This is why we need our facilities to be as local and accessible as possible. We need the FA to be allowed to sell Wembley Stadium and use the proceeds to invest in AstroTurf pitches nationwide and to empower the likes of StreetGames to afford kids from all backgrounds the opportunity to use them safely. We want more teams like Tranmere to have created sports centres and gyms in their facilities that are not prohibitively expensive, as the space would be lying dormant anyway. For private-school facilities to be unlocked as often as possible, and schools like Abingdon to actively encourage their state-school neighbours to use them.

It's easy to look to government, but there is no magic money tree. It is not always easy for cash-strapped, inner-city councils to provide safe areas for the public to play in when budgets are already being pulled in so many directions. There is, however, one other source of opportunity . . .

8. WE'LL STOP MOVING THE GOALPOSTS AND START BUILDING NEW ONES

There's no getting away from the fact that the UK needs more housing. Of course, that comes at a cost to the green fields that we want our children running around on. Developers are increasingly expected to contribute to the communities they are building in, creating more parks and sports facilities, just as they're expected to build certain percentages of affordable housing to broaden access. But it's not always easy to get the balance right, and too often the money doesn't go where it's most needed. Small playgrounds next to 100 new houses are easy to build and tick all the right boxes, but, once the kids are ten years old, they're of little practical use. We need to think bigger.

As we start to recognise that exercise is the cheapest way to reduce NHS pressure and help our kids learn, we will start to see genuine shift in government policy. Just like the London 2012 Olympic Park was built on polluted land and now acts as a physical activity oasis in central London, so we'll start to identify more opportunities to do the same in our towns up and down the country. Plenty of late twentieth-century industrial estates hosting now defunct industries will be taken down for housing, but only if a park is the centrepiece of the design.

Allied to this, we'll start to think more carefully about the role sport can play in revitalising our towns. Many of Britain's town centres were built up on the back of retail and car ownership, and were already teetering pre-pandemic as a result of the dual threat of online retail competition and out-of-town shopping centres. As physical retail chains such as Woolworths, HMV, Carphone Warehouse, Debenhams, Burton and Topshop have collapsed, they have left ghost towns behind.

This represents a significant opportunity. Why can't empty shops be used for indoor carpet-bowl rinks, Jazzercise classes, mini five-a-side pitches for kids, and so on? While this might be utopian in areas where developers and hoteliers are queuing up to buy back precious retail space, there are plenty of areas of Britain where there is little or no demand and the space lies empty. There are opportunities for commercial and public sectors to work together rebuild vibrant town centres, but with exercise and community, rather than retail and the car, at their core. Town centres of the future need to become urban playgrounds.

Changes like this are not only driven by local need, but also by generational shift. As much as buzzing nightlife is still to some extent appealing to twentysomething workers, new generations want to relocate to areas with green space, sports facilities, great restaurants and excellent coffee. Salford Quays, now home to the BBC, is a good example, with running networks galore on Manchester's rejuvenated canals.

Britain has a lot to learn in this space. In fact, even London struggles to hit the Top 50 in the Global Healthiest Cities list. Moving forward, providing facilities to support exercise will be just as important as tax rates, if not more so, in enticing millennials to work and play in Britain. Brexit or no Brexit, we have bred generations of health-conscious global citizens – and will need to create compelling reasons for them to continue to call Britain home.

9. LOCAL SUCCESSES WILL DRIVE GLOBAL CHANGE

Initiatives such as the NHS programmes at Tranmere Rovers and the mental resilience work of Stormbreak are still relatively recent. In isolation these activities are very potent in their local areas, but in combination they can change the way we think about social change. The trick is not only to make these locally powerful, but also to feed the difference they make up to the top levels of influence. This measurement work might take organisations away from the coal face of directly improving individual people's lives, but it is also the key to driving change and government policy across the whole country. Stormbreak needs people to run marathons for it in the short term, but the longer term gift will be to help it prove the value of the work it does so that it can spread its impact as far and wide as possible.

The Beyond Sport Foundation, led by Nick Keller, is on the right track here, aiming to combine organisations with local impact into a genuine global movement for change. The organisation links the work of non-governmental organisa-tions worldwide to Global Goals, a roadmap adopted by world leaders in 2015 to stimulate action in areas of critical impor-tance for humanity and the planet through 2030. This is not token politics: this is the only sustainable way for our planet to survive, let alone thrive. With a broader understanding of the role of sport, it will start to be a principal mechanic used by governments worldwide to drive social change. Organisations like Keller's can capture and share the magic created at the local level so we can learn globally and at pace. When I talked to Nick about his foundation, he told me that 'real change happens in communities, by communities. The only way to make that truly meaningful at scale for our society is for the government or private sector to capture the learning, develop and replicate.'

There will, of course, be roadblocks. Isolationist and extrem-ist leaders are very adept at making climate change, structural inequality or Third World poverty someone else's problem. However, there is always a counter-reaction to extremism. A new generation of leaders is emerging, fuelled by Greta Thunberg's generation reaching the ballot box, who recognise that alternative responses including sport and exercise will be critical components in unlocking a sustainable path for future generations. As we have seen, the next decade will be about arming them with the hard science and data to prove what they already intuitively know.

10. PROFESSIONAL SPORT WILL BECOME ... WELL, PROFESSIONAL

The movement of these tectonic plates at a macro level will change professional sport as we know it. Currently the industry still has the vestiges of a teenage outlook – prone to moments of brilliance and clumsiness in equal measure. However, after the reality check of the pandemic it will start to balance itself out as it matures. It will remain big business – but not at all costs. The new market forces will make that so. 'Change or be changed', remember.

Front of house, new generations of stars will wear their broader responsibilities more heavily – and rightly be rewarded as a result. Pakistan's current prime minister, former cricketer Imran Khan, will not be the last to come from elite sporting ranks on an anti-corruption, centre-ground ticket.

Behind the scenes, the sports industry itself will exit its teenage years with pride in how far it has come, but a slight degree of embarrassment at the lack of diverse personalities, thoughts and actions so far. Board-level diversity will be mandated by the powers that be, but will anyway be good business sense for an industry that will focus its tighter budgets on growth areas like women's sport. Somewhere along the line, natural leaders like Andy Murray, who can argue rationally for change, are bound to play a leading role.

While the biggest sports organisations and leagues will continue to dominate column inches, success at a local level will be driven by clubs, sports and teams rooted in the heartland of their communities. Global events (such as the Commonwealth

Games in Birmingham in 2022) will be a community change programme with a sports event to celebrate, rather than a sports event with a legacy programme tucked behind. That's the only way they will garner enough local support to be welcomed. They will be avidly watched on screens of all sizes, as long as watching is a social experience.

While our lives will still be complex, many of us will use our exercise to get back to outdoor simplicity. Technology will encourage, connect and motivate us, but it will quickly wane unless it genuinely adds to our enjoyment and provides those three key components of personal autonomy, self-belief in individual competence and a sense of community and belonging. Climbing could well be the new cycling, albeit with less Lycra involved. In fact, the climbing wall might well be built on the back of the local professional sports team's main stand as a means of keeping the stadium busy when there are no games on. There will still be mass inner-city marathons, but also gatherings of no particular distance, where families run and then party together.

The forty- and fiftysomethings currently heading up the industry are already working in the knowledge that sport as we knew it in the early twenty-first century is no longer bulletproof. They – we – need to understand that the direction new generations are likely to take with the businesses we built will be very different, and necessarily so. If we are unable to change, very quickly we'll be asked to hand on the baton.

CHAPTER 9 / And so to Tokyo (and Back)

Deep in the recesses of my desk drawer, hidden under broken staplers and laptop cables, is a battered piece of paper covered in scrawled notes. It looks a bit like the history homework I used to churn out – those tasks where you could guarantee a good mark by staining the paper with a teabag to make it look old.

This piece of paper, however, is a genuine relic. At the top, in teenage handwriting, it reads: 'My Sporting Bucket List'. It has yellowed and crumpled naturally over time as, roughly once a year, I've retrieved it and added new ideas.

There are no specific criteria that mean something will make it on to the list. Some are events I would like to watch (the Australian Open tennis tournament for example), others are things I'd love to take part in, such as the mountain marathon around Mont Blanc. I have ticked off a few already but there are plenty more to keep Claire and I out of mischief once we've kicked the kids out of the house to earn a living. There is one in Tokyo, which has been on the list for around a decade. But despite my enduring love for the Olympics, it's not the Tokyo Games.

Instead, pandemic notwithstanding, I hope to find myself in central Tokyo in January 2022. I'll be there to watch the start of the Hakone Ekiden, Japan's biggest annual sporting event. This is a running relay event in teams of ten, starting in the centre of Tokyo, travelling to the foot of Mount Fuji and back. The event is contested by 20 or so teams, each representing a university in Japan. It's 135 miles long, so I'll have to return the following day to watch the finish.

The event itself probably sounds a bit too niche for me to be shining a spotlight on it at the end of this book. But there is a good reason why I've chosen it. *Ekiden* (relay marathon) races really took off in Japan as part of the Second World War rebuilding process. At the time, the country was on its knees. Japan was occupied by the United States; navigating political, economic and social upheaval as it struggled to come to terms with a horrific period in its recent history, which had culminated with the atomic bombs landing in Hiroshima and Nagasaki.

Not only was Japan reeling from the impact of its recent past but also the pace of enforced change driven by the US, not least a swift transition into democracy. Morale among the general public was thus extremely low. The whole country needed rebuilding from top to bottom, which meant the economy needed to get moving. Recognising this, companies set up sports teams as an attempt to boost the morale of their employees. They then organised *ekiden* races between themselves as a means to give their new company teams something to train for.

Very quickly races appeared up and down the country, as running boomed. In the years that followed, this passion was fuelled by new generations who had only ever known hard work, physical activity and democratic freedom in their lives. Running helped give Japanese workers health, vitality and confidence and, in return, these revitalised workers helped drive Japan's recovery.

Today the Japanese *ekiden* continue to be a centrepiece of local sporting culture. There are races up and down the country. The Hakone Ekiden remains the pinnacle, making the London Marathon look like a modest local event. One of the most technologically advanced countries in the world, Japan still stops for two days every new year to watch the racing, tapping into everything sport means to the Japanese and their country. It's not about the race and the winners per se, but a hallowed ritual that continues to place the role of sport at the heart of the nation.

So what makes the Hakone Ekiden such a phenomenon? Well, nobody and everyone. There might be custodians who are responsible for running it but in truth they're not in charge, not really. Without the universities taking time out from teaching to field teams, access to public roads to compete on, roadside supporters to create a spectacle, broadcasters to make it big news and commercial companies to foot the bill, the magic can't happen. And without the magic, kids won't tune in and dream of being a part of the race themselves in future years. If the kids don't dream, they won't pull on their trainers and head out to the same roads the day after the race to emulate the heroes they have seen fly by the day before. And if they do not do that, they'll miss the quickening heartrate, serotonin boost and the sense of mental balance that physical activity gives us.

I want to witness the Hakone Ekiden not just because it would be a great day out, but because it's a movement that has grown up with modern Japan. It was a positive catalyst in horrific times and still today remains fundamental to the renewed identity of a proud nation. Two generations on from the horrors of 1945, the race is still hotly contested, and the next generation is training hard, waiting their turn.

At first glance, the relevance of the inception of *ekiden* races in post-war Japan might seem unclear. But Britain today also needs swift solutions to new problems. Sport is in pole position to make a difference and, as we have seen, has been quietly waiting for its time to come. The barriers have been coming down for a decade now. Employers have started to appreciate – more than they have at any time since the 1870s – that active workers are happier, healthier and more productive. Parents and educators recognise, not a minute too soon, how important physical activity is for children too. Both employers and schools are rethinking the rules out of necessity; starting to challenge their twentieth-century ways of doing things. If the kids respond to yoga more than cross country, then let them do it.

As part of this loosening up, we've started to appreciate that technology and sport – while not always traditionally seen as bedfellows – are learning to get the best out of each other. If you can get a robot to mow the lawn for you, it gives you time to get out for a bike ride. Or do it at home and ride online against the world's top professionals.

Although money still makes the world go around in professional sport, there is increasing appreciation in this still-young industry (younger probably than all but computing and telecommunications as a destination for our hard-earned cash) that it will thrive by being part of the community rather than an unwanted guest. Liverpool FC might be a bigger draw in Asia than Tranmere Rovers, but both clubs – and Everton too – are needed to keep a vibrant Merseyside on the map. And that includes women's as well as men's teams.

As we venture into the 2020s, elite players are finding their voices, and coaches are understanding that, by treating their athletes with more care, they'll play better, and for longer. While there will undoubtedly be the odd regression to the teenage years, Britain is breeding an influential group of young adults to set a path of which our more conventional leaders would do well to take note.

Whether *ekiden*, Stormbreak, London 2012 or This Mum Runs, innovation in our modern world needs partnership. Even if social need is obvious, the state is not able to solve problems alone, with debt mountains to climb (and no bike to do so). Fortunately though, business increasingly recognises it is needed to bridge the divide and that there is opportunity in doing so. Take the examples at Tranmere Rovers – no matter how keen young men might be to attend therapy sessions at football clubs over NHS clinics, Tranmere's mental health support would not be possible without creative funding from an open-minded NHS and a football club prepared to take a risk and try something new. Sport is innovating at pace – we just need to make the best ideas stick. That's where the Sporting Recipe for success comes in.

What this in turn means is that those at the helm of the sports we love will need to be creative and prepared to take risks. Thick-skinned also, given that the media will rightly be unrelenting in their search to hold the industry to account, but often less keen to share news of progress. To make change stick we need a sports industry that is diverse in thought and action, prepared literally to change the rules of the game while respecting the history and formats that made them special in the first place. The Hundred comes from the same team that looks after Test Cricket. The Tour de France partners with Zwift. Tradition blends with innovation. Amateurs with professionals. Even physical and digital in the case of the Drone Racing League.

Ultimately *Jerry Maguire*'s 'Show me the money!' catch-phrase will still be relevant for professional sports but the money is only there if there is an audience who cares enough to pay to watch not only today, but also in decades to come. As generations change, so does demand. Cricket, for example, has been changing formats for commercial gain since it was invented. This time around the challenge for all sports is to be relevant for future generations that consider social equality, diversity and climate change as givens. Challenges like this are unlikely to be solved in pale, male and stale boardrooms.

Assuming sport gets the balance right, it will continue to thrive as the first choice for anyone looking for a break from quotidian pressures, whether that sense of release comes from playing or watching. But really, it should be aiming far higher. The real opportunity is to be a force of revolution not evolution. Prevention rather than cure for the NHS. Bikes rather than cars for cities. Athletics tracks around industrial parks. Sports stadiums as community hubs.

The video is rolling and Britain has pressed fast forward. There's no room for complacency or entitlement but, equally, the opportunity is bigger than it has ever been. We've got everything to play for.

NOTES

1   BARB data, as covered on BBC website
2   https://www.thesun.co.uk/world-cup-2018/6669709/
     gareth-southgate-waistcoat-sales-marks-spencer/
3   https://www.ifs.org.uk/inequality/trends/
4   https://www.sportengland.org/know-your-audience
5   https://www.history.com/
     news/1968-mexico-city-olympics-black-power-protest-backlash
6   https://twocircles.com/gb-en/articles/
     uk-named-world-capital-of-live-sport-following-new-attendance-
     analysis/
7   https://www.statista.com/statistics/282769/
     united-kingdom-uk-national-debt-y-on-y-psndex/
8   https://www.statista.com/statistics/433786/
     fitness-facilities-enterprises-uk-united-kingdom/
9   https://sportengland-production-files.s3.eu-west-2.amazonaws.
     com/s3fs-public/2020-04/Active%20Lives%20Adult%20
     November%2018-19%20Report..
     pdf?BhkAy2K28pd9bDEz_NuisHl2ppuqJtpZ
10   https://sportengland-production-files.s3.eu-west-2.amazonaws.
     com/s3fs-public/2020-01/active-lives-children-survey-academic-
     year-18-19.pdf?cVMsdnpBoqROViY61iUjpQY6WcRyhtGs
11   https://www.kingsfund.org.uk/publications/
     whats-happening-life-expectancy-uk
12   https://activelives.sportengland.org/
13   https://www.lesmills.com/uk/clubs-and-facilities/research-insights/
     audience-insights/generation-active-the-80-your-club-cant-ignore/
14   https://twocircles.com/gb-en/articles/uk-named-world-capital-of-
     live-sport-following-new-attendance-analysis/

15 https://twocircles.com/gb-en/articles/uk-attendance-growth-why-sport-is-prospering/

16 https://time.com/70489/meb-keflezighi-boston-marathon-2014/

17 See https://marathontalk.com/shows/episode-224-boston-marathon-chris-finill/, which includes an interview I did with Martin Yelling about the experience of running the race (47 minutes in).

18 https://www.ft.com/content/c896d066-f0d8-11e9-bfa4-b25f11f42901

19 https://www.theguardian.com/football/2018/jun/02/raheem-sterling-mothers-boy-jamaica-man-england#maincontent

20 https://en.wikipedia.org/wiki/Powerlist_2020

21 https://www.thesun.co.uk/sport/8516897/anthony-joshua-crime-boxing-icon-miller/

22 https://www.englandboxing.org/news_articles/stormzy-inspiration-for-south-london-boxing-led-programme/

23 https://www.theguardian.com/football/2019/aug/17/megan-rapinoe-everything-trump-loves-except-we-are-powerful-women

24 https://www.bbc.co.uk/news/business-45472399

25 https://www.independent.co.uk/sport/football/news/pfa-sporting-chance-mental-health-football-danny-rose-a8942206.html

26 https://www.theguardian.com/football/2020/may/23/frank-lampard-football-stone-age-mental-health-prince-william

27 https://www.theguardian.com/sport/blog/2018/dec/05/parkour-fight-soul-gymnastics; https://www.insidethegames.biz/articles/1101477/ioc-urged-to-reject-parkour-paris-2024

28 https://www.sportspromedia.com/news/liverpool-fc-youtube-revenue-ranking#:~:text=Liverpool%20were%20the%20top-placed,F2%20Freestylers%20(US%20%24716%2C157)

29 https://www.theticketingbusiness.com/2019/09/24/twenty20-blast-hits-record-ticket-sales-2019

30 https://www.ft.com/content/c1178dcc-769d-11e9-be7d-6d846537acab

31 https://www.ft.com/content/fbb1ef1c-7ff8-11ea-b0fb-13524ae1056b

32 https://www.skysports.com/football/news/11679/12113908/raheem-sterling-launches-charity-foundation-to-help-disadvantaged-youngsters

33 https://www.garmin.com/en-GB/blog/the-global-pandemic-and-active-lifestyles/

34 https://www.sportengland.org/news/activity-habits-early-weeks-lockdown-revealed

35 https://www-bbc-com.cdn.ampproject.org/c/s/www.bbc.com/sport/amp/55459593

36 https://www.bbc.co.uk/news/health-52561757?intlink_from_url=https://www.bbc.co.uk/news/topics/c40rjmqdl3jt/obesity&link_location=live-reporting-story

37 https://www.theguardian.com/environment/2020/sep/03/uk-organic-food-and-drink-sales-boom-during-lockdown

38 https://htc.co.uk/supplement-sales-surge-during-lockdown/

39 https://www.bbc.co.uk/news/uk-53242779

40 *Financial Times Weekend*, 12 January 2021

41 https://www.sheffield.ac.uk/polopoly_fs/1.738134!/file/SIVSCE-report_final.pdf

42 https://www.glofox.com/blog/the-future-of-fitspo/

43 https://pubmed.ncbi.nlm.nih.gov/26176993/

44 https://www.gov.uk/government/consultations/advancing-our-health-prevention-in-the-2020s/advancing-our-health-prevention-in-the-2020s-consultation-document

45 https://worldpopulationreview.com/country-rankings/most-obese-countries

46 https://assets.publishing.service.gov.uk/government/uploads/system/uploads/attachment_data/file/664855/Transforming_children_and_young_people_s_mental_health_provision.pdf

47 https://www.sportengland.org/know-your-audience/demographic-knowledge/coronavirus?section=research#page

48 https://www.theguardian.com/business/2020/jun/28/back-us-or-risk-losing-half-uks-public-leisure-centres-industry-warns

49 https://www.wsj.com/articles/SB851552449565409000

50 *Sporting Goods 2021: The Next Normal for an Industry in Flux*, joint initiative between the World Federation of the Sporting Goods Industry (WFSGI) and McKinsey & Company, published 26 January 2021, https://wfsgi.org/sporting-goods-2021-the-next-normal-for-an-industry-in-flux/

51 https://www.bloomberg.com/news/articles/2011-12-14/lego-is-for-girls#p4

52 Interviews with Clare Strange and Peter Norfolk I conducted for the London 2012 Paralympic Games programme

53 https://www.un.org/development/desa/en/news/population/
2018-revision-of-world-urbanization-prospects

54 https://www.sustainabilityreport.com/2020/04/30/reimagining-
stadiums-as-the-nucleus-of-smart-cities/

55 https://www.businessinsider.com/millennials-gen-z-drag-down-
beer-sales-2018-2?r=US&IR=T

56 https://www.theguardian.com/football/2020/jun/07/premier-
league-clubs-turn-to-online-dating-methods-in-the-transfer-
market

57 https://www.bbc.co.uk/sport/football/50674331

58 https://variety.com/2020/biz/news/endeavor-260-million-loan-
ufc-wme-coronavirus-1234603358/

59 https://www2.deloitte.com/uk/en/pages/technology-media-and-
telecommunications/articles/tmt-predictions.html

60 https://www.olympic.org/news/the-gender-of-a-coach-shouldn-t-be-
important

61 https://www.77sportsmanagement.com/

62 Statistics taken from parkrun data resource available at www.
parkrun.com

63 https://hbr-org.cdn.ampproject.org/c/s/hbr.org/amp/2020/12/
want-to-see-the-future-of-digital-health-tools-look-to-germany

64 https://www.youthsporttrust.org/news/
wellbeing-and-location-most-important-factors-parents-choosing-
school

ACKNOWLEDGEMENTS

While this book has been years in the making, it came together very quickly. There's nothing like two locked-down, home-schooling, fridge-raiding children to convince you that hiding in the study for another hour is a sensible decision.

In all seriousness, it wasn't a straightforward time to run the final straight on a project like this. Thank you to my hugely talented co-author Kerry for the massive role she has played. She made the complex simple and the challenging times fun, time after time.

Thanks also to our interviewees, whose commitment and sheer love for their roles shone through. We were privileged to be able to spend time with each of you.

We were fortunate to have a research team as obsessive about the subject area as we were. My dad Martin, co-author for my last book, was consistently able to find the needle of evidence in a haystack of opinion. Kate Brine threw herself into supporting us when the pandemic put paid to her pre-university travel plans.

Our publishing team at Ebury Press, led by Elizabeth Bond and Camilla Ackley, understood immediately what we were trying to do. Their belief and fresh perspective have been pivotal in bringing this book alive.

We wrote this book because sport matters far beyond the field of play. Dave Rayner, Trevor Whitby and Pat Roberts, my own early sports coaches, taught me as much about myself as the sport I was trying to master. Dr Challoner's School, Amersham, and Fitzwilliam College, Cambridge, both gave me a chance and taught me to work hard but play harder. I clung on to that philosophy with sports agency Two Circles, set up by my wife Claire and I alongside our great mate Gareth Balch. From Chertsey Town to Chelsea FC – this book has many authors.

I am fortunate that my very first five-a-side team – my family – was impossible to beat. I cannot say enough about my mum and dad, whose own ongoing passion for sport and desire to go the extra mile for their kids influences me daily. Also to my sisters, Em and Lou. As I was tucked away in lockdown, Em was continuing to lead veterinary clinics while simultaneously supporting in NHS COVID-19 wards. Lou was working as a respiratory physio in an NHS intensive care unit and developing a specialism in supporting patients coming back from long COVID. I am in awe of you both.

On the subject of awe – to my wife, Claire. Here's to many more sporting adventures.

Index